Social Theory and Religion

Many aspects of religion are puzzling these days. This book looks at ways of improving our understanding of religious change by strengthening the links between social theory and the social scientific study of religion. It clarifies the social processes involved in constructing religion and non-religion in public and private life. Taking illustrations of the importance of these boundaries from studies of secularisation, religious diversity, globalisation, religious movements and self-identity, James A. Beckford reviews the current state of social scientific knowledge about religion. He also assesses the strengths and weaknesses of a wide range of theoretical attempts to account for religious change and continuity. The discussion goes in two directions. The first is towards identifying ways in which studies of religion would benefit from taking better account of themes in recent social theory. The second is towards identifying reasons for social theorists to pay more attention to the findings of empirical investigations of religion. The book will be of interest to social scientists, philosophers, theologians and specialists in religious studies.

James A. Beckford is Professor of Sociology at the Department of Sociology, University of Warwick. His previous publications include *The Trumpet of Prophecy. A Sociological Study of Jehovah's Witnesses* (1975), *Cult Controversies. The Societal Response to New Religious Movements* (1989), *Religion and Advanced Industrial Society* (1989), and *Religion in Prison. 'Equal Rites' in a Multi-Faith Society* (with S. Gilliat, Cambridge, 1998).

Social Theory and Religion

James A. Beckford

CAMBRIDGE
UNIVERSITY PRESS

PUBLISHED BY THE PRESS SYNDICATE OF THE UNIVERSITY OF CAMBRIDGE
The Pitt Building, Trumpington Street, Cambridge CB2 1RP, United Kingdom

CAMBRIDGE UNIVERSITY PRESS
The Edinburgh Building, Cambridge, CB2 2RU, UK
40 West 20th Street, New York, NY 10011–4211, USA
477 Williamstown Road, Port Melbourne, VIC 3207, Australia
Ruiz de Alarcón 13, 28014 Madrid, Spain
Dock House, The Waterfront, Cape Town 8001, South Africa

http://www.cambridge.org

First published 2003

Printed in the United Kingdom at the University Press, Cambridge

Typeface Plantin 10/12 pt.   *System* LATEX 2$_\varepsilon$ [TB]

A catalogue record for this book is available from the British Library

Library of Congress Cataloguing in Publication data
Beckford, James A.
Social theory and religion / James A. Beckford.
    p.   cm.
Includes bibliographical references (p. 221) and index.
1. Religion and sociology.   I. Title.
BL60.B34   2003   306.6 – dc21   2003043583

ISBN 0 521 77336 9 hardback
ISBN 0 521 77431 4 paperback

To my family

Contents

Preface

This book has been a long time in the making. I have been fortunate to receive support and encouragement from many people who have helped me in various ways to complete the project. First, my good friend in Chicago, Fritz Huchting, dignified it from the beginning with the title of *The Summa*. My much younger colleague in Århus, Lene Kühle, kept chipping away at the initial weaknesses in one chapter. Meanwhile, Danièle Hervieu-Léger extended to me the generous hospitality and the intellectual stimulation of the Ecole des Hautes Etudes en Sciences Sociales in Paris. Further encouragement came from Françoise Champion, Jean-Paul Willaime and Véronique Altglas at the Ecole Pratique des Hautes Etudes in Paris. Finally, the Study Leave Committee of the University of Warwick supported the work at a crucial stage.

Colleagues at the University of Warwick have kept me well supplied with good ideas and entertaining distractions. Bob Jackson, Danièle Joly, Mike Neary, Eleanor Nesbitt, Jonathan Tritter, Charles Turner and Simon Williams all deserve special thanks. The genial company, embodied and electronic, of 'the Perfect' – Eileen Barker, Meredith McGuire, Jim Richardson, Cynthia Richardson and Jim Spickard – has been an inspiration. In addition, I am deeply appreciative of the interest in my work shown by generations of my graduate students in Chicago and Warwick and by members of the International Society for the Sociology of Religion.

Without the initial encouragement of Camilla Erskine and the tolerant support of Sarah Caro at Cambridge University Press this book would not have seen the light of day. Nick Ye Myint helped to reduce the number of errors.

As ever, I owe the greatest debt of gratitude to the members of my family who have displayed exactly the right blend of curiosity, forbearance and love to keep my motivation high.

Abbreviations

ACM	Anti-cult movement
CCC	Celestial Church of Christ
CIRF	Commission on International Religious Freedom
IRFA	International Religious Freedom Act
ISKCON	International Society for Krishna Consciousness
ISSR	International Society for the Sociology of Religion
MILS	Mission Interministérielle de Lutte contre les Sectes
NGO	Non-governmental organisation
NRM	New religious movement
NSM	New social movement
RCT	Rational choice theory
SGI	Soka Gakkai International
TM	Transcendental Meditation
UCKG	Universal Church of the Kingdom of God
YMCA	Young Men's Christian Association

Introduction

This book begins at the point where my *Religion and Advanced Industrial Societies* (1989) ended. My main argument there was that religion had been at the very centre of the first generation of sociological and anthropological classics but that, over the course of the twentieth century, it had moved into a marginal position.[1] I offered two explanations of the processes that led to religion's insulation against, and isolation from, the principal currents of social scientific thinking. The first explanation was based on some aspects of the ways in which religion had been conceptualised as an object of study. The second relied on changes that had taken place in what counted as religion. My conclusion was that

Religion has come adrift from its former points of anchorage but is no less potentially powerful as a result. It remains a potent cultural resource or form which may act as the vehicle of change, challenge, or conservation. Consequently, religion has become less predictable. The capacity to mobilize people and material resources remains strong, but it is likely to be mobilized in unexpected places and in ways which may be in tension with 'establishment' practices and public policy . . . The deregulation of religion is one of the hidden ironies of secularization. It helps to make religion sociologically problematic in ways which are virtually inconceivable in the terms of the sociological classics. (Beckford 1989: 170, 172)

It seems to me that, since the end of the 1980s, the balance of social scientific evidence has confirmed my analysis. Indeed, the trend towards the de-regulation of religion in some countries, disputes about what counts as religion, and attempts to devise new ways of controlling what is permitted under the label of religion have all increased. This is not the complete picture, of course. Continuity in the beliefs and practices that qualify as 'religious' is also apparent – as is slow, organic change. And there are spurts of intense innovation and originality from time to time.

The point of good social science is no less to keep the short-lived, eye-catching upheavals in proportion than to avoid being mesmerised by what appears to be timeless tradition. This balancing act is always difficult but it can be made considerably easier if the focus of analysis is on the social processes whereby phenomena are categorised as variously

1

'not religious', 'religious but unusual' or 'religious and traditional'. From this point of view, sociological studies of, for example, the ordination of women as priests in Christian Churches, the participation of members of the Japanese government in Shinto ceremonies to honour military personnel killed in wars, Hindu nationalism, and the framing of laws concerning religious freedom in formerly Communist lands all exemplify the constant process of framing and re-framing phenomena as 'religious', 'non-religious', 'acceptably religious', 'unacceptably religious', and so on.

Attentive readers will have noticed that these remarks are phrased in a deliberately oblique fashion. In fact, they are not directly about religion as such. They are about *changes in the conceptualisation and regulation of what counts as religion.* I shall explain my reasons for adopting this approach more fully in Chapter One, but it is important to give an early indication of the strategy that will be adopted in this book. The starting-point is the assertion that, whatever else religion is, it is a social phenomenon. Regardless of whether religious beliefs and experiences actually relate to supernatural, superempirical or noumenal realities, religion is expressed by means of human ideas, symbols, feelings, practices and organisations. These expressions are the products of social interactions, structures and processes and, in turn, they influence social life and cultural meanings to varying degrees. The social scientific study of religion, including social theory, aims to interpret and explain these products and processes.

The social scientific approach that underlies this book is only one, necessarily limited, perspective on religion. It is not concerned with the reality status or the truth claims that are made about the objects of religious beliefs. Nor is it concerned with questions about the authenticity of personal experiences attributed to religion. And, while religious texts may provide valuable evidence of religious ideas, neither the exegesis of texts nor the creation of theological systems is directly relevant to my social scientific project. This is not to assert the priority of the social over the sacred; nor is it to consign all things religious to the status of epiphenomena. John Milbank's (1990) criticism of social theorists for tending to assume that religion is only an artefact of social life is certainly applicable to some extreme cases of sociologism. But his criticism misses the point that putatively divine or sublime forces can only be communicated among human beings through cultural media. Consequently, the social and cultural conditions that help to shape the ideas, experiences, texts and intellectual systems that are widely regarded as having divine origins or a religious character *are* central to any social scientific perspective on religion. In addition, the social scientific perspective ideally involves a radical shift of focus. It means abandoning the tendency to regard religion as a relatively well-defined object. It also means examining critically the social processes whereby certain things are counted as religious. No less interesting to social scientists are the processes whereby prevailing concepts of religion are extended, challenged or rejected. Finally, it means taking seriously the changes that occur over time in everyday conceptualisations of religion.

The approach that I am taking to the social scientific study of religion is, broadly speaking, a 'social constructionist' one. Let me try to be clear about my use of this phrase. It recurs frequently in the language of social scientists and students of culture, but there is wide variation in how it is used (Velody & Williams 1998). Radical constructionists may claim that social reality consists of nothing but text and discourse – the 'universal constructionism' that John Searle (1995) dismisses for good reason. There is nothing more real or accessible than the tissue of language and discursive practice, according to this position (see, for example, Gergen 1999). By comparison, a more modest use of 'constructionism' implies only that human beings create or construct meanings when they interact with each other. Thus, public order, disorder, panics and confidence are constructed as emergent products of myriad human interactions. The meaning that I want to attribute to 'construction' in this book lies somewhere between these two extremes. Without denying the existence of anything other than text and discourse – and building on well-established insights into the constructive and destructive possibilities of social interaction – I seek to analyse the processes whereby the meaning of the category of religion is, in various situations, intuited, asserted, doubted, challenged, rejected, substituted, re-cast, and so on.

My version of social constructionism leaves entirely open the question of whether human beings, universally or selectively, experience religion in forms that are not pre-constructed by human culture. I am certainly not denying *a priori* the possibility that religion is some form of 'basic' – in the sense of anthropologically necessary – impulse or need, although I do not find the evidence put forward to support such a view persuasive. In any case, it seems to me that the question is irrelevant from a social scientific point of view. For, if religious forces can somehow trump, subvert, bypass or dispense with human agency, then it follows by definition that social science has no way of taking them into account. Nothing can be done about this situation except perhaps to follow the sublime path into mysticism or theology – or, better still in my opinion, to follow Wittgenstein's advice to place a full stop at the point where nothing can be said. 'The ineffable is ineffable' seems to be a logical conclusion of regarding religious forces as beyond human culture. But, since we *are* human beings who live in the medium of meanings, contested as well as shared, we are on firmer ground if we limit our investigations to what we can know about the social construction of religion as process and product. Although very few social scientists claim to have the last word to say on religion, their investigations of the ways in which human beings 'do religion' can still be interesting and provocative.

The priority that I assign to 'construction' is not necessarily related to any particular assumptions about ontology ('what there is') or epistemology ('what can be known'). It is merely an analytical strategy, that is, a device or a method employed for the purpose of analysing a phenomenon – in this case, the construction of religion as a complex and variable category of human knowing, feeling, acting and relating. Indirectly, my strategy also asks how the category of 'non-religion' is socially constructed. There is no assumption on my part that the category of either religion or non-religion is any more natural, given or unproblematic than the other. I want to show how the boundary between these two categories is staked out, defended, deployed, attacked, smudged, re-defined or even dissolved. It is a boundary zone that is heavily, perhaps essentially, contested.

I find it strange that social scientists have shown relatively little interest in the 'frontier wars' and skirmishes that occur throughout the border zone (but see Greil & Robbins 1994). They seem to prefer to act, instead, as if there really were separate spheres or domains and as if their task were to capture the differences between them in words and thereby to map the 'real' line of division. It makes no difference to my argument whether their aim is to distinguish between religion and non-religion, sacred and profane, holy and unholy, and so on. All such dichotomies indicate belief in the real existence of non-overlapping spheres or domains.

It makes very little sense, in my view, to think of religion as an object or a subject that could exist independently of human actors and social institutions. Religion does not 'do' anything by itself. It does not have agency. Rather, it is an interpretative category that human beings apply to a wide variety of phenomena, most of which have to do with notions of ultimate meaning or value. The sedimented meanings associated with religion in the course of social life constitute authoritative guides not only to usage of the term but also to social action. The category of 'religion' is an abstraction from, or distillation of, these meanings and actions. As such, the category of religion is subject to constant negotiation and re-negotiation. Its meaning must therefore be related to the social contexts in which it is used.

The central theme of this book is that disputes and conflicts about the social meaning of religion remain lively in the early twenty-first century, whereas discussion of religion in social theory tends to be relatively dull and poorly informed about these particular disputes and conflicts. My aim is, therefore, to create a more fruitful relation between the major changes that are taking place in the social and cultural phenomena categorised as 'religions' and the theoretical interpretations of them.

It would quickly become tedious if I had to adorn every use of the term 'religion' and its cognates with inverted commas in order to emphasise my claim that they do not denote anything fixed or essential beyond the meanings that they carry in particular social and cultural contexts. I shall, therefore, omit the inverted commas for stylistic reasons, but readers will understand that, in my view, 'religion' is a social and cultural construct with highly variable meaning.

Let me put some descriptive flesh on these dry, analytical bones by means of a timely example. There is no shortage of social theorists prepared to claim that the growing popularity in advanced industrial or late-modern societies of so-called New Age spiritualities and therapies is evidence of various fundamental shifts. A common claim is that the underlying, or 'master', shift is from modernity to late-modernity. The claim is that New Age beliefs and practice represent the advent of reflexive self-monitoring, which is supposedly indicative of significant departures from modern modes of social and cultural life. This particular theoretical 'move' involves the interpretation of beliefs and practices as different as astrology, crystal healing, channelling, yoga and numerology as indicators of a retreat from typically modern ways of being religious or spiritual. Moreover, these late-modern forms of religion and spirituality are supposed to bear a strong family resemblance to new social and cultural forms of work and employment, leisure activities and intimate relationships. The argument is that a particular logic or dynamic is at work in transforming modernity into late-modernity. The implication is that religious changes are merely an effect or by-product of causes that lie in the very long-term evolution of rationality, science and nation states.

However, the level of interpretive ambition and theoretical abstraction is so high in this particular approach to social theory that little consideration is given to the detailed aspects of New Age phenomena. Intricate debates about the meaning of the term 'New Age' are ignored. Empirical studies of the bewildering patterns of interaction between 'modern' and New Age practices are overlooked. Evidence about the distinctly 'modern' forms of organisation and commerce that have grown up around the New Age receive no acknowledgement in the characterisation of late-modernity. And, most importantly, the theory takes little account of the plentiful evidence that New Age forms of religion and spirituality, far from displacing more conventional or modern forms, are merely one small but colourful feature of a much more complicated picture of religious change. In other words, the concept of late-modernity offers an interesting interpretation of New Age phenomena but, unless it is combined with the findings of careful empirical research, it represents a highly selective and uncritical perspective on these phenomena and on their meaning in relation to other religious continuities and changes that do not fit easily into the depiction of late-modernity.

What is to be done? My proposal is, first, to explore the tension between the interests of high-level social theory and the interests of scholars who study the social aspects of religion. Second, I advocate scrutiny of the points of tension with a view to improving the conceptual building blocks of the theory, the internal relations between them and the empirical evidence with which to assess the concepts' value. By comparison, I shall devote little space to questions of research strategies and methods. In addition, I plead guilty to the charge that my discussions take relatively little account of religion or social theorising outside the confines of advanced industrial democracies.

Ideally, then, the choice of topics for empirical investigation would be informed by conceptual and theoretical knowledge; and the process of refining and elaborating theoretical understanding would, in turn, take proper account of empirical knowledge. Mutual interaction between theory and empirical investigation does not, of course, resolve all intellectual puzzles or put an end to all disagreements. Nevertheless, it can generate new insights and fresh perspectives simply by exposing to criticism the bases on which existing claims to knowledge are founded. In some cases it may even allow researchers to replicate previous studies (see Van Driel and Richardson 1988; Beckford and Cole 1988).

Even when the outcome of replication fails to produce agreement between different sets of researchers, there is still value in the procedure whereby each 'side' makes explicit its initial assumptions and its justification of methodological choices. A prime example is the on-going debate about the association between religious diversity and religious vitality. Starting with Finke and Stark's (1988) attribution of the USA's high rates of church attendance to the absence of a religious monopoly and to the strength of religious pluralism, the debate prompted a sceptical response from Breault (1989) on technical grounds, an alternative approach to interpreting the history of church participation in the US from Land, Deane and Blau (1991) and from Blau et al. (1992), an insistence from Chaves and Cann (1992) on the relatively strong impact of State regulation on levels of pluralism, critical comments from Olson (1998, 1999) on regional differences in the impact of pluralism, and energetic attempts by Bruce (1999: 159) to show that 'choice undermines faith'.

At some junctures Finke and Stark (1998; and Stark and Finke 2001) have responded to some of these criticisms by attempting to place their ideas in a broader context.

It would be an exaggeration to suggest that this occasionally ill-mannered and acerbic debate has produced progress in the social scientific understanding of the relationship between religious diversity and religious vitality in the USA. Rather, positions have hardened to some extent, and a self-defensive mood has settled on some of the disputants. Yet, the process of stating assumptions and justifying analytical inferences has undoubtedly clarified many of the issues that were less clear at the beginning. The disagreements still outweigh the points of agreement, but the debate has given social scientists a better understanding of what is at stake in questions about religious diversity, pluralism and vitality. In my opinion, this represents the common pattern of development in social scientific studies of religion. For, amid all the disputes about the validity of data, the reliability of measurements, the comparability of cases and the appropriateness of measures of statistical significance there is also discussion of historical contexts, cultural meanings and conceptual boundaries. It may even be possible to clarify high-level theoretical propositions and to identify testable hypotheses in some cases. This is all theoretical work, and it is one of the main aims of this book to indicate the importance of theoretical ideas to a social scientific understanding of the meanings and uses of religion.

Chapter One lays the groundwork for the longer chapters that follow on the topics of secularisation, pluralism, globalisation and religious movements. It does so by establishing that social scientific perspectives on religion are sceptical towards common sense definitions of religion. I argue that, ideally, social scientists distinguish between the 'first order' notions of religion that actors deploy in everyday life and the 'second order' constructs that serve analytical purposes. In both cases, ideas of what counts as religion are constructed, negotiated and contested. My aim is to show that, far from being a fixed or unitary phenomenon, religion is a social construct that varies in meaning across time and place. It is the task of social science, in my view, to study the processes whereby the social construction of religion takes place at all levels of the social world and with varying degrees of formal authorisation. Of course, first order and second order constructs of religion also meet with resistance and rejection. Agreement on what counts as religion is never universal. Disagreements are sometimes violent and destructive. The following chapters discuss the capacity of the social constructionist approach to enhance the social scientific understanding of change and continuity in some key issues affecting religions today.

My discussion of ideas about secularisation in Chapter Two comes early in the book. This may give the impression that I regard secularisation as the key to social scientific understanding of religion. This would be a misleading impression, however. My reasons for dealing with secularisation ahead of the other principal topics are twofold. First, the volume of commentary on secularisation is so great that it deserves special attention. Second, the arguments that rage around ideas of secularisation and de-secularisation bring to light many broader issues concerning the social construction of religion. Consequently, secularisation is 'good to think with'. The first half of the chapter discusses the deep philosophical and ideological wellsprings of the widely differing ideas that bubble up in arguments about the decline of religion. The second half of the chapter analyses in detail the six main clusters of ideas that I detect in these arguments. They range from the claim that secularisation consigns religion to insignificance as a force in social life to the opposite claim that the eclipse of religion is simply inconceivable. The middle of the range contains attempts to show that religion is not declining but is merely undergoing various metamorphoses. My conclusion is that debates about secularisation are highly revealing about the underlying ways of constituting religion as an object for social scientific analysis and that studies of the social construction of religion in everyday life promise to deliver fresh insights into the struggles to distinguish between the religious and the secular.

The word 'struggles' appears in the previous sentence because I want to emphasise the fact that the social construction of religion and non-religion is, in some cases, the outcome of intentions, policies, strategies and campaigns. Human beings and social agents contend with each other to determine what counts as religion and where the boundary lies between acceptable and unacceptable forms of religion. Chapter Three is an extended critique of the tendency of some social scientists to conceal these struggles behind a problematic use of the term 'pluralism'. The main argument begins with the claim that 'pluralism' conflates three things that should be kept analytically separate: religious diversity, the extent to which the practice of a variety of religions is acceptable, and the positive evaluation that is widely given to religious diversity. I argue that this conflation has its origins in the particular ways in which pluralism was associated with ideas about secularisation in the mid-1960s. The argument goes on to show that more recent work on the management of religious diversity illustrates the need to take seriously the political opportunity structures within which individuals and collectivities compete, and sometimes conflict, in their attempts to determine the limits of religious tolerance and acceptability. A case study of the 'political economy' of prison chaplaincy demonstrates some of the struggles that occur over access to prisoners, resources and respect. The conclusion discusses some of the objections that social scientists have raised against insufficiently critical notions of pluralism as an analytical concept and as an ideological position. The chapter urges social scientific students of religion to pay close attention to relations of power and conflict between religious groups, for these issues are all too easily masked by uncritical usage of 'pluralism'.

The main theme of Chapter Four is that much of the social theorising about globality and globalisation is problematic because it fails to do justice to the subtlety, variety and complexity of religious phenomena. This is not a pretext for abandoning all notions of the global, however. On the contrary, it is a plea for conceptual clarity and for greater familiarity with the findings of research into religion under conditions of globality. The first phase of the argument establishes that religions have long been 'vehicles' of ideas about globalisation, although social theorists do not usually take sufficient account of these ideas. In fact, a review of four influential works on globalisation shows that their analyses of religion are deficient in several respects. In addition to displaying widespread confusion about basic concepts, there is a strong tendency for social theorists to simplify, and to exaggerate the significance of, religious fundamentalisms. They also neglect evidence of the complex interweaving of globalisation and non-fundamentalist forms of religion. The concluding section discusses a range of anthropological and sociological studies that demonstrate the usefulness of thinking critically about the mutual connections between religion and globalisation. The conclusion is that, if social theorists accepted the challenge of explaining these varied connections, the social scientific understanding of globalisation would be significantly enhanced.

The focus of Chapter Five is on the challenges that religious movements represent for social theories. The main argument is that there has been an imbalance between the impressive volume of empirical investigations and the comparatively meagre amount of attention to their theoretical significance. A critical review of normative functionalist, phenomenological and Marxist approaches shows that social scientists have tended to regard religious movements primarily as marginal or deviant phenomena. What is more surprising is that the sociological literature on new social movements also tends to categorise religious movements as having little significance for an understanding of the major fault lines, grievances and conflicts of late modern societies. But there are three sets of theoretical ideas that have proved capable of throwing explanatory light on religious movements *and* of showing how the waxing and waning of religious movements can help to explain aspects of societal change. The roots of these theoretical ideas lie in the resource mobilisation model of social movements, rational choice theory and a variety of approaches to culture and identity under conditions of post-modernity. The findings of research embodying these ideas show that developments in religious movements are closely associated with patterns of social and cultural change. The challenge is for social theorists to take better account of the evidence of these developments and thereby to realise that religious movements, far from being necessarily deviant or marginal, are an integral part of social and cultural change. At the same time, social scientists would benefit from examining major developments in social theory to see how far they can enhance our understanding of religious movements.

The concluding chapter explains how a social constructionist perspective throws new light on the topics of secularisation, globalisation, religious diversity and religious movements whilst also forging closer links with social theory. The contested frontiers and boundaries between religion and non-religion are central to each topic. It is also argued that recent developments in theoretical ideas about the self and society in late modern conditions can enhance our understanding of religion's continuing significance – especially in conjunction with ideas of self-reflexivity, post-modernity, rational choice, 'postemotionality' and embodiment. Paradoxically, the parallel themes of individualisation and standardisation are shown to run through many attempts to capture late modern developments in the social construction of religion. Only a social constructionist approach, it is argued, can do justice to these kaleidoscopic developments.

Although this book advocates the use of a social constructionist approach to the social scientific study of religion, I do not discount other theoretical approaches. On the contrary, I recognise that it is compatible with, if not required by, many other approaches. My aim is not to be exclusive but inclusive – in the interest of fomenting dialogue. I also recognise that the social constructionist approach has its limitations and is not immune from criticism. On balance, however, I am confident that it is an approach that throws into sharp relief some of the most intriguing and challenging aspects of what counts as religion today.

1 Religion: a social constructionist approach

"Wise is he who recognises that Truth is One and one only, but wiser still the one who accepts that Truth is called by many names, and approached from myriad routes."[1]

Introduction

This book will examine a wide range of theoretical ideas that have a bearing on topics central to the study of religion today – secularisation, pluralism, globalisation and religious movements. These ideas are associated with concepts as diverse as identity, gender, self-reflexivity and post-modernity. In turn, these concepts take their meanings from broad frameworks of theoretical ideas. That is, the frameworks act like scaffolding or codes that structure relations between the concepts, thereby lending them distinctive meaning and significance. Social theory, in my sense of the term, consists primarily of frameworks of concepts configured in such a way as to offer accounts of social phenomena at a relatively high level of generality.

Some theoretical frameworks consist of logically interrelated assumptions and propositions from which testable hypotheses can be derived. Others are much looser assemblages of concepts that merely sensitise social scientists to interesting ways of interpreting the social world. For my purposes, they all belong to the broad category of social theory, regardless of whether the theorists who create them believe that the frameworks are true depictions of reality (and of what makes it real) or merely helpful devices for casting light in dark corners. Nicos Mouzelis (1995) labels these two attitudes to the purpose of social theory respectively 'end-product' and 'tool'. I would add that there are also meta-theoretical ideas about the kinds of theoretical frameworks that social scientists employ. But my interest here is mainly in ways of using theoretical ideas as tools for helping to identify precisely what it is about the social aspects of religion that causes me surprise or puzzlement. In addition to alerting me to questions that call for answers, theoretical ideas can also suggest ways of constituting the topic in researchable forms. Furthermore, theoretical ideas colour the interpretations that I place on the findings of my investigations. Eventually, the findings may re-shape the theoretical ideas with which my research began. Theoretical ideas are therefore indispensable tools at every twist and turn in the process of reflecting on what I know, what I want to know, and how I can claim to know it.

Theoretical ideas about religion in relation to social life had a strong influence on social theory in the formative period of sociology (O'Toole 1984; Beckford 1989), anthropology (Morris 1987) and, to a smaller extent, psychology (Bowker 1973). Indeed, social theorists of a variety of eponymous persuasions – Marxist, Weberian, Durkheimian, Simmelian and Parsonian – accounted for religion in terms of, for example, its origins, its functions and its affinities with other social phenomena. In the last quarter of the twentieth century, however, social theorists tended to overlook religion unless, like Peter Berger and Niklas Luhmann, they happened to have a particular interest in it (Featherstone 1991). A more dramatic description of the situation is Craig Calhoun's (1999: 237) observation that religion 'has been banished to the sidelines in the contemporary field of theoretical struggle'. Charles Lemert's (1999: 241) reference to 'our theoretical sins of omission on the subject of religion' is even more colourful. And there is no shortage of reminders from specialists in various disciplines associated with the study of religion that religious phenomena are becoming more, rather than less, important in late modernity. Phillip Jenkins (2002: 1), for example, asserts confidently that 'it is precisely religious changes that are the most significant, and even the most revolutionary, in the contemporary world'. Without necessarily agreeing with these far-reaching claims, I intend to show that it is a mistake for social theorists to overlook religion; and I shall argue for the usefulness of a social constructionist approach to understanding religion. Yet, my advocacy of this approach does not exclude others. In fact, as I shall argue in Chapter Three, my preference is for theoretical pluralism in the sense of openness to the possibility that social scientific studies of religion benefit from employing a variety of theoretical perspectives. I shall begin by making the case for a social constructionist approach.

What counts as religion?

Human societies and cultures have taken widely differing forms. The catalogue of the different ways in which people have provided for such things as their livelihood, physical protection, child-rearing, property ownership and transmission, dispute settlement, control of sexual relations and artistic expression is vast. The patterns of social relations and of meanings generated are far from being random or haphazard but they are bewilderingly varied. They change over time and they vary from place to place. This is virtually taken for granted today, but these generalisations become more interesting when they are subjected to methodical examination. For, on closer inspection, it becomes clear that the broad patterns of social and cultural life that we call, for example, 'work', 'family', 'politics', 'property', 'childhood', 'law', 'marriage', 'war' and 'art' are not simply variations on basic themes. They are also social and cultural constructs, the meaning of which has changed over time, has differed between social classes and has never been universally agreed. In other words, the meaning of these concepts is not fixed once and for all time. The meaning of these everyday aspects of the social and cultural world can be contested, rejected, modified or confirmed. This commonly happens when, for example, parents and their teenage offspring disagree about whether the latter are still 'children'. An example of the more formal institutional construction of the meaning of basic categories of social life concerns the way in which taxation authorities and social welfare agencies identify 'family' or 'partner' for their particular purposes. There may be general agreement on the dictionary definitions of 'child' or 'partner', but skirmishes take place along the boundaries of these terms in everyday social life. And formal debates about them occur in courts of law and legislatures when boundary disputes erupt about, for example, the age at which children become responsible for any criminal acts that they commit. 'Negotiation' is an aseptic term that refers to the frequently heated, if not violent, arguments that occur about the practical meanings attributed to the basic categories of social life.

Religion is not just another example of a contested concept. The history of disputes about what counts as religion or 'true' religion is long and bloody (McGuire 2003). Religion is also a particularly interesting 'site' where boundary disputes are endemic and where well-entrenched interest groups are prepared to defend their definition of religion against opponents. The history of anti-witchcraft movements in many parts of the world, particularly the Inquisition, is powerful evidence of the deadly lengths to which some interest groups go to enforce their definition of 'true' religion. To make matters even more interesting, legal and conventional regulation of what is permitted in the forms of religion has been getting weaker in many countries, thereby leading to some fascinating controversies. Competition for admission to the increasingly de-regulated 'space' or 'market' for religion is therefore increasing. At the same time, resistance to de-regulation and competition is gathering strength in some places. The result is that the questions of 'What is religion?' or 'What is really religious?' remain contentious and are still capable of stirring

up controversy in public life. Agencies of the State and international organisations find themselves drawn into disputes about the boundaries of
religion.

The fact that the right to hold religious beliefs or non-religious beliefs
enjoys protection in the constitutions of many sovereign countries and in
authoritative international declarations and codes of human rights may
appear to have lessened the likelihood of disputes about religion. Moreover, the high degree of similarity in the ways in which constitutions and
codes frame religion for the purpose of defending the right of individuals
to hold religious beliefs, and in some cases to practise them, also suggests
that the problems of defining religion must have been solved. Yet, this
form of juridification, whilst undoubtedly asserting the privileged character of individual beliefs, does not make it any easier to decide what
counts, or what should count, as religion. Indeed, in some respects the
codification of the right to hold religious beliefs can actually exacerbate
situations in which disputes about religion already exist. For, the protagonists and the antagonists alike may feel obliged constantly to block their
opponents' attempts to benefit from codes of rights in order to protect
their own interests. Of course, legal and philosophical disputes about religion are unquestionably preferable to violent conflict. And there is always
the hope that, in time, disputes about the right to believe certain religious
things will have the effect of defusing tensions. In the short term, however, litigation and less formal struggles over religious rights often help to
prolong and to intensify disputes about the meaning of religion by high-
lighting the difficulty of deciding between 'real' or 'true' religion and,
for example, bogus or fake religion. Codes of rights rarely supply the
explicit criteria by which such decisions can be made. Nor do they offer
unconditional protection of the right to put religious beliefs into practice.
The shortfall between the right to believe and the right to act on what is
believed is the source of many grievances.

This is not a new situation, of course. Religious disputes have left a
bloody mark on the history of most peoples and territories. Some disputes
have broken out between factions of one religion or of one particular
religious organisation. Others have pitted the followers of entire religions
against one another. And the battle between the Scientific Atheism that
was practised in the former Soviet Union and *all* religions, which was
a major feature of State Socialist and Communist regimes in Eastern
Europe, still remains a live issue in Cuba, North Korea and China. But the
current situation in many countries, including those formerly dominated
by Communist regimes, represents a relatively new development. The
dominant features today are competition for the designation of 'religion'
or 'real religion' and concern about the possibility of abuse on the part

of religious and would-be religious actors. This was especially evident in the sometimes anguished discussions that took place in public and private about the motives of those who planned and executed the attacks on the World Trade Centre and the Pentagon on 11 September 2001. Could they possibly have acted out of 'really' religious motives? Should any motive to kill other people, except in self-defence, ever be called 'religious'? Could anyone have the human right to take other people's lives deliberately in the name of religion?

Not dissimilar questions of principle arise on a daily basis about the limits to which the definition of religion is, or should be, subject in relation to justifications of men's exploitation of women, attacks on facilities where abortions take place, and opposition to the inclusion of evolutionary theory in school curricula. Each of these complex disputes turns, in part, on the meaning attributed to 'religion' and on the notion that it is a human right to hold religious beliefs which may lead to actions that are objectionable in the eyes of critics and opponents. This contestable character of religion presents a challenge to social theory because it does not fit easily into the theoretical categories employed by those social theorists and empirical investigators of religion who regard religion as a relatively simple, unitary institution or practice.

The main reason why some social theories have tended to be less than convincing in their accounts of religious phenomena is that they have framed religion as an object of social scientific or scholarly study in unhelpful ways. I mean that all too often theorists have taken religion as a relatively unproblematic unitary and homogeneous phenomenon that can be analysed and compared across time and space without proper consideration of its multi-faceted and socially constructed character. Talal Asad (1993: 29) refers to this conception of religion as a 'transhistorical essence'. There is no mystery about the reasons why religion has been taken as such a relatively straightforward object for social scientific analysis. The fact is that powerful agents in every known human society have made claims about the sacred significance of certain beliefs, objects, practices and people. The investment of hope, material resources and time in furthering their claims and in embodying them in would-be permanent institutions has been huge. The task of formalising, intellectualising and teaching them in the form of theologies has, at times, been a major social activity involving countless numbers of religious professionals and specialists. By the time at which sceptical social science began to emerge from various movements of Enlightenment in Western Europe and North America, the presumption that religions were taken-for-granted phenomena that were given in the nature of human cultures and societies had become virtually impregnable. Moreover, the academic study of theology, philosophy of religion and religious history had long been established at the heart of universities. Against this background it has been difficult for social scientists to justify an approach that would put aside the strongly institutionalised assumptions about the generic givenness of religion in favour of an investigation into how human beings produced, reproduced, modified, challenged and rejected what they regarded as religion.

Is religion generic?

To put my argument in its most radical form, I doubt whether it is helpful to theorise about 'religion', as if it were a generic object, when the aim is to produce social scientific analysis of the astonishingly varied phenomena to which people have historically attributed religious significance. From a social scientific point of view, it would be better to abandon the search for, and the assumption that there are, generic qualities of religion and, instead, to analyse the various situations in which religious meaning or significance is constructed, attributed or challenged. Susan Budd (1973) proposed a similar approach to the sociological understanding of religion but, as far as I know, she never developed her argument more fully. Her analysis of various definitions of religion suggested that 'religion is not a single phenomenon and consequently that research to establish what religion "is" or "does" is vain' (Budd 1973: 82). It follows that talk of the 'the role of religion in society' is unhelpful for two reasons. The first is that such a phrase masks the complexity and variety of things that count as religions. The second is that it obscures the complexity and variety of ways in which people *use* what they define as religious. To claim that there is a 'role' for religion is to simplify religion, society and human actors to such a degree that any generalisations about such a role run the risk of being either trite or indefensible in empirical terms.

A closely related argument against any attempt to seek a universal definition of religion is at the centre of Talal Asad's (1993) important project of uncovering, in the manner of genealogical research, the discursive processes through which definitions of religion have been framed differently over time. He stresses the way in which the exercise of power in many different areas of society has contributed to changing conceptions of religion, for 'Even Augustine held that although religious truth was eternal, the means for securing access to it were not' (Asad 1993: 35). This is why Asad attaches so much importance to the 'authorizing discourses' that, amongst other things, rejected 'pagan' practices from medieval Christianity, authenticated miracles and shrines, and regulated the creation of religious Orders. Modern authorising discourses in Christianity are centred, rather, on the authentication of, for example, individual vocations, individual beliefs and, most recently, individual rights – all of which are indirect reflections of changes in the State, in science, in law and in philosophical notions of the individual person. The implication of Asad's thesis is that any claims about the essential nature of a religion like Christianity are of dubious value because they obscure the historical development of the ways in which what counts as 'really religious' or 'truly Christian' are authorised, challenged and replaced over time. It also follows that historical changes in how the category of religion has been socially constructed affects, in turn, the interpretations that the holders of any particular notion of religion have about phenomena that they categorise as religious or not religious.

Some of the situations to which religious meanings are attributed involve the actions, feelings or ideas of human beings as individuals or in groups. Other situations involve the meanings and rules sedimented in institutions, organisations and communities. In practice, it is often beneficial to scrutinise the interaction between the meanings attributed to religion by individuals and groups *within* the confines of institutions and organisations. A good illustration would be the potential for tension that is experienced by military chaplains when their personal or professional sense of religious values and duties sits uneasily with the orders issued by their military superiors. A much more commonly experienced form of tension between individual and collective constructions of religious meaning occurs when individual members of religious organisations find that they cannot, in good conscience, comply with the organisations' codes of conduct. Those Roman Catholics who practise 'artificial' forms of birth control are a good case in point. Jehovah's Witnesses who deviate from the Watch Tower Society's prohibition against blood transfusions are another example. In neither of these illustrations is much to be gained from referring to the supposedly generic characteristics or functions of religion. Rather, each situation calls for explanation in terms of competing or clashing notions of religious truth, integrity, authority, obedience and so on. The exercise of power is at issue in each case.

Admittedly, the methodical analysis of how notions of religion are socially constructed and used in everyday life is likely to lead to inferences about *patterns* of conduct, thought and emotion. Indeed, rigorous observation, classification, comparison and testing may give rise to claims about the statistical probability of certain patterns. Nevertheless, there is rarely sufficiently convincing evidence to warrant generalisations about religion in all the varied settings in which its significance is claimed and successfully established. Yet, some social theorists tend to generalise about religion as if it were a single, invariant object that operates independently of human agents and agencies. In my view, however, social scientific analysis cannot safely go beyond the investigation of the *uses* to which notions of religion are put in social life. In case this creates misunderstanding, let me immediately add that I am not referring exclusively to individual uses of religion. I am also arguing that the notion of religion is constructed and used for all kinds of purposes by many *collective* agents such as the institutions of law, the State, the mass media, school education, health authorities and so on. Collectively warranted or legitimated constructions of religion operate in many areas of social life. They are often uncontroversial, but it is not uncommon for clashes to occur between competing criteria of religiousness and differing notions of what is acceptable in the name of religion. Heated disputes therefore occur in some countries over the question of whether students in State schools are permitted to wear any symbols of their religious identification or to conduct anything resembling prayer meetings on school premises. In other countries the disputes are about whether any religious activities other than those of the single authorised faith are permissible in public. There are also virtually ubiquitous disputes about the permissibility of appeals to religious reasons for dispensation from laws and contracts governing health treatments, use of drugs, scheduling of days of rest from paid work, divorce, child rearing practices, military service, and so on.

Now, you may object that there is nothing wrong with making theoretical statements about religion's essential properties or functions because such statements are merely short-hand or convenient ways of avoiding the need to specify precisely what 'religion' means for social scientific purposes. It would indeed be tedious, as well as stylistically awkward, if a moratorium were placed on the use of the word 'religion' unless it was always qualified with a phrase such as 'socially constructed notions of'. Simplicity and parsimony are at a premium in social theory. But my intention is not to legislate for the use of terms: only to encourage a better awareness of what is at stake when the term 'religion' appears in the writings of theorists and social scientists. I am advocating a form of prophylaxis that will help to keep social scientific discourse about religion to some degree free from the assumption that religion is an easily delimitable, invariant object that has a single, common sense meaning in everyday life. Against this view I want to argue that social scientists' analyses are all the more insightful and persuasive for being sceptical about common sense. Ideally, such analyses are critical, conceptually clear and rooted in sound evidence. This requires a sceptical attitude towards essentialist definitions of religion as well as towards high-level generalisations about religion and its supposedly generic properties. It also calls for clarity about the precise aspects of the phenomena regarded as religious that are under discussion – beliefs, feelings, actions, relationships, organisations and so on. In everyday life this high level of scepticism and precision would be entirely inappropriate, but it is essential for the purposes of social theorising and of studying the social aspects of what counts as religion at particular times and in particular settings. This line of reasoning is modelled on Max Weber's (1964: 118–19) warning against the use of high-level collective concepts such as 'family' and 'State' unless supportive evidence is available about the attitudes and actions of individuals and groups.[2]

The everyday and the scientific

What is the point of insisting that, for social scientific purposes, generic concepts of religion are unhelpful? Why do I think that it is necessary to stress the socially constructed character of religious phenomena? Part of my answer has to do with the need to establish a distinction between the social scientific approach and the everyday, relatively unquestioning acceptance that religion constitutes a generic object that exists in most societies under a variety of names such as Judaism, Sikhism, Islam or Christianity. While I do not wish to deny that generic similarities can be discerned between these complexes of beliefs, actions, emotions and organisations, my point is that their common status as religions does not go very far towards explaining how their followers think, feel and act, how other people regard their organisations, or how well their values influence social life. To answer these questions about social significance, it is necessary to descend from the generic level in order to examine precisely what each religion actually means in terms of social interaction and social significance at particular times and places. It may turn out, on closer inspection, that the differences between religions in terms of their expression in social life outweigh their supposedly shared characteristics. If so, then it might be more productive for explanatory purposes to focus on categories of, for example, ideology, world-view, culture or ethnicity. Thus, the fact that Shinto and Christianity conventionally belong to the category of religion may actually obscure the differences between their respective modes of operation in Japan. Specialists in comparative religion, history of religions and theology may take it for granted that religions constitute discrete objects sharing generic properties. Indeed, part of the professional mission of these specialist scholars is to elaborate the specific differences that occur within the generic type. In my view, however, social scientists do not need to make these assumptions and should be open to the possibility that the conventional boundaries between, say, religion, politics and ideology could be re-drawn in order to better understand particular situations.

Another reason for suspending belief in the idea that religion somehow exists independently from its social constructions is that there is little agreement on the meaning of the term 'religion'. Academic specialists in the study of religion are no less divided about its meaning than are members of the lay public. Admittedly, there is a measure of agreement these days about such things as belief in super-empirical entities or perception of the 'felt whole'. But this tendency to focus on the cognitive criteria for deciding what counts as religion is a modern and originally Western disposition. It is a historically and culturally specific tendency and, consequently, not a sound basis on which to mount claims about the universal meaning of religion. Moreover, the points of disagreement about definitions of religion are stubbornly persistent. In these circumstances, I can see no reason for social scientists to act as if 'real' religion existed somewhere beyond all the observable confusion and disagreement. The alternatives are either to stipulate a definition for religion in an intuitive fashion or to draw up a long list of defining characteristics or family resemblances. The former option has the advantage of being neat and tidy; but it also suffers from being more or less arbitrary. The latter option is more firmly rooted in evidence of social usage; but it runs the risk of giving rise to a template, a lowest common denominator or an 'average type' of religion. Both the stipulative strategy and the listing of defining characteristics can be useful for certain purposes, although neither of them is likely to impress true believers in the possibility of knowing the essence of religion. It is better, in my view, to recognise that an all-purpose, universally acceptable definition of religion is unattainable.

I would go further and argue that such a definition is not necessary for social scientific purposes. Given the wide extent of uncertainty and disagreement about what counts as religion in everyday life, it would be unwise for social scientists to intuit or to impose a definition of their own making, especially if it were restrictive. A better strategy is to map the varieties of meaning attributed to religion in social settings, to discern the relative frequency of the prevailing meanings and to monitor changes over time. In this way, the twin dangers of arbitrariness and narrow essentialism would be avoided. This strategy also offers the advantage of maintaining a close connection between everyday uses of the term 're-ligion' and the identification of religion as an object of social scientific study. I agree, therefore, with Susan Budd (1973: 84) that a good way forward is 'to try to discover what is "religious" and what is "secular" for each society and each group'. In short, the field or the topic of religion would follow the contours of existing usages but without making any assumptions about the possibility that 'real' or 'essential' religion might be lurking inside or behind these usages. Let me emphasise that my position is not one of nominalism. I am not prepared simply to nominate a meaning for 'religion'. On the contrary, I am advocating an approach that remains attentive to the uses that individual and collective actors make of the term.

If there is an objection to my strategy on the grounds that it fails to demarcate the boundaries of religion with sufficient clarity, my response is that the everyday practice of giving meaning to religion is itself unclear. The confusion or uncertainty in many people's minds is real and is not necessarily the result of faulty reasoning or misperception. And there is very little prospect that scholarly research into religion is going to remedy the uncertainty. Uncertainty about metaphysical issues is common among human beings who are fully capable of constructing meaning but who lack all the information that would be required to achieve metaphysical certainty. In other words, uncertainty about what religion really is does not pose a problem to social scientists: it merely challenges them to understand how so many human beings still manage to navigate life without achieving certainty about religion or religious issues. Judging by the huge efforts made by social scientists to make sense of the extreme *certainty* that large numbers of religionists display about their religious convictions, it seems to me that certainty about religion is even more of a challenge than uncertainty. Nothing can be taken for granted or at face value. Social scientists therefore search for clear and robust reasons for the strong religious convictions that they observe in some cases. Neither religious confusion nor religious certainty can be regarded as natural or given in the nature of things.

A further reason for being sceptical about the view that religion somehow exists independently of human constructions of its meaning is that the concept of religion is a second-order concept. It is an observer's construction that is supposedly based on the first-order beliefs, practices and experiences of human actors. To put this point more simply, many human actors have beliefs and experiences associated with, for example, the power of deities to influence human affairs or the sense of being in the presence of a supernatural power. Actors do not have generic or 'contentless' religious beliefs and experiences: they have beliefs and experiences with *particular* contents. Only in reflective moments do actors sometimes apply the label of religion to these beliefs and experiences. Similarly, social scientists do not observe religion directly: they analyse evidence of various beliefs, actions and experiences that they separately choose to categorise as religion. In short, the meaning of religion is not given in itself. It has to be attributed by human beings and is therefore variable. Incidentally, this argument is also connected with the reluctance of some Buddhists and others to accept that their particular philosophy of life amounts to a religion, as this term is commonly understood. They resist the application of this second-order construct to their first-order beliefs, experiences and practices because they have reasons for believing that conventional concepts of religion are not sufficiently discriminating. Many Hinayana Buddhists object to being lumped together with systems of belief in gods and spirits, claiming that the basis for their own convictions is not faith but reason and experience.

To sum up, debates about how to frame the concept of religion have a long history and are likely to persist into the foreseeable future, but I believe that, from a social scientific point of view, some of the debates have tended to go in unhelpful directions. This is, first, because the search for an all-purpose, 'correct' conceptualisation is not only in vain but also unwise in view of the immense variation in the meanings attributed to the term in everyday life. Second, the allure of a once-and-for-all concept may tempt some scholars into imposing their own formulation regardless of how well it actually accords with observed patterns of beliefs, experiences and practices. Third, it is important to guard against the danger of regarding definitions as mini-explanations. This occurs when explanations appear to follow 'by definition' from the characteristics of which the definition is composed.

The strategy that I am advocating avoids these difficulties (a) by insisting on a clear conceptual distinction between first-order and second-order notions of religion and (b) by aligning religion as an object of social scientific analysis with its usages in everyday social life and in institutional settings. The raw material that social scientists have to analyse consists mainly of social interactions, reported experiences, structures and practices for which religious meanings have been claimed or contested. There is no necessity for a more restrictive or inclusive approach, for nothing turns on this particular way of demarcating what counts as religion. Any claims about the distinctiveness of religious phenomena will therefore have to be based on evidence that is not just an effect of how religion is conceptualised or defined.

There is clearly a risk that my strategy will produce a totally relativistic and solipsistic view of religion. If I am suspending judgement about the essential meaning of religion and if I am identifying the field of religion with the meanings attributed to it in everyday life and institutional settings, it might seem as if 'anything goes'. Is there not a danger, then, that the term 'religion' could mean something different in every situation where it occurs? This would make it relativistic in the sense that its meaning was relative to the situations in which it was used. If this is so, might there not also be a danger that, by a process of *reductio ad absurdum*, entirely idiosyncratic and arbitrary uses of the term 'religion' would have to be taken as seriously as any others? For, if there is no reliable or Archimedean point of shared reference for the meaning of 'religion', perhaps one person's idiosyncratic idea is as good as any other. The risks of relativism and solipsism certainly have to be taken seriously, but they have no fatally damaging consequences for my social constructionist approach.

This is because, in the first place, I begin by making an analytic distinction between first-order and second-order constructs, thereby giving priority to evidence of the first-order meanings attributed to religion by individuals, groups, organisations and institutions. This means that the risk of absolute relativism and solipsism is strongly reduced by my insistence on taking evidence of *social* usage as my main point of reference. It follows that what counts as religion does not have arbitrary or solipsistic boundaries but is strongly aligned with a variety of social practices and arrangements that reflect the meanings commonly attributed to religion. A second reason why I do not believe that charges of relativism and solipsism will fatally undermine my approach to the social scientific study of religion is that I am careful to make a distinction between, on the one hand, claims that there must be a once-and-for-all essential concept of religion and, on the other, claims that it is possible to understand how differing notions of religion are generated, negotiated, warranted and reproduced in the course of social life and across time. For the purposes of social science, what is needed is sensitivity to the various forms of religious expression and the skill to relate them to features of the social and cultural contexts in which they occur. Questions about the 'real' meaning of religion can be safely left to philosophers, theologians and mystics, for there is no implication in my approach that the accumulation of social scientific insights into the ways in which people use religion will lead directly to claims about the essence of religion.

Another potential objection to the social constructionist approach that I am advocating to the social scientific study of religion is that it may give undue prominence to subjective thought and feelings about religion. Is there not a danger that, in focusing on evidence of the meanings attributed to religion in everyday life and institutional settings, the subjective opinions of individual human beings will dominate the picture, thereby ruling out the possibility of discovering anything worthwhile about the *collective* dimension of religion? Without wishing to deny that an excessively subjectivist approach to the study of religion might be problematic, I would argue that the shared meanings attributed to religion can be detected in many social and cultural processes, structures and products. They range from the most formal, legal determinations of what is allowed to count as religion for particular purposes to the much more informal assessments of how far certain beliefs or practices belong to one or more religious traditions. Religion is therefore 'real' in the sense of producing effects on some human lives and societies.

At the formal extreme, the United States Supreme Court interprets the US Federal Constitution with a view to ruling whether, say, the Commonwealth of Virginia's requirement that State schools should begin each day with a minute's silent reflection amounts to a breach of the First Amendment's establishment clause. Likewise, the British Independent Television Commission lays down standards governing the definition of religious organisations suitable for placing advertisements on commercial television broadcasts. Moreover, the Mexican Vice-Ministry of Religious Affairs makes decisions about which organisations will be officially designated as 'religious'. And my own research has uncovered the long drawn out processes whereby various prison services have come to stipulate that officers conducting searches of prisoners' belongings should treat religious artefacts with special respect.

At the other extreme, individuals sometimes have to decide whether a particular course of action falls inside or outside the boundary of what counts as their religion. How far are new reproductive technologies, for example, perceived as compatible with the basic teachings of various schools of Islam? What exactly counts as 'work' for Orthodox Jews who try to observe the prohibition on work after sunset on Fridays? In what ways is participation in Brazilian spiritist activities compatible with being a sincere Catholic? These examples show that ordinary people in their everyday lives have to make decisions about the categorisation of things as religious or not religious in particular circumstances. This does *not* mean that the decision-making is necessarily difficult or distressing. It is merely a fact of life that the question of where the boundary lies at any given moment presents itself with varying degrees of importance and urgency.

The social constructionist approach goes a long way towards averting the unhelpful consequences that flow from assuming that religion is a clearly demarcated object with generic properties. This approach is also in close alliance with the tendency of many social and cultural anthropologists to reject the idea that religions, like strong notions of culture, necessarily produce uniform effects on their practitioners. Instead of assuming that all members of faith communities think or act alike and that they do so because their religion somehow predisposes or programmes them in deterministic ways, the approach that I am advocating has an entirely different starting-point. It begins from the assumption that human beings are capable of learning to attribute meaning to the world around them and that in this venture some of them draw on what they consider to be religious resources. But there is nothing necessary or automatic about this interpretive process. In other words, the uses of religion are situational and highly variable. It would be wrong, therefore, to try to read off people's dispositions or sympathies merely from the knowledge that they are members (by birth, conversion, marriage or deception) of any particular religions. It would be safer and more rewarding to investigate precisely what they count as religious resources and how they translate them into beliefs, dispositions and actions *in particular situations*. The willingness to adopt a religious interpretation of events is likely to vary in strength from situation to situation. Similarly, the readiness to emphasise religious identity or religious values is not necessarily a constant: it also varies with the situation. And there are even variations in how the most devout people choose to foreground their religion. Yet, this does not mean that the 'performance' of religion is always a cynical matter of identity management. It merely means that giving expression to religion involves subtle and complex choices that respond, in part, to the perceived situation, the actions of significant others and the actor's stock of religious resources.

Moreover, the subtlety and complexity of the processes involved in the use of religious resources are not only in the eye of the social scientific beholder but can also be in the consciousness of actors. For example, numerous studies have examined the ways in which young Muslims *knowingly* select and apply elements of Islam and of their parental cultures to everyday situations in France (Khosrokhavar 1997; Césari 1998) and the UK (Jacobsen 1998; Butler 2001). Their adaptations and innovations, far from being imposed on these young people or merely reproduced in a mechanical fashion, are actually the subject of discussions and dispute with parents, kin, friends and community leaders. Young Muslims are aware of their own efforts to construct images of Islam and ways of being Muslim which are appropriate to different situations in France and Britain without compromising the idea of being Muslim. They cultivate Muslim identities, but it would be misleading to refer to the result as if it were 'a Muslim identity' that was necessarily shared by all Muslims (Vertovec 1994). In other words, their own sense of belonging to a group may be at odds with the criteria that other people use to categorise Muslims. The distinction between 'group' and 'category' cannot be rigid, however, since a dialectical relation operates between self-identity and external categorisations (Jenkins 1997: 55).

Careful research would investigate precisely how, in particular situations, actors negotiate a balance between identity based on a sense of belonging to a group and identity based on the categories employed by others and selectively adapted by self. The experience of tension between group and category can be disturbing, as I discovered among ex-members of controversial new religious movements (Beckford 1985a). My informants often talked enthusiastically and with a strong sense of nostalgia about the other members of the small cliques and friendship groups to which they had belonged. They tended to regard their participation in these small groups as a valuable contribution towards their self-identity. Yet, they expressed strong reservations about the way in which leaders of the movements and outsiders categorised them as members. They objected to journalistic categorisations of them as brainwashed zombies; and they were uneasy with the leaders' categorisation of them as deployable and compliant workers. The consolations of identification with a group were powerful enough to keep some of these ex-members active in their movements for several years, but disillusionment and defection set in quickly when their small groups collapsed or were deliberately disbanded. The ex-members were not prepared to put up with unwelcome categorisation unless it was offset or underpinned by a group identity. The tension between group and category was more easily bearable in some situations (such as fund-raising in small teams) than in others (such as domestic work in leaders' homes). This is because fund-raising was usually a 'team' activity involving close relations among team members for many hours a day and over long periods of time. Each team's sense of group identity also depended on how well it performed in comparison with other teams competing for the highest rates of success, as measured by the donations received.

Other research that I have conducted on prison chaplaincy (Beckford & Gilliat 1998) shows that the dialectic between group-identity and categorisation does not always favour the small group. For example, the Prison Service of England and Wales allocates each prisoner to one of many religious categories or to the category of 'no religion'. This categorisation, based on prisoners' answers to a question about the religion to which they belong, does not permit membership of more than one religion; nor does it allow for differences between the 'sects' or 'schools', with the exception of Christianity, that exist in all major religions. To put it crudely, 'a Buddhist is a Buddhist is a Buddhist' as far as the Prison Service is concerned, regardless of the different types of Buddhism that prisoners practise, whereas Christian prisoners can register as, for example, Jehovah's Witnesses, Methodists or Anglicans among others.

Another reason for challenging the apparently commonsensical idea that religion is a clearly demarcated object that determines many aspects of its practitioners' lives is that phenomena widely considered religious are not confined within the boundaries of particular institutions or organisations. Yet, not only common sense but also the findings of many empirical research projects have tended to reinforce the image of religion as a generic object by reducing it to its most visible expressions in the

form of institutionalised beliefs and practices. To regard religious organisations and their members as the sole source of evidence about religion
has methodological advantages in the sense that social scientists do not
have to waste time deciding what is to count as religion. It is highly convenient to be able to limit, by definition, the category of religion to visible organisations. This is because churches, denominations, synagogues,
gurdwaras, mosques, and temples usually monitor changing levels of participation in their activities and can, therefore, provide reliable statistical
evidence of, for example, membership, attendance and financial donations. They seem to represent religion in an unproblematic fashion. And
this is true in many respects. But what is convenient is not necessarily
helpful in terms of sensitising social scientists to the religious significance
attributed to beliefs and actions that bear, at best, a distant relation to
organised religions. This was the central point of Thomas Luckmann's
(1967) criticism of those sociologists of religion who were so preoccupied
with 'church oriented religion' that they could not see the religious significance of phenomena lying outside the control of religious organisations.
Subsequent inquiries into 'implicit religion' (Bailey 1997, 1998), 'folk religion' (Clark 1982), 'common religion' (Towler 1974) 'diffused religion'
(Cipriani 1989), 'conventional religion' (Towler 1984) and 'customary
religion' (Hornsby-Smith, Lee and Reilly 1985) have reinforced the wisdom of Luckmann's belief that studies of churches could not exhaust all
the interesting expressions of religion.

Another way of raising questions about the 'invisible religion' or the
diffusion of sacred sites in late-modern societies is to examine the content of consumer culture, popular culture and mass culture. In a variety of
attempts to break away from intellectualist assumptions about the necessary centrality of belief to religion, sociologists and anthropologists have
sought evidence that religious and sacred significance can be attributed to
moments of collective effervescence such as rock music festivals (Mellor
and Shilling 1997), moments of collective solemnity such as the funeral
of Diana, Princess of Wales (Walter 2001) and even the consumption
of commodities. According to Featherstone (1991: 121) 'consumer culture has not resulted in the eclipse of the sacred by a debased materialism'. Indeed, everyday life continues to generate what Luckmann (1990)
calls 'little transcendences' outside the confines or the control of religious organisations. This area clearly offers scope for more fruitful cross-
fertilisation between studies of religion and studies of the uses made of
non-elite cultures.

I am not criticising social scientists for studying religious organisations
and other institutionalised expressions of religion. On the contrary, such
studies are the core of research into religion. The point that I am making here is different. It is simply that 'organised religion', in the form

of, for example, activities conducted in denominations, synagogues, fraternities and mosques is not the entire picture. The label of 'religion' is applied to a vast range of social arrangements and practices partially or wholly outside the sphere of religious organisations. Moreover, the study of religious organisations runs the risk of implying that all participants in these organisations think, feel and act alike. Careful research minimises this risk, but there are still practical and methodological advantages in focusing social scientific investigations on the most visible and accessible 'sites' of religion. For example, interest is currently high among some social scientists in the religious and/or ethnic identity of migrants from less prosperous regions of the world to advanced industrial societies. It makes good sense to focus such research on so-called ethnic congregations where researchers can easily gain access to informants and their social networks (Warner & Wittner 1997). Invaluable information about complex patterns of continuity, change and conflict in religious and ethnic identity has flowed from studies grounded in ethnic congregations of Christians and in analogous organisations in other faith communities (Williams 1988; Ebaugh & Chafetz 2000).

Yet, by definition, such research projects struggle to do justice to the experience of migrants and settlers who do *not* associate with 'community' organisations or who leave them after a short interval. Since there is no convenient way of reaching them through ethnic congregations; and since their numbers are too small to show up in samples of the general population, they become virtually invisible to researchers.

This discussion of theoretical approaches and research methods has been lengthy, but it is essential to be clear about the central issue. The apparently commonsensical and methodologically convenient practice of focusing research on organised groups of religionists has two unfortunate effects on social scientific studies of religion. The first is that it systematically downplays the significance of the religious beliefs, practices and identities that are not expressed through formal groups. The second is that it distracts attention from questions about the representativeness or numerical significance of religious organisations. This problem is not entirely unique to the sociology of religion but it is aggravated by the fact that it is extremely hard to obtain funding for research on aspects of religion that lie outside the boundaries of religious organisations.

Conclusion

I would like to conclude by clarifying the sense in which I use 'social construction' in this book. There is no intention to deny *a priori* the possibility that the divine or supernatural powers on which most religious faith is usually said to rest actually exist. My position is closer to that of the methodological agnostic who argues that, in the absence of compelling proof of the existence of these powers independently of human agents and agencies, the best course of action is to put aside questions about the reality of their existence and to concentrate, instead, on less problematic questions about the uses that human beings make of religion. This approach leaves open the possibility that divine or supernatural powers may affect human life directly. For sound methodological reasons, however, my approach limits its scope to the analysis of the ways in which human beings express what they regard as religious ideas and sentiments in social and cultural forms. Finally, I would like to emphasise the fact that my approach differs markedly from the approach of Peter Berger and Thomas Luckmann. Their work rests on assumptions about the 'anthropological necessity' for human beings to fend off chaos by socially constructing sacred frames of meaning. It posits a phenomenology of mental categories that are supposedly constitutive of all human meaning. These issues fall outside the scope of this book.

2 Secularisation

Introduction

If theories are defined in rigorous terms, then *social* theories are rare; and social theories of *religion* are even rarer. But what are 'theories'? A widely accepted, if dated, view is that theories are sets of assumptions, initial conditions and logically interrelated propositions from which testable hypotheses can be derived. This is an admittedly extreme example of how to define theories. It is fairly representative, however, of ideas that dominated the philosophy of science and, by extension, the philosophy of social science in the mid-twentieth century. It was fashionable then to assume that the intellectual power of the 'hard' sciences such as physics and chemistry depended on the continuous process of formulating, testing and reformulating theories (the hypothetico-deductive method) in the desire to make their generalisations applicable to more and more phenomena. Leaving aside all variations in the understanding of these so-called propositional theories (but see Zetterberg 1965), the opinions of philosophers and historians of science have subsequently become much more divided about the status and character of theory in scientific work.

Although the popularity of rigorous propositional theories was never strong among philosophers of *social* science, there is a lingering respect, if not nostalgia in some places, for at least the ideal of being able to state important generalisations about social phenomena in the form of logically interrelated propositions (see, for example, Wallace 1969; Stark & Bainbridge 1987). Of course, there is no need to claim that social scientists actually conduct research in accordance with the hypothetico-deductive method, but there is no doubt that clarity of expression and rigour can be served by the discipline of having to present theoretical ideas in logically sound sequences.

In fact, the second half of the twentieth century witnessed a steady erosion of reliance on propositional theories outside the disciplines of economics and the field of game theory in political science and international relations. For a wide variety of reasons justification of social science as an intellectual enterprise came to rest less on models originating in physics and chemistry and more on interpretative strategies with roots in historiography, literacy criticism, linguistics, and humanistic psychology. 'Theory' in these contexts tended to favour sensitivity to human values, meanings and intentions rather than the search for law-like generalisations that transcended social particularities. Following the 'cultural turn' that deeply affected social sciences in the 1960s, the meaning of social theory moved in two different directions simultaneously. On the one hand, there was a partial revival of 'grand theories' in the sense of high-level constructions of the master characteristics or driving forces of social formations. This was accompanied in some cases by metaphysical speculation about the nature of human societies and the corresponding methods of studying them. On the other hand, theory confined itself to the elaboration of concepts, with little or no attempt to arrange them in logical sequences. Indeed, feelings of suspicion towards propositional theories were strong, on the grounds that they systematically abandoned evidence of social differences, cultural richness and playfulness for the sake of defending rigorous, but possibly trite or sterile, generalisations.

The treatment of *religion* in social theory conforms in many respects with my rough and ready presentation of change in the meaning attributed to 'theory' in the social sciences. 'Grand' social theories continue to take account of religion with varying degrees of seriousness and reliability, although it is uncommon for religion to be as near the centre of such theoretical preoccupations as it used to be in the late nineteenth and early twentieth centuries. Propositional theories have been extremely rare, but the hypothetico-deductive model of social science nevertheless remains implicit in the design and presentation of research that typically uses questionnaire surveys or the secondary analysis of quantitative data about reported religious beliefs, practices and opinions. By comparison, the elaboration and critical refinement of concepts is a major aspect of theorising about religion – sometimes in conjunction with analyses of empirical evidence and at other times as a free-standing enterprise.

Theories about religion in terms of its social characteristics (which is a more accurate label than 'social theories of religion') have often involved ideas about the *decline* or negation of religion. This indicates a major difference from the social scientific study of, say, health or education. Whereas interest is high in the social distribution of poor health and low standards of educational provision, the eclipse of health or education as forms of social activity is not a common topic for research. By contrast, one can sometimes gain the impression that the social scientific study of religion is *centrally* concerned with the decline, erosion or eclipse of religion. Indeed, the prospect of its decline seems to motivate some researchers to study religion. An influential article by Jeffrey Hadden (1987) argued that 'secularisation' had never amounted to a testable theory but had simply been a taken-for-granted ideological reflex of antagonism towards religion and rationalist assumptions about modernity. It was allegedly a 'doctrine' and an 'ideological bias' that was 'deeply internalized in the minds of our European and American founding fathers' and 'is still firmly entrenched in the minds of contemporary sociologists' (Hadden 1987: 595). Many other commentators have remarked on the irony that religion appears to call for systematic study precisely because it is doomed to extinction. This is supposedly one of the main reasons why the subject of secularisation lies so close to the centre of sociological approaches to religion. Anthropological and psychological approaches show less interest in secularisation. But what does 'secularisation' actually mean?

It would be completely at odds with the spirit of this book if I tried to stipulate a definition of secularisation that would resolve all the disputes about the concept's meaning and application. It is undoubtedly necessary to have a preliminary agreement about the boundaries of the phenomenon in question, but it would be counterproductive to go further at this stage. Let me make it clear, then, that for my purposes studies of secularisation have tended to assess the extent to which, and the ways in which, the influence of religion has declined over time in one or more of the following areas: the lives of individuals, culture and social institutions. At this stage in my argument, very little depends on this stipulation. It merely marks the outer limits of the debates about secularisation without biasing or prejudicing any of the points in contention. Nevertheless, as my argument unfolds, it will become apparent that many of the terms used in my stipulation can be contentious in certain circumstances. The fact is that there is no neutral language in which all terms are innocent or not freighted with connotations that are objectionable in the opinion of some critics. In other words, 'secularisation' is one of those essentially contested concepts (Gallie 1955) that are simultaneously central to academic debate *and* inherently problematic. My response to this difficulty is neither to turn my back on disputes about secularisation ('a plague on all your houses') nor to seek a way of avoiding them by adopting an apparently less problematic term ('religious change'). Instead, I intend to explore and to lay bare the variety of conceptual strategies and logical moves that have been made in discussions of secularisation as a way of demonstrating how challenging the study of religion can be to social theorists.

I shall outline the historical roots of the concern with secularisation before mapping the principal contours of recent debates about secularisation in the social sciences. My aim will be to show that secularisation became, and remains, of interest to social theorists because of contextual ideas about the nature of the social upheavals and transformations that have taken place in many societies since the late eighteenth century. Continuing debates about the scope, speed and direction of major social changes have kept the issue of secularisation alive, albeit in some new and unexpected forms. While some aspects of debates about secularisation strike me as unpromising if assessed solely in terms of their capacity to spark off rewarding research, other aspects present some interesting challenges that may lead to valuable insights into the changing uses of religion in the early twenty-first century. Following the 'social constructionist' line of reasoning developed in Chapter One I shall argue that one of sociology's most important tasks is to investigate the changes in meaning attributed to 'secularisation' at different times and places. The boundary between the religious and the secular is by no means clear, fixed or impermeable. It is a highly contestable social construction. My conclusion will nevertheless be that notions of secularisation, suitably clarified and situated in the contexts from which they arose, have an important heuristic role to play in social theorising about religion. In short, secularisation may be good for social theories of religion.

History of the concept

'Secularisation' is akin to many key notions in social science in the sense that it has been adapted from usage that can be traced back to Roman civilisation and to subsequent applications in the law governing the medieval Catholic Church. Indeed, the adoption of Christianity as one of the religions of the late Roman Empire was an early proof of the separation of religious and political authorities, thereby setting the scene for subsequent elaboration of the idea that the category of the secular could be distinguished from that of the sacred. And the Church employed the term 'secular' to designate priests ordained to work outside the authority of religious orders.

Whereas the term 'secularisation' had previously referred to the process of releasing priests from their vows, the new meanings that it took on in the early modern period referred to relations between religious institutions and the spheres of politics and commerce, which were gaining independence from religious control at that time. There was nothing inevitable about this evolution, but it is not difficult to trace the course of the many currents of ideas that eventually flowed into the main streams of social scientific thinking about religion and secularisation. I stress the plurality of streams. And some of them flowed against the others. Moreover, the relations between the sacred and the secular were far from being the sole preserve of elite thinkers; they were the very stuff of practical politics throughout the medieval period of European history and were evident in the history of some regions of Asia as well.

It was in the territories where variants of Protestantism became dominant that the early modern State found its strongest political and religious justification. Lutheran doctrines of the Two Kingdoms and the more radical doctrines that developed in Holland and England concerning the sovereignty of groupings based on social contracts or binding covenants indirectly made it easier to conceive of a distinction between the realms of religion and the secular. The English State, under Henry VIII, forcibly removed property, functions and status from the Catholic Church (and from what became the Church of England) by acts of 'secularisation', thereby stamping a modern meaning on the term and establishing legal boundaries between what was in the sphere of religion and what was not.

When seventeenth-century philosophers and legal theorists in Europe formulated ideas about the relation between Churches, monarchy and the early modern State, many of the present-day problematics of secularisation began to take shape. The revolutionary possibility of constituting nations as collectivities of citizens, freely contracting to unite under the rulers of their own choice and within the law, helped to create the conditions in which the separation in principle between religion and non-religion became not only thinkable but also allegedly essential to the well-being of countries as different as the USA, France and, much later, the Soviet Union. Even today, however, controversy surrounds any attempt to argue that these instances of deliberate secularisation, or laicisation, necessarily depressed the level of religious belief, feeling and practice among the populations of these three countries.

Advances in scientific thinking in the late eighteenth century also contributed strongly towards new ways of conceptualising the boundary between religion and non-religion. Radical atheism was still confined to a tiny minority of thinkers and remained politically risky in view of the laws that continued to require religious conformity in some European countries as a condition of access to civil liberties and participation in the emerging public sphere. But in the course of the nineteenth century, and particularly under the auspices of positivism, socialism, theories of evolution and liberal biblical criticism, the idea that religious and secular views of the world were *opposed* to each other gathered momentum. The subsequent influence of ideas shaped by Marx, Nietzsche, Freud and relativistic theories of physics further sharpened the religious/secular opposition, thereby taking the distinctiveness between the religious and the secular one stage further.

It is highly significant from my point of view that the first programmatic attempts to identify secularisation, in the sense of the declining
significance of religion, as a key feature of societal development in the
mid-nineteenth century, occurred in the context of ambitious efforts to
characterise the novelty of industrial, capitalist or modern societies. It
was as if secularisation, in its many different formulations, had been
the midwife or the catalyst of what, for the sake of simplicity, I shall
call 'modernity'.[1] A recurrent theme, in the otherwise widely differing
accounts of the causes and concomitants of the transformations that
had supposedly taken place in the foundations of societies undergoing modernisation, was the progressive widening of a gap between the
religious and the secular spheres. Secularisation was not incidental to
the main vectors of change: it was pivotal in some accounts. Moreover,
agreement about the central significance of secularisation was not confined to theoretical schemes that welcomed the decline of religion's social significance as a condition of progress or improvement. Even the
ideological opponents of secularisation felt obliged to account for the
declining significance of religion. Yet, there were widely differing interpretations of the meaning of religion and secularisation, and the lineal
descendants of these variations are still discernible in today's sociological
debates.

A detailed analysis of all the formative currents of thought about religion and secularisation is not necessary in this context (see Tschannen
1992). A more productive way forward for my purposes is merely to identify some of the most influential strands of social thought without paying
attention to the ways in which thinkers packaged them as distinct theories. These strands overlapped and formed complicated patterns within
the broader fabric of theories about social change. I have grouped them
under the six headings of structural differentiation, empiricism and scientific ideas, inner dynamics of religion, liberal visions, Marxism and
Freudianism.

1. The first strand of thought about religion and secularisation that was
to be influential for the development of social theory centres on the notion
of *structural differentiation* as the motive force of evolutionary change. Despite their differences, Henri de Saint Simon, Auguste Comte, Herbert
Spencer and Emile Durkheim all subscribed to variations on the theme
that human societies and cultures pass through various stages of evolution. The direction of change is from the relatively simple to the relatively
complex. The consequence of evolutionary change for religion is that it
ceases to function as the regulatory code for all social life and becomes, instead, an increasingly separate institution with the more limited function
of explaining and legitimating the prevalent form of society.

2. A second, influential strand of thinking about religion and secularisation centres on a variety of claims about the capacity of *empiricist and scientific ideas* to demonstrate the implausibility and weaknesses of religion and to replace it with ways of thinking grounded in confirmed experience and reason. The mixed pedigree of this triumphalist view includes the French Encyclopaedists and the Scottish Enlightenment thinkers. David Hume's faith in human reason was perhaps emblematic of this approach. Anticipating the theory of cognitive dissonance, Hume attributed belief in miracles to an illogical refusal to abandon religious dogma in the face of inconvenient facts. Far from breaking the laws of nature, he argued, the evidence of putative miracles merely confirmed the laws. Nor did he believe that the law-like regularities of the natural world supported belief in a God-like designer. On the contrary, he claimed that there were many freaks of nature; and the effects of natural forces were not overwhelmingly benign from the point of view of human beings. He conceded that it is understandable for the human mind, which is accustomed to looking for cause-effect relations, to infer the existence of a divine intelligence capable of bringing about the regulation of nature. But Hume doubted whether the evidence on which such an inference could be soundly made was convincing. He would go no further in his *Dialogues Concerning Natural Religion* than admitting the possibility of an analogy between the causes of natural order and the intelligence of human beings. Moreover, he was reluctant to accept that belief in a monotheistic deity fostered sensible and tolerant politics. His argument in *The Natural History of Religion* was that monotheistic religions tended to be associated with irrational fanaticism and intolerance towards minorities. A similar expression of disdain and mockery towards the harmful effects of strongly held religious convictions was also characteristic of the most outspoken freethinkers who contributed to the French *Encyclopédie* in the mid-eighteenth century.

Yet, one of the surprising features of sociological debates about secularisation is that

they have tended to overlook, omit or deliberately ignore the significance of both organised and diffuse attacks on religion. It is as if the progress of secularisation could be adequately accounted for in terms of the effect of abstract social and cultural forces, such as class struggle or functional differentiation, without consideration of the agents and agencies that actively campaigned for secularism and secular societies. Given that a wide range of campaigns, movements and voluntary associations promoted secularism, rationalism, atheism and humanism in Britain and elsewhere, it is important to consider their direct and indirect contributions to secularisation *and* to interpretations of secularisation. (Campbell 1971)

Susan Budd (1977) claimed that atheist and agnostic organisations have never been large or socially influential, but that the ideas on which they are based 'are for the most part very dominant in our society' (Budd 1977: 2). This apparent paradox is resolved by acknowledging that many 'ordinary people' accepted irreligious ideas without needing to be persuaded by irreligious organisations. In other words, secularisation had already affected culture in the UK to the point where it was no longer necessary for secularist organisations to be large and publicly prominent. The spread of free-thought is the centrepiece of this approach to the social construction of the boundary between the religious and the secular.

3. A third influential strand of social theory concerns the inner *dynamics of religion*, particularly Christianity. Drawing on specialised studies in the history of religions, comparative religion, historical linguistics and theology, Max Weber and Ernst Troeltsch explored the complex interaction of cultural and material factors that explained ideal-typical developments in religions. They shared a common fascination with the social dynamics of religion in general and with the specific issue of the 'conservation of religious energy' in particular. This is my inelegant way of characterising their concern with the ways in which religious inspiration and enthusiasm are institutionalised, are revived from time to time, but are eventually routinised in forms which compromise their vitality or purity. In Troeltsch's case, this concern with what could be called 'religious entropy', or a tendency towards disorder and inertness, related to the fate of liberal Protestantism, especially its social ethics, in the early twentieth century when he correctly perceived a growing threat from relativism, nihilism and other extreme positions (Séguy 1980). In Weber's case, a central preoccupation was with the close but ironic relationship that he detected between religions and rationality.

4. A fourth, and closely related, strand of thinking about secularisation had its origins in *liberal visions* of social and political order, individual rights and Christian theology. To be more accurate, many different, and not always mutually compatible, strands of liberalism have contributed towards various narratives about the weakening hold of religious ideas and of religious organisations on the lives of individuals. To go back no further than the late seventeenth century, John Locke gave reasoned expression to ideas about the benefits that he expected to flow to individuals and to collective life from honouring what he regarded as the natural right of human beings to choose their form of polity, their political rulers, their ways of making a living, and their religion. Religious toleration was therefore a condition and a consequence of Locke's influential liberalism. By the middle of the nineteenth century, John Stuart Mill could argue that

a liberal state had no right to impose any particular form of religion on individuals and that it should remain neutral towards all religions. The spirit of Mill's liberalism continues to animate the 'in principle' opposition to, for example, Church–State alliances and compulsory religious education in schools.

5. A *Marxist* strand of thinking about religion and secularisation has been heavily influential in some places but virtually unknown in others. There were, in fact, two separate threads in this strand. The first had its philosophical roots in radical Hegelianism and reflected the belief that the rational human spirit was progressively unfolding or realising itself in history through the combination of reason and Christianity. The aim was to strip away the theological and religious obstacles to the full realisation of human reason's power to explain and to improve the world. In effect, idealistic philosophy was to be the instrument for changing the world. The second, much more materialist, thread held that religion had been corrupted and co-opted by the ruling classes of every social formation but that, after the destruction of capitalism, the mysteries of religious ideologies would no longer be necessary or credible in social formations lacking class exploitation and division. Marx expected that the transparency of social relations under socialism would dispense with the need for religious mystification. The instrument of these changes was to be a dynamic combination of self-critical socialist theory and socialist practice – the liberal philosophical approach could not deal with the root cause of human distress and injustice, namely, social class oppression.

Secularisation was not an original or necessary component of Marxist ideology in the nineteenth century, but the political implementation of Marxist-inspired state socialism and communism ensured that the significance of religions in both the private and the public spheres would be greatly reduced. To adapt Chadwick's (1975) comment, Marxism was among the powerful assaults on religion in the twentieth century. Yet, it is also necessary to add that various neo-Hegelian-influenced currents of Marxist philosophy have continued to underwrite intellectual and practical initiatives such as the Worker Priest movements, Liberation Theology and Theologies of Struggle.

6. A good case could be made for including *Sigmund Freud's* ideas under the heading of the empiricist and scientific strand of thinking, but this would not do justice to the distinctiveness of his position. This is not only because his approach to religion owed very little to empiricism but also because his account of religion introduced notions of depth psychology and psychoanalysis that were alien to many other scientific critics of religion. Indeed, Freud introduced a largely novel dimension, the realm of the

unconscious, into studies of religion. Moreover, his insistence on relating the development of the individual's conscious *and* unconscious mind to psycho-sexual experience before birth and during childhood seemed to preclude the possibility that religion could be grounded in any other cultural or social (to say nothing of supernatural) reality. Freud's approach to religion was therefore radical in several different ways; and its implications for understanding the future of religion at the level of human societies as well as individual psychology were drastic.

His work also happened to open up entirely new perspectives on the reasons for the persistence of religion in human cultures and on the reasons for its survival in the minds of individuals. Yet, Freud never concealed his personal and professional preference for a state of affairs in which religion would cease to operate at both the cultural and the individual level. This left him vulnerable to, but never defensive about, the charge of being ideologically biased against religion in all its manifestations. 'He had been a consistent militant atheist since his schooldays', according to Peter Gay (1988: 525–6) 'mocking God and religion, not sparing the God and the religion of his family . . . All his life he thought that it was not atheism that needed explaining but religious belief'. The critical responses to Freud's ideas about religion have therefore become an integral part of the debates about secularisation, even though he did not seek to make a direct contribution to them. Nor did he favour the incorporation of his views on religion into systems of theology or into religiously inspired therapeutic practices. This has not, however, deterred theologians and therapists from constructing systems of thought that combine elements of religion and Freudian psychoanalysis. In a curious way, then, Freud and the hugely varied group of specialists who have made theoretical and clinical applications of his work are part of the 'data' about secularisation: not just commentators on it. By the very act of keeping Freud's ideas alive they have become part of the evidence about the decline or the persistence of religion. At the level of psychological generality, Freud offered a series of insights into the function of religion to permit expression of tensions and conflicts in the unconscious mind of individuals. Religion, as one of the neurotic by-products of the conflict between the unconscious and conscious realms of mind, held considerable interest for Freud because it provided a valuable insight into common responses to psychological conflict and into the conditions in which neuroses could either become intolerable or be overcome. The search for the deep conflicts that allegedly give rise to religious forms of neurosis is at the centre of the psychoanalytical method of exposing the conflict and its repressions in order to strengthen the personality and improve psychological health.

A third level of Freudian analysis deals with religion in culture and society. Starting from the view that religion is 'the universal obsessional neurosis' Freud and, more importantly, many of his followers attempted to understand the persistent hold that religion still exercised over large numbers of people. The main argument articulates, on the one hand, deep psychological conflicts between unconscious drives and devices for repressing them with, on the other, social and cultural forces that tend to suppress potentially destructive patterns of thought and conduct. Features of modern, industrial society were regarded as exceptionally suppressive and therefore productive of neuroses, including religion.

Freud believed that, with maturity and rationality, human beings were capable of outgrowing and therefore overcoming their neurotic dependence on religious fantasies and myths. Likewise, at the level of social relations and culture, Freud believed in the possibility of evolutionary developments that would relegate religion to the status of a minor weakness. Freud's view that science was antithetical to religion in both individuals and societies therefore contributed directly and positively not only to broader currents of thought about secularisation but also to anti-religious sentiment. Moreover, Freud's legacy is not just a theoretical reflection on secularisation: it is also, and more importantly, a mainstay of extremely widespread, albeit contestable, assumptions and practices that help to shape the daily lives of countless people in many societies. In this respect, Freudian psychology is one of the forces undermining the social and cultural significance of religion.

It should be clear from this selective survey of the meanings associated with 'secularisation' in the formative period of social theory that the concept was integral to some widely differing ideas about social change and its religious concomitants. A number of general points emerge from the survey.

1. Concern with the *conceptualisation* and definition of religion was relatively low in these general accounts of religious change. For most purposes, the term 'religion' was used interchangeably with 'Christianity', 'Christian beliefs' or 'Christian churches', although some writers sought to make analytical distinctions between popular religion and formal religion, or between religious belief and religious practice.

2. None of these currents of thought assigns *priority* to religion or to religious decline as the motive force of social and cultural change. In most cases, religion is treated as a function of its social and cultural environment or as a product of psychological processes. Only in work on the inner dynamics of religious systems is there a more even-handed approach to the capacity of religion to act independently on its environment.

3. Although 'secularisation' and its cognate terms appeared frequently in some of these accounts of social change, the focus of analysis was primarily on *other issues* – except in the work of Weber, Troeltsch and the later writings of Durkheim. The principal issue was the nature of the changes that seemed to be transforming many aspects of life in societies that were coming to be labelled 'industrial', 'capitalist' or 'modern'. Even Freud's preoccupation with civilisation transcended the boundaries of individual and group psychology.

4. The interest in social transformation and religious change was not purely intellectual or theoretical. On the contrary, with the exception of Max Weber, many of the major contributors to discussion about these issues were involved in *political and practical schemes* to clarify, obstruct or assist the decline of religion's significance. What was at stake was not simply a dispassionate theoretical understanding of religious change but, more importantly, an opportunity to affect the pace, direction and outcome of change.

In sum, the modern notion of 'secularisation' never had a unitary meaning and was not the central focus of any rigorous study of religious change. Concern with the putative decline of religion was a mainly incidental effect of much broader questions about the character of industrial, capitalist or modern societies. In some cases, these questions were inseparable from debates about the value of religion and campaigns for its control and/or its suppression. The 'stakes' were immensely varied, even going to the heart of political struggles for power in some countries. For example, programmes of 'laïcité' in early twentieth-century France imposed a settlement on long-running difficulties in relations between the Catholic Church and the State (Poulat 1987; Baubérot 1990a). In these circumstances, and in countries such as Brazil, Mexico and Italy, where religion-State relations were also difficult and occasionally violent in the formative stages of statehood, there was very little incentive to try to make careful distinctions between the factors affecting religious change.

It is important to emphasise the point that notions of secularisation originated in philosophically disputatious and ideologically charged settings. There was never a moment in the formative period of the social and human sciences when questions about the trajectory of religious beliefs, practice and influences did not carry, explicitly or implicitly, a strong ideological charge. These questions were at the very centre of debates and disputes about relations between modern States, especially republics, and the societies that they controlled. They were also integral to the complex controversies about the growing authority of science, scientific institutions and organisations representing the professions. And they were inseparable from arguments about the scope for individual judgement in matters of social reform, personal morality and self-responsibility.

Consequently, the suggestion that it is somehow illicit nowadays to allow an ideological bias to creep into uses of the concept of secularisation seems ironic. In my opinion, the term has been suffused with ideological significance, positive *and* negative, from its earliest usage.

Secularisation took on the appearance of an ideologically neutral concept only in the mid-twentieth century when, largely under the influence of attempts to produce would-be universal sets of theoretical concepts for depicting modernisation and modernity, empirical evidence was adduced in support of the idea that religion was bound to decline in countries following the pattern of political, economic and social development displayed by the advanced industrial societies. Notions such as 'the logic of industrialism', 'the convergence' of industrialising societies on the model of the USA, and the reportedly timeless 'functions' of certain social institutions all contributed towards a sense of confidence that social scientists had finally discovered some universal regularities in social life.

I believe that this was a misguided project because it wrongly assumed that religion was a unitary phenomenon, the strengths and weaknesses of which could be, in principle, gauged at any moment in time. It also ignored the fact that notions of the religious and the secular were social constructions that did not represent a fixed reality lurking behind the concepts. Empirical investigations of secularisation cannot therefore escape from the web of variable meanings that it carries in different theoretical perspectives. There is no archimedean point from which to judge the superiority of one concept over the others. But there are many ways of testing the coherence of concepts and of assessing the degree of support that they receive from information that counts as evidence from their own point of view.

It was in the 1960s, then, that the first methodical attempts were made to work out the implications of the logic of advanced industrial societies for religion and secularisation. At the same time, some sociologists sought alternative ways of constituting religion as an object of sociological analysis, either in a critical reaction against the prevailing views of modernity or in pursuit of new perspectives on it.[2] The next section will review the loose clusters of theoretical ideas that have guided the search for the truth about secularisation since the 1960s. Some of them bear the marks of their descent from grand theories of modernity. Others present relatively novel ways of charting the contours of religion and its decline, responding to alternative views in social theory about modernity and its successor(s). The clusters are arranged in a sequence that begins with the clearest indication of religious decline and ends with arguments for the indispensability of religion.

Main clusters of ideas about secularisation

A number of *conceptual maps* or overviews of the territory already exist. They help to indicate the extent to which the notion of 'secularisation' has been interpreted in different ways. These conceptual maps take a variety of forms, but among the earliest influential maps was Larry Shiner's (1967) six-fold classification of the meanings commonly attributed to 'secularisation' in empirical research: decline in religion; conformity with 'this world'; disengagement of society from religion; transposition of religious beliefs and institutions; desacralisation of the world; and movement from a 'sacred' to a 'secular' society. Although Shiner considered it unlikely that researchers would simply abandon secularisation because of the term's ambiguities, he still hoped that the term would be retained as a catch-all or covering concept under which the separate meanings would be kept distinct for the purpose of empirical investigation.

A significantly different approach to conceptual mapping was taken by Peter Glasner (1977) in his attempt to expose what he called 'the sociological myth' of secularisation. The mythic status allegedly derives from the ideological bias of social scientists against religion. Moreover, they supposedly adopt methods of empirical investigation which are likely to generate evidence that can only confirm the irresistible progress of religious decline. As a result, processes of secularisation can be analysed on the bases of the particular way of defining religion that each of them embodies – institutionally based, normatively based or cognitively based. Glasner's central recommendation was that it would be more productive for sociologists to focus their investigations on the more inclusive topic of religious change, within which careful attention could still be given to evidence of religious decline where it existed.

David Martin's (1978) mapping exercise threw into sharp relief the distinctive contours of the religious and the secular that had been shaped by social and cultural mechanisms in countries that had undergone certain crucial historical experiences. Using as his main criterion the question of whether a vicious or a beneficent spiral developed in any given society between religious and political forces, he discerned three basic patterns of secularisation (understood as the decline in [a] the power of religious institutions and [b] the acceptability of religious beliefs)[3] and resistance to secularisation. The basic generalisation holds that 'Where there exists one religion possessed of a monopoly, society splits into two warring sides, one of which is dedicated to religion. Similarly, where there are two or more religions (or distinct forms of the same religion) this does not happen' (Martin 1978: 17).

Martin's analysis is a complex and nuanced interpretation of the multiple factors influencing the public and private significance of religion (or better Christianity) in Europe and North America since the sixteenth century. Secularisation emerges from this analysis as a contingent and possibly reversible product of particular historical forces. Martin's approach was an influential attempt to scotch the myth that secularisation was a universal, unilinear process.

It was left to Karel Dobbelaere (1981) to make a creative synthesis of the varied approaches to secularisation and to offer a solution to the logical difficulties that haunted the concept. In effect, he helpfully perceived three analytically separate but overlapping dimensions of the phenomena often bundled together as secularisation: laicisation, religious change and religious involvement. The first refers roughly to the declining significance of religion in society; the second to changes in the theology and organisation of churches as well as the beliefs of individuals; and the third to changes in the relationships between individuals and religious organisations. The question of how these three dimensions are interrelated remains open, and there is a distinct possibility that they can vary independently of each other. But my reading of Dobbelaere is that he regards laicisation as the most important dimension but that, at the same time, he denies that it is a unilinear or irreversible process.

Finally the debates about secularisation can be shown to conform with Thomas Kuhn's (1962) notion of a scientific 'paradigm' in the sense of shared philosophical assumptions, a set of agreed findings, and widely used methods for resolving intellectual puzzles within a community of like-minded scholars. It is not a theory but a set of shared practices for making sense of the world in the light of the examples and exemplary studies that are most influential within particular scientific communities. Olivier Tschannen's (1991, 1992) application of Kuhn's ideas to sociological studies of secularisation emphasises the importance of key individual exemplars and a key organisation – the ISSR[4] – in fashioning what is widely referred to as a 'theory of secularisation'. In this way, the twists and turns of debates about secularisation take their place within a consensus characterised by a shared image of the world that is applied by analogy to virtually all intellectual puzzles. The resulting map of the major contributions therefore comes close to depicting them as satellites revolving around a mass of ideas that determines their trajectories.

These various attempts to map the concept of secularisation show two things. The first is that there is very little agreement about the term's meaning and even less agreement about how it should be used in social scientific research. The second is that it is no less difficult to re-arrange the different meanings and usages of 'secularisation' into a small number of basic categories or dimensions. In my view, this difficulty stems from the questionable assumption that secularisation, like religion, is a complex but unitary phenomenon that simply requires conceptual explication or better specification as a measurable reality.

Since no conceptualisation is likely to impose itself over the others, however, my response is to concentrate on identifying the different and/or competing logics that are at work in this field. For it is clear to me that social scientific uses of 'secularisation' are so diverse that it is fruitless even to look for the hidden thing that they might have in common. Instead, it is better to analyse the family resemblances among different uses of the term in order to identify their separate rationales and modalities without making any assumption that there are necessarily any underlying similarities among them. Since my focus is on the underlying logics, the level of detail about the contributions of particular scholars is relatively low, especially in the first three sections on differentiation, rationalisation and modernisation. This is partly because the main contributions are already well known and partly because excellent analyses and summaries are available in, for example, Fenn (1978), Dobbelaere (1981, 1987), Wilson (1985, 1992), Tschannen (1991, 1992), Willaime (1995) and Bruce (2002).

(i)   *Differentiation*

The first main set of ideas about secularisation clusters around notions of social systems, social institutions and processes of social differentiation. Starting from the assumption that human societies can be represented as systems of functionally integrated institutions such as kinship, economy, law, polity and religion, a series of analytical questions comes to the fore. They ask about the conditions in which one or more institutions determine how the overall system develops, how relations between the institutions are regulated, and how the integrity of the system is maintained in the course of interaction with other systems. This particular perspective on human societies pays special attention to the processes of differentiation that occur when systems face inner tensions or external competition and challenge.

As far as religion and secularisation are concerned, questions about differentiation have produced several influential responses. Religion in advanced industrial societies is believed to have lost or abandoned its former function of supplying a sense of ultimate values and legitimacy for the entire social system. It is also said to have become less effective

at one level has no necessary implications for other levels of the social system. This is one of the reasons why disagreements about the social significance or impact of religion cannot be simply resolved by taking more, or better, evidence into account. Moreover, all assertions about the functions of social phenomena are meaningless if they do not specify (a) a particular time scale in which the putative functionality can be assessed and (b) a particular level of the social system at which the phenomena are supposed to be functional.

A radical response to the baggage of functionalism that seems unavoidably to accompany a focus on the differentiation of social institutions is Mark Chaves's (1991) insistence that it is mistaken ever to think of religion as more than simply one institution among others. At a stroke he tries to de-pathologise the effects of societal differentiation on religion. Furthermore, finding the notion of 'religion' too vague and the notion of 'secularisation' as the decline of religion even vaguer, Chaves makes the interesting move of framing 'secularisation' as the declining scope of religious authority structures[5] (understood as organised attempts to control access to salvation or to the reassurance of salvation). He operationalises this concept in terms of data about attendance in American denominations between 1939 and 1990.

This is certainly a promising approach to sociological questions about the organisational and individual levels of religion, and it has borne valuable fruit in studies of change in American denominations (Chaves 1997). But this approach arbitrarily excludes from consideration all those religious phenomena that fall outside the sphere of formal organisations such as American denominations and does not, therefore, lend itself readily to application to more informal or unofficial expressions of religion. Indeed, the link that Chaves makes between the concept of 'religious authority structure' and the empirical indicator of church attendance is debatable. Still, the claim that 'Secularisation occurs by a weakening of religious authority, not by a decline in religion' (Chaves 1991: 96) deserves serious scrutiny.

(ii) Rationalisation

Ideas about the differentiation of social systems overlap extensively with ideas about the rationalisation of industrial and advanced industrial societies. Many writers on religion treat the two sets of ideas as virtually coterminous but, since it is conceivable that some societies could be differentiated without being rationalised, and vice versa, I shall analyse them separately. For my purposes, the process of rationalisation is defined as the methodical pursuit of efficient relations between means and ends. In some cases this may also mean the pursuit of efficiency as an end in itself. Many social scientists believe that rationalisation corrodes and erodes religious faith by calling into question beliefs and practices that are revered as values in themselves or as part of ways of life that are justified and warranted by sacred tradition.

Rationalisation is said to pave the way for secularisation in many respects. They include: challenging the intellectual basis for truth claims made on the strength of sacred and/or revealed knowledge; substituting scientific knowledge for sacred knowledge; calling into question the authority of religious specialists; scrutinising supposedly sacred forms of organisation in terms of rational efficiency; doubting the capacity of religious agencies to compete successfully with secular agencies; exposing religious ideas as mystifications or expressions of false consciousness; and weakening the intellectual and symbolic resonance of cultural symbols.

The force of the argument about the secularising effects of rationalisation depends heavily on the assumption that rational and religious ways of thinking are mutually exclusive – or, at least, that they are locked into a winner-takes-all competition. Thus, substantiated claims about the replacement of ways of thinking and acting that used to have religious meaning by ideas and practices that were shown to be merely efficient and effective amount to evidence of secularisation by rationalisation. For example, the growing authority of rational, scientific ideas about the world of nature, cosmogony, disease, education, work and so on has tended to replace or to marginalise religious authorities on the same issues.

Some of the most interesting topics in the sociology of religion concern the 'border disputes' that occur in areas of life where the ascendancy of rationality over religion is either unclear or contested. This is the case with, for example, disagreements about the criteria for deciding precisely when human life begins and ends, about the admissibility of religious testimony in courts of law (Fenn 1981), and about the acceptability of religious contents in public broadcasting. To the extent that attempts to exert religious authority over these areas are rejected, the advocates of the rationalisation perspective on secularisation count it as evidence that supports their position.

In response, it is open to those who are sceptical about the effect of rationalisation on religion to offer several counter-arguments. One is that there is no necessary incompatibility between religion and rationality. In theory, at least, rational inquiry, empirically confirmed scientific knowledge and the pursuit of efficiency can all be accommodated within a world-view based on religious faith. A variant on this argument holds that rational scientific world-views may actually fulfil some of the same functions as religion, such as providing a sense of ultimate reality, reasons for having faith in the order of nature, and grounds for feeling confident about predicting the future. Faith in computers has even given rise to 'cyber-religion'; Brasher 2001; Dawson 1999) and a religious culture of technology.

A second response is to turn the tables on rationality by arguing that it can never provide a satisfactory basis for social and moral order in itself because it is inherently relativistic. That is, an efficient relation between means and ends may be helpful in many situations; but it can easily become counter-productive if it helps to promote ends that are dangerous, destructive or de-humanising. Since, in other words, the rational value of rationality is dependent on the ends to which it is oriented, there is always the possibility that the pursuit of rationality for its own sake will create the conditions in which the need for religious perspectives, as a source of values, will be re-asserted.

A third response is to acknowledge that rationalisation is rampant in the public sphere but that individuals and groups can still choose to follow religious principles in their private life and in the interstices of formal organisations. Indeed, in the manner of participants in 'subterranean' spiritual disciplines as diverse as Third Order Franciscans, Opus Dei or certain New Age training programmes, there is encouragement to be methodical about influencing the life of apparently secular institutions and organisations. This is not so much a question of *resisting* the rationalising aspects of secularisation as of co-opting and working with them to establish or to maintain the influence of religious values in places where they may be effective.

As we saw with arguments about secularisation as differentiation, there is no easy way of resolving the disagreements about the effects of rationalisation to the satisfaction of both the protagonists and the antagonists of the idea that rationalising forces somehow weaken the significance of religion. The two groups begin from different assumptions, regard different things as evidence, and make different inferences on the strength of what each side regards as the 'evidence'.

(iii)   Modernisation

A third cluster of ideas emerges from the mixture of differentiation and rationalisation with pluralisation. This mixture amounts to modernisation. By this, I mean a complex configuration of social, legal, economic, political and cultural processes of change that favour (a) the strengthening of states within an increasingly co-ordinated system of international states; (b) the systematic pursuit of economic productivity and power at national and international levels; (c) the application of theoretical knowledge and practical skills to the enhancement of productivity; (d) the establishment of democratic forms of politics and government; (e) the valorisation of education and freedom of thought and expression; (f) the dominance of urban centres of residence and work, and; (g) the cultivation of notions of individual subjectivity, dignity and rights. This is an admittedly 'thin' selection of modernising processes, and there is no implication that they all unfold without resistance or at the same pace. Nor am I suggesting that modernisation has a clear beginning or end. Rather, the processes are open-ended and immensely variable in respect of their patterning.

What these processes have in common is the idea of a break with traditional bases of authority and an accelerating rate of change in many areas of life (Yack 1997: 35). Given the close association between religion and many pre-modern centres of authority, the effects of change were widely expected to have adverse effects on religion. And there is no shortage of evidence from around the world that processes of modernisation have indeed undermined, for example, the 'parochial civilisation' of French Catholicism (Lambert 1985), the emotional attachment of city dwellers in Japan to Shinto shrines (Morioka 1975), the 'female piety' and the 'pietised femininity' on which modern British religious practice had heavily depended until their precipitous collapse in the 1960s and 1970s (Brown 2001), and the virtual desertion of Canadian Protestant churches in the same era (Bibby 1987). But as I shall show in later sections, the dramatic impact of modernisation on many religious beliefs, practices and institutions does not exclude the possibility that religion could assume new forms and exercise new types of influence in the midst of modernity or late modernity.

For my purposes, the importance of much of the highly diverse theorising about modernisation is that it bears directly or indirectly on questions about secularisation. For example, the relaxation or abandonment of religiously inspired controls over politics, law, culture, the economy and social relationships can be thought of as a pre-condition or concomitant of modernisation. As it happens, social scientists of religion have tended to place particular importance on the implications of modernisation for shaping a strong sense of the subjective identity of individuals and of their freedom to entertain a wide variety of ideas. Thus, early modern notions of toleration, in conjunction with growing familiarity with 'other' cultures, contributed towards a diversification of religions and of non-religious world-views.

As I shall argue in Chapter Three, the most celebrated account of the relations between modernisation and religion is Peter Berger's (1969).

The priority that he assigned to 'pluralism'[6] gave the impression that modernisation was necessarily corrosive of religious faith because the juxtaposition of diverse religions induced the belief that there could be no single source of absolute truth. Two points need to be made about Berger's thesis on pluralism. The first is that there is a logical *non sequitur* in his argument that pluralism necessarily leads to strong relativism. I shall discuss this at greater length in Chapter Three. The second point is that Berger has revised his own thinking about the relation between pluralism and secularisation:

> If I look back on my earlier work, I would say that I was wrong about secularization, but right about pluralism. I misunderstood the relation between the two: the latter does not necessarily lead to the former (*vide* the American case). What pluralism does (and there I was right) is to undermine all taken-for-granted certainties, in religion as in all other spheres of life. But it is possible to hold beliefs and to live by them even if they no longer hold the status of taken-for-granted verities. In other words, I would now say that pluralism affects the *how* of religious belief, but not necessarily the *what*. (Berger 1999: 196)

This position is compatible with the belief that a 'new paradigm' is gaining force in the sociology of religion (Warner 1993) and that the diversity of religions currently on offer in countries like the USA is much more likely to produce religious vitality than secularisation (Stark & Finke 2000). It is also in line with ideas about 'religious modernity' and 'European exceptionalism', as I shall explain later in this chapter, which are intended to rebut strong versions of the equation between modernisation and secularisation.

By contrast, the 'orthodox model' (Wallis & Bruce 1992) and the 'inherited model' (Wilson 1985) of secularisation insist on a causal relation between modernisation and religious decline. These models contend that religion loses its plausibility and its capacity to legitimise the social and moral order in conditions of modernity. Religion allegedly becomes privatised and marginalised at the same time. The significance of religion for 'the operation of the social system' (Wilson 1992: 199) is therefore said to decline, regardless of fluctuations in levels of religious belief and practice – and regardless of the many attempts to bring religious ideas or sentiments to bear on politics, morality, the economy or social policies. The advocates of secularisation theory, in its undiluted state, will not be persuaded to abandon it unless cogent evidence is forthcoming that the major social institutions are again guided by religious values. They do not claim that secularisation is a universally active process; nor do they assert that the process is inevitable. In fact, Wallis and Bruce (1992) and Bruce (1999) argue that the advance of secularisation may be retarded in circumstances where religion serves as an important marker of collective identity for groups undergoing major cultural transitions (for example, during large-scale migration) or defending their culture against perceived threats.

(iv)   Metamorphoses

Enthusiasm for explicitly grounding arguments against secularisation in the functional requirements for social order, moral coherence or cognitive understanding of ultimate reality has largely subsided in the social sciences. But a more implicit version of this way of thinking about religion is currently enjoying popularity. It takes a number of different forms, but the underlying theme is constant. It holds that evidence of declining support for conventional forms of religious beliefs, practices and organisations does not necessarily indicate secularisation. Instead, this decline is taken as evidence that religion is metamorphosing into new and different forms at various levels. In other words, the appearance of secularisation is regarded as deceptive. Moreover, according to David Lyon (2000: x), 'the idea of secularisation, if taken to refer beyond institutional religiosity to the attenuation of all forms of faith, spirituality, and belief, is plainly mistaken'. What is really happening, according to a wide variety of scholars, is that religion is being assembled, packaged and experienced in new forms, some of which bear little resemblance to previously taken-for-granted expressions of religion.

The idea that decline in the empirical indicators of religious activity does not necessarily equate to secularisation is far from novel. To take just one example, it has been a recurrent theme in Robert Bellah's work since the late 1960s. Recognising that change was endemic in religion he nevertheless claimed that, 'The modern world is as alive with religious possibility as any epoch in human history. It is no longer possible to divide mankind into believers and non-believers. All believe something' (Bellah 1970: 228). Secularisation amounts to nothing more than the decline of traditional religious belief and the erosion of 'the external control system of religion'. 'But religion, as that symbolic form through which man comes to terms with the antinomies of his being, has not declined, indeed, cannot decline unless man's nature ceases to be problematic to him' (Bellah 1970: 227).

Relying more on the evidence of empirical research than on Bellah's impressionistic assessment, Hadden (1987: 603) nevertheless came to a similar conclusion about the balance between change and continuity in religion:

[R]eligion is changing within a context of broad stability. There is a general absence of indicators which would support the long-term secularisation hypothesis. Religion is dead in the minds, hearts, and feet of large sectors of American society. But just as certainly, religion is alive for other broad sectors. There is no evidence to support a decisive shift either toward or away from religion.

Echoes of this assessment can be heard in many, more recent attempts to depict the changing shape and character of religion in the late twentieth and early twenty-first centuries. I shall select three for detailed examination.

(a) A popular starting point for recent arguments about the metamorphosis of religion is the idea that the decline in the number of young people who regularly participate in mainstream Christian churches in Western Europe is not matched by a corresponding decline in levels of reported subscription to broadly Christian values. Grace Davie's formulation of 'believing without belonging', originally intended to apply to the UK alone, has come to represent this deceptively simple idea: 'religion and religious values are not so much disappearing among young people as being redirected' (Davie 1990: 462). The credibility of this idea rests not only on statistics concerning indicators of 'belief' and 'belonging'[7] but also, in more recent formulations (Davie 2001b, 2001c), on observations about the continuing significance in public life of religious organisations at a time when other comparable, non-religious voluntary associations are failing to retain members or to exercise influence in the public sphere. This twin-pronged response to crude arguments in support of secularisation is therefore unusual in so far as it accepts without demur many of the statistical claims about declining rates of participation in religious organisations whilst, at the same time, insisting that many people no longer belong to churches, but nevertheless continue to hold religious beliefs of some kind. Even the widely available evidence of declining rates of belief in central Christian doctrines is accommodated by this thesis. It holds that religious beliefs, unless checked by the discipline of participation in collective worship or study, are likely to be individualistic and unorthodox (see also Gill 1993, 1999). This style of reasoning displays many continuities with early and mid-twentieth century theorising about the shift from ascribed to achieved identities; from particularistic values to universalistic ones; and from collectivism to individualism.

This approach to a re-interpretation of empirical findings that have often served to support the idea of secularisation is also compatible with the argument that declining rates of participation in mainstream churches are more or less unique to Western Europe. The case for 'European exceptionalism' (Warner 1993; Berger 1999; Davie 1999, 2001b) denies that the trajectory of mainstream churches in Europe is necessarily a faithful guide to the development of churches in other parts of the world. It is the particular character of Western Europe's social, cultural and political history which has allegedly favoured 'believing without belonging', whereas circumstances outside Europe have had a less corrosive effect on church participation.

The thesis of 'believing without belonging' has helped to force a reconsideration of 'the inherited model' (Wilson 1985) of secularisation and has been instrumental in encouraging a more subtle interpretation of empirical indicators of religious belief and participation in religious organisations. Indeed, refinements have also occurred in the thesis itself. For example, instead of focusing analysis exclusively on individuals' beliefs and levels of participation, Davie (1999, 2001c) takes account of 'vicarious religion' in Western Europe. This refers to the apparently widespread 'tacit understanding' that the mainstream churches are able to continue playing important roles *on behalf of* both nominal and practising Christians because enough 'nominal' Christians are still attached, at least emotionally, to their churches. Yet, research into the role of the Church of England as a 'broker' not only for inactive Christians but also for the growing proportion of active participants in Islam, Hinduism and Sikhism in the UK (Beckford & Gilliat 1998; Gilliat 1998; Gilliat-Ray 1999) raises doubts about the long-term prospects for this form of vicarious religion.

Nevertheless, it is reasonable to claim that 'An evident fall both in religious practice and in religious knowledge in the postwar period does not lead to a parallel loss in religious sensitivity (the data quite clearly suggest otherwise) or to the widespread adoption of secular alternatives' (Davie 2001c: 110). What is less clear is whether 'religious sensitivity' represents a dilution of the notion of 'believing' that was central to the original thesis. For it seems to me that a thesis about the persistence of religious sensitivity or spirituality, as some authors prefer (Wuthnow 2001), places considerable strain on the argument that religion is merely being restructured or redirected. To resolve this question, it is essential to conduct empirical studies of continuities and changes in the meanings attributed to 'religion' and 'spirituality'. This would mean examining the *re-conceptualisation* of what counts as religion in public and private life: not the restructuring of something putatively unchangeable and indispensable.

A number of other difficulties confront these attempts, in the name of 'believing without belonging' or 'vicarious religion', to challenge stronger versions of secularisation thinking. First, it is not clear how evidence of the declining levels of subscription to the central doctrines of Christian churches and of the rising levels of subscription to religious and spiritual beliefs not rooted in 'official' Christianity can be reconciled with the claim that the balance between believing and belonging is merely being adjusted. According to Hornsby-Smith (1992: 128), for example, only about one third of Catholics in England and Wales 'could be regarded as orthodox both in terms of weekly mass attendance and in terms of a measure of orthodox belief' in the late 1970s, whilst a further one quarter fell into the category of 'believing without belonging'.

A second difficulty with the 'believing without belonging' thesis is that the analogy between Christian churches and non-religious voluntary associations in Western Europe is questionable. This is partly because some Christian churches enjoy constitutional privileges in many countries as a consequence of concordats and other legal provisions. And it is partly because of the complicated interweaving of churches into the social fabric of many geographical communities, especially but not exclusively in rural areas. Consequently, evidence indicating that participation in Christian churches is not declining faster than for comparable voluntary associations should be treated with caution.

Uncritical use of the 'believing without belonging' thesis could create a third problem if it is allowed to distract attention from the growing popularity, albeit on a modest scale in Western Europe, of conservative evangelical and Pentecostal churches, as well as certain expansive sectarian movements, many of which display an unmistakably clear and close relation between the strict disciplines of both believing and belonging. These forms of Christian collectivity not only tend to insist on the integration of belief and practice but they also monitor the orthodoxy of belief carefully and take disciplinary action to control deviance or dissidence if necessary. The thesis of 'believing without belonging' is not, therefore, unproblematic but it will no doubt continue to stimulate interesting debate not just about the robustness of secularisation theory but, more importantly, about changes in the meanings attributed to 'religion'.

(b) The second major strand of the argument that the 'metamorphosis of religion' is a more accurate and appropriate depiction of religious change since the mid-twentieth century is associated with Danièle Hervieu-Léger (1986, 1993, 1999). Her work, as well as that of the many scholars who have followed her example, shares many aspects of the 'believing without belonging' thesis but is nevertheless different in its initial assumptions and emphases. Reflecting the cultural dominance that Catholicism enjoyed in France, despite the constitutional separation of religion and state, Hervieu-Léger's analysis is rooted in the recognition that a virtually obligatory mode of believing and belonging (or at least practising) has lost its grip on the majority of the population. In place of the formerly monolithic collective practice of Catholicism, sanctioned by a parochial civilisation, the French have adopted a set of more disparate and individualised world-views and expressions of religion. The collapse or enfeeblement of many of the Roman Catholic Church's organisational structures, notably its religious orders and priesthood is a key part of this transformation. But Hervieu-Léger insists that it is indeed nothing more than a transformation or restructuring of religion and is not necessarily confirmation of the triumph of secularisation. The choice of metaphors and other images for depicting this situation ranges from 'the changing contours in the modern religious landscape' (2001: 112), to 'the religious logic of modernity' (1989: 73) and to 'institutional deregulation' (2001: 117). But the constant theme is that evidence of decline in many aspects of religious belief and practices is counterbalanced in others by evidence of religious vitality, creativity and resurgence.

The basis for the explanation of what I call this 'theory of the conservation of religious matter' is the assumption that the declining authority of religious institutions, in accordance with the dictates of modernity, leaves individuals exposed to the *need* to make their own sense of their lives and of the rapidly changing world in which they live. Echoing Peter Berger's phenomenology of religion as the collective attempt to ward off the threat of chaos, Hervieu-Léger claims that individuals have nowadays acquired 'a colossal measure of freedom' as a result of the collapse of collective codes of meaning and morality. The ideal-typical figures who embody this autonomous response to modern freedom are the pilgrim and the convert (Hervieu-Léger 1999).

These ideal-typical religious actors, far from being static, are figures in movement against a background of religious currents that are also flowing in various directions. The only landmarks in this confusing panorama are the great religious traditions, to which reference can be made if the powers of cultural memory are strong enough. The images of fluidity and mobility are clear, then, but there is some doubt about their bearing on the question of whether religion is declining or reviving. Religion is undoubtedly in movement, according to Danièle Hervieu-Léger, but the direction and the velocity of the movement are still to be ascertained. In particular, the number of pilgrims and converts needs to be estimated so that their proportion among other types of religious actors can be gauged. Only empirical investigation can resolve these questions by revealing, to preserve the hydraulic metaphor, how far pilgrims and converts represent 'tidal waves', 'major currents' or mere 'eddies' and 'ripples' on the surface of religion. Research conducted in Switzerland (Campiche *et al.* 1992) goes some way towards meeting the need for empirical investigation of the thesis that the practice of Christianity has become individualised in the course of restructuring. Moreover, the Swiss findings give no support to the idea that religion is 'privatised' in the sense of being confined to the personal sphere. On the contrary, even the most individualised believers made connections between their personal beliefs and issues of social and collective concern.

At the same time as theoretical ideas about the restructuring of religion depict individuals as needing to make their own, personal 'portfolio' of religious beliefs on the model of the pilgrim-type or the convert-type, they also claim that religion, at a collective level, exercises a powerful influence over culture. This perspective therefore has an individual *and* a collective dimension, again mirroring Peter Berger's confidence that, outside Western Europe, religion continues to be a powerful force in public life. Even in the fiercely laicised world of French politics there is evidence that Catholicism still permeates public culture and individual mentalities. The influence is not exerted directly but indirectly by means of the categorisations and symbols bequeathed over centuries to French people, most of whom no longer regard themselves as practising Catholics. Support for this view of the restructuring of religion in public culture comes from empirical studies of, for example, French attitudes towards such bioethical issues as genetic manipulation and assisted reproduction (Ladrière 1985), towards the religious character of the setting in which the late President Mitterand's state funeral took place (Hervieu-Léger 1996), and towards the visit of Pope John Paul II to France in 1986.

The notion of 'collective memory' is integral to most of these claims that religion is somehow being 'restructured' (Hervieu-Léger 1993). The argument seems to be that, despite superficial changes in the forms in which they express their religion, French Catholics can still draw on a heritage of cultural memories handed down across the generations. Faith consists of these lineaments of belief. The critical question that Meštrović (1997) would probably ask is whether these memories are 'authentic' or 'recycled' and 'manufactured'. He would want to know how authentic memories of the sacred could survive in a 'postemotional' era. The collision between the claim that memory is the vehicle of faith and the argument that 'postemotional' memory cannot be authentic could ignite a fruitful debate about religion and social theory.

(c) A third basis for rejecting the idea that secularisation is inevitable rests on a variety of claims about the persisting importance of *unofficial* religious forces that are not fully under the direction of formal religious organisation. This line of reasoning contributes to the broader argument about the re-structuring, rather than the decline, of religion. It does so by documenting the resilience and the continuing evolution of beliefs, dispositions, values and practices that undoubtedly articulate religious views of the world but without forming part of the activities of religious organisations. The range of such phenomena is extremely wide, extending from religious superstition and folk religiosity at one end to the diffuse influence of Catholic values still detectable in some societies at the other end. Terms such as 'customary religion' (Hornsby-Smith, Lee and Reilly 1985), 'implicit religion' (Bailey 1997) and 'diffuse religion' (Cipriani 1989) have all captured aspects of this subterranean religiosity. What they have in common for my purposes is the capacity to lend religious meaning to everyday life without necessarily being closely associated with the patterns of believing and belonging advocated by religious organisations. And, as socio-historical investigations have shown, the boundary between 'official' and 'informal' or 'unofficial' expressions of religion is not given in the nature of things or fixed once-and-for-all: its location is the result of centuries of struggle between religious leaders, secular elites and popular interests.

From a sociological point of view, there is no reason to regard official, formally organised religion as the sole or even normal repository of truth. Consequently, it is unhelpful to consider unofficial religion as merely a residue of mistaken, degraded or inauthentic phenomena. Unofficial religion amounts to a set of expressions in parallel with, and sometimes overlapping, formal religion. From this point of view, then, questions about the decline of religion cannot be safely answered with reference only to those aspects that happen to have been socially constructed as 'official'. It is not as if unofficial religion is necessarily a second-best option or an instance of last resort when official religion loses some of its power or social significance. Rather, it is a realm of meaning in its own right, the significance of which may appear to increase in proportion to the declining rates of participation in 'official' religious organisations. But the fact that certain religious beliefs and practices are largely outside the control of formal religious organisations does not, *ipso facto*, render those beliefs and practices individualistic. I am even more reluctant to classify them as 'privatised', *pace* Wallis and Bruce (1992: 22).

The findings of research conducted in South America (Parker 1998) also call into question the tendency to equate low levels of support for official religion with secularisation. Again, the argument is that unofficial religious beliefs and practices, far from being a residue of 'proper' religion, represent a distinctive style of religious expression in their own right. The fact that this unofficial religion is not articulated by formal organisations does not mean that it is inconsequential for the conduct of life. On the contrary, Cristián Parker has documented its continuing capacity to shape the social and cultural life of the many people who nevertheless show few signs of believing and belonging in the manner required by the Roman Catholic Church.

The case of Japan is even more difficult to fit into any of the secularisation scenarios because, leaving aside the periods when registration with local Buddhist and Shinto associations was obligatory for reasons of political control, formal religious organisations have rarely been able to impose or to induce particular requirements for beliefs and practice. As a result, the informal traditions of honouring local Shinto deities and spirits or conducting Buddhist funerary rites and commemorative ceremonies constitute the closest approximation to a religious mainstream.

The fact that 'unofficial' religion continues to adapt to the rapidly changing conditions of life in the twenty-first century is further evidence for some theorists that 'metamorphosis' of religion is a better characterisation of religious change than is 'secularisation'. On the other hand, it is unlikely that scholars who define secularisation in terms of the declining social significance of religion will regard the persistence of unofficial religion as being incompatible with their argument.

(v)   Continuing vitality

Critics of the 'orthodox model' of secularisation have sometimes overlooked the fact that occasional outbursts of religious fervour and relatively high levels of participation in religious organisations in some countries are actually compatible with a central argument of the thesis about the decline of religion's significance for the ordering of societies. Taken to extremes, this argument in defence of the idea of secularisation could mean that evidence about levels of participation and religious belief is simply beside the point. The point is really about the capacity of religious values to influence the conduct of individuals and the policies of the institutions and organisations that effectively control public life. The advocates of strong versions of the secularisation concept still insist that religion is losing, or has already lost, this capacity to shape and control societal development.

Challenges to the strong thesis of secularisation nevertheless take the line that the level of religious vitality in many countries is too high to be dismissed as evidence of merely occasional eruptions or recreations of religious fervour without social significance. Indeed, there is also support for the view that the significance of organised religion is strong enough in some places to affect societal development either directly through a change in shared values or indirectly through the work of religiously responsive politicians, social movements, campaigns or political parties. Indeed, David Martin (1999: 49) concluded a review of the political implications of the upsurge of evangelicalism in many regions of the world with the prediction that

The Evangelicals' most potent contribution will be the creation of voluntary associations and the multiplication of social and political actors in the public arena . . . [T]he cultural characteristics of Evangelicals – participation, pragmatism, competition, personal discipline – ought in the long run to foster democracy.

Thus, although Evangelicals are unlikely to pursue the aim of instituting religious monopolies over political power, in the manner of Catholic integrism or some versions of Islamic fundamentalism, Martin's argument is that they can seek to exercise influence over public life by fulfilling the role of critical commentators on the moral quality of society.

Another challenge to strong versions of secularisation theory also turns on the claim that Christian churches remain capable of influencing public life. But José Casanova's (1994) argument is more ambitious than David Martin's. It denies that religion has necessarily been 'privatised', and therefore marginalised, in the course of modern history. The philosophical anthropology that underlies his position is in part phenomenological, with a heavy reliance on Peter Berger's and Thomas Luckmann's writings, but it also draws on aspects of humanistic Marxism and critical theory. Casanova's principal thesis is that, contrary to Enlightenment expectations and to the central tenets of theories of modernisation and secularisation, religion has not been confined exclusively to the sphere of private life. Despite the evident differentiation and rationalisation of modern societies, which have transformed the relations that most people have to religious organisations, the 1980s witnessed the 'deprivatisation' of religion in some areas. This means that a variety of collective actors, in rejection of the marginal position to which modernity was supposed to have consigned religion, have successfully reasserted the relevance of religious values to the spheres of politics and public morality. Thus,

Religions throughout the world are entering the public sphere and the arena of political contestation not only to defend their traditional turf, as they have done in the past, but also to participate in the very struggles to define and set the modern boundaries between the private and the public spheres, between system and life-world, between legality and morality, between individual and society, between family, civil society, and state, between nations, states, civilizations, and the world system. (Casanova 1994: 6)

Perhaps the most distinctive feature of Casanova's approach is his denial that processes of secularisation were necessarily unavoidable in late-medieval Europe and necessarily irreversible in the modern world. In his opinion, it was the 'caesaropapist embrace of throne and altar' or 'the very attempt to preserve and prolong Christendom in every nation and state' (Casanova 1994: 29) that undermined churches in Europe but not in the USA. In other words, societal forces of differentiation and rationalisation weakened Christianity in modern Europe because the main churches clung to political power for too long, thereby precipitating an avoidable clash with emerging secular nation states and churches resisting structural change. Not surprisingly, then, Casanova considers the established churches and the state churches that survive in Europe to be in a weak position because they are allegedly unable to exercise independent leverage on political power or state authorities. He argues that religiously motivated campaigns and political movements that are *unconnected* with established churches are nowadays in a strong position to deprivatise themselves and to influence public values and policies in civil society (understood in a Habermasian mode as a sphere of discursive freedom independent from the state, the economy and political society).

'Deprivatisation' means challenging the secular liberal consensus on the location of the public/private boundary and showing that modernity can create the conditions in which religious values are able to address public issues and structural forces and thereby to influence individual consciousness. Thus, while structural differentiation and the declining capacity of religious organisations to retain the unquestioning loyalty of large sections of society seem to be irreversible trends of modernity, Casanova regards the deprivatisation of religion as a mere 'option' on the path of history: not a trend. The result, in his view, is that differentiation and the decline of religious beliefs and practices are well-documented features of secularisation, but that privatisation *can* be avoided or reversed if collective religious actors actively engage with debates in the sphere of civil society. The interventions that religious actors can make in civil society represent, for Casanova (1994: 220), 'new types of immanent normative critiques of specific forms of institutionalisation of modernity'. But, just as he refuses to consider privatisation as a necessary trend, so he also warns that there is nothing inevitable about the deprivatisation of religion. The evolution of the Catholic Church in Spain serves as his example of a recent failure to take advantage of an opportunity for deprivatisation.

In short, Casanova's approach is not so much a rebuttal of secularisation theory as an attempt to extract privatisation from it and to show how some transnational religious traditions can be revitalised and reformed, especially in conditions of globalisation, if they seek to replace failed secular ideologies with new normative ideas in the public sphere. The three main forms of deprivatisation are (a) religious mobilisation in defence of traditional life-worlds against forms of colonisation by states or markets (b) challenges to the dominance of states and markets, and

(c) the maintenance of visions of a common good to offset the prevailing individualism of modern liberalism. This comes close to regarding deprivatisation as a rationalised programme for completing the Enlightenment project without falling victim to the Scylla of pre-modern traditionalism or the Charybdis of post-modern irrationality.

Casanova's approach is distinctive and original in a number of respects. First, it offers no support for theories of the recurrent return of the sacred in response to some self-limiting characteristic of secularity. Second, it does not challenge the controversial view that many societies have been secularised as a result of processes of structural differentiation and the declining interest in religious beliefs and practices. He regards these developments as historical trends within modernity. Third, he appears to limit the scope of religious revitalisations of civil society to religious currents that have already accommodated themselves to the Enlightenment critique of religion, thereby excluding obscurantism, fundamentalism and world-renunciation. Consequently, he argues that only transnational, global religious organisations such as the Roman Catholic Church seem capable of fostering the ideological motivation to intervene in the public sphere of civil society and thereby to enjoy revitalisation. On the other hand, Casanova (2002) has recently come to entertain the possibility that Islam may also be capable of shaping a civil society and democratic institutions in certain countries such as Turkey, Iran and Indonesia. He argues that these hypothetical developments could only occur, however, if religious authorities abandoned theocratic ambitions and if the State protected pluralism and the human right to freedom of religion or no religion.

Casanova's argument leaves a number of questions unanswered, however. For example, it is unclear whether his thesis could apply to transnational Protestant churches or to Islamic movements if they have had no experience of trying to influence the public sphere in the past. It is also questionable whether the development of the Catholic Church in Poland since the early 1990s really justifies Casanova's belief in its capacity to help forge civil society without abusing its numerical dominance and without retreating into a separatist position in Polish society. Yet, probably the most debatable aspect of Casanova's thesis is his readiness to equate the privatisation of religion with its marginalisation. In fact, the contrast that he draws between the private and the public is too sharp, for it seems to exclude the possibility that the force of privatised religious views could exercise influence over public opinion, public debates in the sphere of civil society and, possibly, strategies in the political sphere. Evidence that this is indeed happening in the early twenty-first century comes from countries as diverse as the USA, Spain and Turkey. The problem with

Casanova's argument is that it tries to apply a would-be universal distinction between the private and the public, whereas the definition of these concepts and of the boundary between them varies from society to society. He is clearly receptive to the possibility of 'multiple modernities', but his notion of the public/private distinction appears to be irremediably modern in a Western sense. What is needed is a careful analysis of the processes whereby the definition of the private and the public is constructed, contested and constantly re-negotiated in different places and circumstances. Ideally, these processes would be the topic of analysis: not an uninspected tool of analysis.

In sum, there is persuasive evidence of the continuing capacity of some forms of institutionalised religion to influence debates in civil society and, indirectly, action in the public sphere of supposedly secular societies. On the other hand, the case that Casanova makes for deprivatisation exaggerates the distinction between the public and the private and is not fully supported by the recent evolution of public religion, even in the societies for which his argument was designed. Yet, empirical evidence of religious vitality at the *grassroots* level of societies in Latin America (Martin 1990; Lehmann 1996), Southern Africa (Prozesky 1990; Besier 1999), the Middle East (Ayubi 1991; Kepel 1994) and South Asia (Juergensmeyer 1993; Bhatt 1997) could support Casanova's denial that privatisation is necessarily the fate of all religion in modernity. His analysis of the capacity of transnational religious organisations, principally the Roman Catholic Church, to influence public debate and public life through political channels does not exclude the possibility that other expressions of religion could also be capable of shaping debates in the public sphere (Westerlund 1995; Brouwer, Gifford & Rose 1996; Haynes 1998).

An important variation on the theme that religion remains important in the public sphere of some societies concerns diasporic and migrant communities. Extensive research in the twentieth century brought to light evidence of the pivotal role played by a wide variety of religious organisations in aiding *migrants* to adapt to new circumstances and, in some cases, to generate higher levels of religious practice than those to which they were accustomed in their places of origin. Formative studies of migrants to the industrial cities of North America (Fauset 1944), New York City (Poblete 1960) or Guatemala City (Roberts 1968) tended to emphasise the functional value of religious participation for the mundane purpose of finding employment and housing. But the tendency of more recent studies is to regard 'religious diasporas' (Coward, Hinnells & Williams 2000), 'new ethnic and immigrant congregations' (Warner & Wittner 1998) or simply 'immigrant congregations' (Ebaugh & Chafetz

2000) as important sources of personal identity and collective insertion into civil society. According to Kurien (1998: 37) 'How to "fit in" but still maintain one's cultural and personal integrity is the challenge that most immigrants in the United States face in their transition from immigrants to ethnics'. Thus, immigrants to the USA from India and from Iran (Feher 1998) regard Jewish Americans as a good model to follow because they are well integrated into mainstream American society but have not lost their distinctive religion, culture and close-knit communities.

The rapidly growing body of social scientific knowledge about 'ethnic' and 'immigrant' congregations provides clear evidence of pockets of religious vitality, but it is questionable whether the findings paint a reliable picture of the level of religious activity among all migrants or minority ethnic categories in the United States. The methodological strategy of focusing on relatively stable 'congregations' and formal organisations runs the risk of exaggerating the extent to which they really represent the experience of immigrants in general. Ideally, these findings of congregational vitality would be considered alongside information about the proportion of immigrants who have little or no involvement in congregations or who leave them after a relatively brief interval. In short, there is a question about how far the undoubted evidence of congregational vitality is an accurate reflection of the level of religiosity among all immigrants and settled migrants to the United States.

Research into the religious practices of people who are the second or third generation descendants of cross-national migrants has also generated evidence of religious vitality. One might have expected that life in advanced industrial societies would reduce levels of participation in organised religious activities, and there is no shortage of evidence to this effect. But there are also signs of a disposition, especially among young members of some minority ethnic and religious communities, to take more seriously the religion of their parents and grandparents. In fact, some evidence shows that 'As religion becomes less than taken for granted under the pluralistic and secular conditions prevailing in the United States, adherents become more conscious of their tradition and often more determined about its transmission' (Warner 1998: 17). This may involve adaptation of familial and communal traditions in favour of more self-conscious identities and practices. According to Jessica Jacobson (1997: 239), for example, young British people of Pakistani descent show 'a growing tendency to emphasize a distinction between religion and ethnicity as sources of identity' and to give priority to their religious identity.[8] Comparable findings emerged from Farhad Khosrokhavar's (1997) study of young Muslims in France.

Finally, support for the idea that levels of religious vitality are high in many parts of the world comes from a theoretical approach and a series of associated studies that are based on assumptions that human beings are both rational *and* in need of religion. A more extended discussion of what is widely known as the rational choice theory of religion will appear in Chapter Five, but for present purposes it will be necessary only to introduce the underlying assumptions about human psychology and social dynamics.

Early versions of what has become an elaborate and sophisticated form of propositional theory include Stark and Bainbridge (1985, 1987), while a more recent and refined statement can be found in Stark and Finke (2000). The proponents of what these authors now prefer to call an approach based on 'subjective rationality' formulate the key principle of human rationality as follows: 'Within the limits of their information and understanding, restricted by available options, guided by their preferences and tastes, humans attempt to make rational choices' (Stark & Finke 2000: 38). They argue that this principle applies as much to choices in religion as to choices in any other areas of social life. In conjunction with other assumptions about, for example, the willingness of human beings to accept that scarce rewards may be obtainable only in the distant future and that otherworldly rewards are available only in an unverifiable, non-empirical context such as the afterlife or some other supernatural realm, this theory seeks to explain how and why humans believe that they can enter into exchange with deities. It also spells out the implications of these assumptions for a wide range of religious activities and forms of organisation. For example, religious groups that live in a high degree of tension with society are said to be likely to experience high rates of growth in the number of their members and material resources, particularly if they prevent congregations from becoming too large to sustain dense social networks among members and if they restrict the growth of church bureaucracy.

Stark and Finke (2000) bring the numerous assumptions, definitions and propositions that constitute their theory of rational choice in religion to bear on many issues, among which the conditions of religious vitality loom large. For example, the relatively high and constant rates of membership growth in the Church of Jesus Christ and Latter Day Saints, as well as the Watch Tower Society, are explained in terms of factors such as their exclusiveness, the high demands placed on members, the policy of splitting congregations in two when they reach a critical size, and so on. Conversely, the same theoretical approach serves to explain the relatively low rates of membership growth in liberal Protestant denominations and the declining number of female vocations in Catholic orders and dioceses that have failed to preserve the exclusivity and distinctiveness of the religious life. In other words, high-demand or 'expensive' religious groups tend to foster high levels of satisfaction and retention of members (within certain limits).

The rational choice approach does not assert that religious belief is universal; nor does it deny the existence of irreligion. Yet, its findings support the view that, notwithstanding countries with state churches or other systematic obstacles to the free market of religious choice, religious vitality is widespread. The findings also claim that the notion of secularisation has no foundation in empirical fact. Religious decline is therefore dismissed as a myth (Stark and Finke 2000: 61) and a product of secularist ideology or wishful thinking. One might expect, then, that other critics of the theory of secularisation would enthusiastically welcome the support of rational choice arguments. In practice, however, there seems to be reluctance on the part of sociologists advocating ideas such as 'the restructuring of religion', 'vicarious religion' or 'the deprivatisation of religion' to make common cause with rational choice theorists. As I shall explain in Chapter Five, some of the reasons for this reluctance lie in misgivings about the theory's psychological underpinning and its assumptions about the depressive effect of religious traditions and mainstream churches on religious vitality.

(vi)   Universality of religion

A final cluster of ideas has formed around the notion that evidence of secularisation can only ever be superficial because the need for religion is *universal*. These ideas range from, at one extreme, a blanket denial that religion could ever lose its social significance to, at the other, a belief that some decline may be occurring but without rendering religion insignificant. The range is therefore wide, but it makes sense for me to assemble these ideas in a single category because they are all opposed to the thesis that secularisation is an inevitable or irreversible process of decline. Instead, they tend to frame developments in terms of religious change or re-structuring. As with the differentiation and rationalisation arguments, however, relatively little attention is given to questions about changes in the conceptualisation of religion. The assumption is that a fixed definition of religion as a unitary phenomenon can serve as the basis for social scientific analyses of the changing functions that religion fulfils. Put differently, this approach treats the meaning of religion as constant while regarding its place in social and cultural life as changeable.

The most distinctive argument for the universality of religion and the logical impossibility of secularisation rests on psychological assumptions. For example, it is assumed that the human mind is structured in such a way that religious concerns are a psychological or even biological constant. This assumption means that it makes no sense even to take the possibility of secularisation seriously. According to this approach, human beings are, by definition, religious. Thus, although individuals may vary in the extent to which they are aware of, or willing to acknowledge, the 'fact' that they are essentially religious beings, it is not natural for them to live without religion. For example, David Hay (1990: 9) claims that 'the religious quest . . . is a biologically natural phenomenon' which is 'built into us in a way analogous to linguistic competence'. A more 'cultural' version of the argument about the necessity for religion is Robert Bellah's (1970: 206, 223) assertion that 'Somehow or other men must have a sense of the whole if they are to live; they must have something to believe in and to commit themselves to . . . [R]eligion is a part of the species life of man, as central to his self-definition as speech'.

There are sociological and anthropological perspectives on the universality of religion that parallel the arguments about the essentially religious nature of human beings. They are mostly variants on the theme that the experience of being socialised into human societies gives rise to a sense of the sacred that, in turn, finds expression in religious ideas and practices. Fustel de Coulanges (1864), W. Robertson Smith (1889) and Emile Durkheim (1964), developed these ideas about the socio-genesis of religion both with regard to the history of particular forms of religion and with regard to each individual's acquisition of religious sensibilities in the course of everyday social life. Georg Simmel's (1905) insight into the supposedly religious quality of interpersonal interaction added a further dimension to the case for claiming that religion is an anthropological universal. In more recent times, the case against secularisation has also come to rest on the argument that the rationalised banality of much of human life in advanced industrial societies is still pierced on occasion by outbreaks of collective effervescence (Mellor & Shilling 1997). Even the 'carnal' character of the effervescence has a religious character, according to this neo-Durkheimian view, since it re-establishes forms of ritualised sacred inter-connectedness among humans.

This line of reasoning against the most extreme forms of thinking about secularisation took a more phenomenological and cognitive turn at the hands of Thomas Luckmann (1967), Peter Berger (1969) and Hans Mol (1976). In their different, and not always mutually compatible, ways they argued that the human search for meaning and security, in the face of an otherwise threatening world of chaos and nothingness, was an anthropological necessity. Processes of human socialisation induced a sense of belonging to a universe of shared meanings and feelings that transcended the mundane world, according to Luckmann, and thereby rendered the possibility of secularisation virtually inconceivable. Berger's view was less sanguine. For him, a sacred cosmos was a functional requirement if individuals and human societies were to stave off the terrifying prospect of nothingness, but secularisation remained a possibility if the cultural and social structures that sustained the plausibility of belief in the sacred cosmos somehow failed. However, evidence of such failure has not yet persuaded Berger to change his mind, although his confidence seemed to wobble in the late 1960s. By the time of his article on 'Second thoughts on defining religion', Berger (1974) had already begun to distance himself from functionalist arguments whilst finding other reasons to believe that secularisation was not inevitable.

Berger's recent criticisms of the way in which some sociologists of religion tend to use 'secularisation' follow two different directions. On the one hand, he claims that the concept applies at best to Europe alone. Indeed, he has coined the expression 'Eurosecularity' for this very purpose (Berger 2001: 194). On the other hand is his claim that empirical evidence of religion's vitality in the USA and many regions of the world renders the term 'secularisation' inappropriate. According to Berger (2001: 194), the world is 'full of massive religious explosions'.

By comparison, Hans Mol's (1976) position has never wavered. The functional necessity for belief in a sacred dimension of human life has always been axiomatic for Mol, but he insisted that conventional or institutional religious beliefs and experiences were not necessarily destined to be the sole vehicles of the sacred. Secularisation was unthinkable in his terms, even though the significance of religious beliefs and organisations might go into serious decline. Other symbols of the sacred would simply replace them in the never-ending process of human meaning–construction.

Conclusions

Disputes about secularisation show no sign of abating. This is mainly because the disputants conceive of religion and its decline in radically divergent and incompatible ways. Awareness that the category of religion is itself a product of continuing social construction and disagreement is low. As a result, so-called debates about secularisation are a dialogue of the deaf. The antagonists talk past each other and cannot agree on ways of resolving their differences. Theoretical opinions are more divided now than they were in the 1960s. They can be summarised as follows:

(a) Some believe that the disputes can be resolved only by refining the empirical indicators of religious decline, by making more accurate measurements or by interpreting the empirical evidence more honestly.

(b) Others, by contrast, claim that the functional need for religion is virtually a pre-requisite for individuals to become humans or for societies to be viable. Consequently, the notion of decline cannot apply to religion, in their view.

(c) Some concede that the evidence of declining support for institutionalised religion is incontestable, while also insisting that the expression of religion is taking new forms or is being restructured. Privatised religion is supposed to have largely replaced the public forms of religious believing and/or belonging.

(d) Another argument is that privatised religion is not necessarily the fate of all religion, despite the fact that levels of support for institutionalised beliefs and practices have undoubtedly declined. There is still an important opportunity, according to this way of thinking, for religion to be the inspiration and basis for the mobilisation of normative values in the public sphere. The claim is that 'deprivatised' religion or 'vicarious' expressions of religion, articulated by mainstream religious organisations in the sphere of civil society, could thereby be significant influences in society and culture.

(e) A further variation on the theme of partial secularisation holds that, despite evidence of institutional decline, religion continues to be important by virtue of being implicit in everyday life or by continuing to diffuse distinctive values through social institutions.

One response to the complexity of these theoretical ideas is to try to put it aside with the argument that 'secularisation' has solidified into a 'myth' or an expression of ideology that merely pre-empts empirical investigation of the facts. But this is to miss two important points. The first point is that social scientific concepts are invariably contestable and under-supported by indisputable facts. There is always disagreement about their meaning and, consequently, about what can count as evidence in support of them. Judgements always have to be made about the adequacy of fit between concept and evidence. And opinions can change over time. Of course, a kind of intellectual inertia might dispose some social scientists to cling on to concepts, the meaning of which is no longer as clear as it used to be. But, *pace* Glasner (1977), even this does not amount to myth making. Any reluctance to modify the meaning attributed to a concept, or to abandon it altogether, in the light of fresh evidence or cogent reasoning is more likely to stem from the fact that it is embedded in a field of interlocking concepts. Piecemeal adjustments to a single concept are therefore improbable. The second point that is often missed in claims that secularisation is an ideological myth sustained by anti-religious scholars is that, as Wallis and Bruce (1992) argued, the motives of researchers are irrelevant to the truth value of their claims.

The debates about secularisation reveal very few cases of willingness to abandon fundamental points of view or, except in rare cases, to take account of the known arguments. Instead, it is more common for social scientists to defend their particular concepts and interpretations, in the face of arguments that are allegedly fatal to them, by re-specifying the meaning with which they invest their concepts. In this way, criticisms can be parried or side stepped. The possibility that fresh evidence might actually persuade social scientists explicitly to abandon a concept such as secularisation is almost inconceivable.

There is nothing abnormal or shocking about this. And it is certainly not an aberration of the sociology of religion alone. Similar 'dialogues of the deaf' have long taken place around notions such as 'rationalisation', 'modernisation', 'class conflict' or 'privatisation'. These theoretical ideas are of such a high level of abstraction that the social scientists who structure their view of the world in terms of them are unlikely to be persuaded to give them up simply because they appear to be incompatible with some 'facts' generated within different views of the world. High-level abstractions operate like compressed narratives and, as such, can be re-written or re-interpreted to accommodate facts or ideas that might appear to be inconvenient. This does not mean that the narratives are entirely fictional or mythical. They rest on a basis of facts that are deemed to support the narratives. But the relationship between adherence to the narrative and openness to the 'evidence' is loose and generally weak. The relationship is extremely elastic.

Does this mean that it is fruitless to conduct empirical investigations with the intention of resolving differences between the competing narratives about secularisation? Will additional facts not make a difference? My answer is in two parts. On the one hand, high-level, narrative conceptions of what is really going on in society are not usually vulnerable to evidence that their critics consider to be sufficiently damaging to render the conceptions untenable. In this sense, the best efforts of their critics and opponents rarely undermine commitment to high-level concepts such as secularisation. On the other hand, however, much of the empirical investigation that is supposed to undermine acceptance of opposing concepts does serve the useful purpose of clarifying the concepts in which it is rooted. As a result, empirical research helps to refine and strengthen conceptual thinking about the assumptions on which it is based; but it rarely gives rise to findings that fatally weaken support for these assumptions.

It would be churlish, then, to deny that sociological thinking about secularisation has changed. On the contrary, successive elaborations of basic concepts and repeated empirical investigations have brought many new things to light and have cast new light on many taken-for-granted things.

This has done very little, however, to bridge the gulf between the basic interpretative positions for and against the various ideas of secularisation.

From my point of view, this is not a pathological failure on the part of sociologists of religion – and certainly not a consequence of inadequate effort. It merely signifies that human societies are founded on a variety of shared meanings or views of the world which are not always mutually compatible. These world-views give rise to categories, boundaries and criteria that shape our perceptions and experiences of reality. The processes of constructing and contesting these meanings are the stuff of social life. The task of social and human sciences is not, therefore, to uncover a world of objective reality lurking behind the social constructions. Instead, the task is to understand how a sense of objective reality is socially constructed and changed – ideally including the self-reflexive process of doing social science itself.

There are welcome signs of a determination to step outside the conventional approach to a sociological understanding of secularisation and, instead, to pursue a social constructionist approach in Jay Demerath's (2001) idea of an oscillation between secularisation and sacralisation. Refusing to abandon the concept of secularisation simply because of the confusion that attends its usage, Demerath nevertheless insists on avoiding the triumphalist excesses both of those who regard secularisation as an inevitable master trend of modernity and of those who choose to deny that secularisation could ever occur. His own strategy is to focus on what he describes as one of the basic dynamics of culture, namely, the process of oscillation between secularising and sacralising tendencies. He implies that the process is never entirely predictable or irreversible. In other words, the oscillation is an open-ended process which, under the influence of numerous factors, gives rise to a variety of provisional states or scenarios. Demerath's (2001: 215) major argument is that tendencies in the direction of secularisation and sacralisation 'generally check each other to ward off all-or-nothing extremes of either sort'. Moreover, these outcomes are not solely to do with the fate of religious beliefs, practices or institutions but are also associated with developments of culture in general. At the heart of these developments are 'shifting conceptions and locations of the sacred' (Demerath 2002: 21). My particular gloss on this approach is that these shifts are best understood as the products of social processes in which the interests of human groups are at stake. They are not the outcome of deep structural forces within culture but can be traced back to struggles between ideas, values and material interests as articulated by human beings.

One aspect of the sacred that is currently undergoing re-location is the relationship between conceptions of religion and spirituality. Medieval and early modern notions of spirituality tended to emphasise personal discipline and the intensification of commitment to institutional teachings and practices. Yet, spirituality has come to refer to the quality of individuals' relations with the divine or 'a sense of awareness of a suprareality that goes beyond life as ordinarily experienced' (Wuthnow 2001: 307). Indeed, it is common for Christians to construe their spirituality as a freely chosen expression of their 'real selves', thereby accentuating the difference from externally controlled religion. The re-drawn boundary between popular conceptions of spirituality and religion is associated with broad changes in culture and social relationships, including patterns of religious belonging, believing and practising.

Wuthnow's (2001: 318) argument about the need for more careful investigations of the cultural resources on which people now draw in constructing their own spiritual practices is well taken. It is fully in keeping with the social constructionist approach that I am advocating towards debates about secularisation. I must add, however, that I prefer to take account not only of shifts in personal opinions and practices but also of legal, political, economic and other circumstances that favour locating the sacred in ideas of personal spirituality rather than in organised religion. In other words, societal forces and conditions are involved in shaping the view that subjective or individualistic forms of spirituality are appropriate and authentic forms of expression in late modernity. Religion and spirituality are clearly not unusual in this respect, for the assumption that individualism is taken-for-granted as 'normal' in advanced industrial societies is evident in fields as diverse as consumer behaviour, health care and education. It is only in situations where resolutely collective expressions of religion remain dominant, for example in some energetic religious movements, that critics raise questions about authenticity and acceptability.

3   The vagaries of religious pluralism

Since the 1960s it has been almost an article of faith for sociologists of religion to describe advanced industrial and late-modern societies as 'pluralist'. As we saw in the previous chapter, the notion of pluralism is inseparable from some influential versions of secularisation theory. In addition, it is intimately associated with ideas about the subjectivisation and the privatisation of religion. Pluralism is therefore one of the theoretical ideas that have helped to shape the sociology of religion; but criticisms have also been voiced (Flanagan 1990; Riis 1999; Champion 1999).

My intention is not to dismiss the idea that today's advanced industrial or late-modern societies are pluralist. Instead, I want to argue that the concept of pluralism is much more complicated and problematic than the term seems to imply. I also want to show that a more nuanced approach to pluralism can help to make sociological sense of many aspects of religious change today.

In order to enhance the importance of the topic of 'pluralism' in the sociological analysis of religious change I will need to do three things. The first is to explicate the term's current meanings. The second is, having exposed some problems with the most influential uses to which sociologists of religion have put the term 'pluralism', to propose a new term for some of the ideas that presently come 'bundled with' pluralism. And the third is to outline what seems to me to be a productive way of exploring pluralism today. This will require going outside the confines of the sociology of religion in order to adapt concepts that have shown themselves to be helpful in explaining the complexities of societies with growing diversity of culture and religion. My broader aim is not only to examine the uses to which sociologists of religion have put 'pluralism' but also to advocate a pluralistic approach to the scientific study of religion.

Conceptual clarification

My starting point is that there has been a tendency for sociologists of religion to conflate three separate aspects of religion in public life under the general heading of 'pluralism'. First, societies differ in the extent of their religious *diversity*. Second, the degree to which various religious groups enjoy *acceptance* or recognition in the public sphere varies from country to country. Third, support for the moral or political *value* of widening the public acceptance of religions is also variable. This third sense of the term is an ideological or normative commitment that I shall call 'pluralism'. There are undoubtedly close connections between these three phenomena, but for my purposes it is important to distinguish as clearly as possible between them.

(a)   Diversity in religion

'Diversity' is such a common term in everyday language as well as in the social sciences that it may seem surprising that I want to analyse the range of its meanings. But religious diversity can take many different forms, and dominant ideas about religious pluralism reflect only some of them. In the interest of conceptual hygiene, then, it is important to distinguish analytically between the following five forms of diversity in religion.

(i) It may appear as if the most straightforward indicator of religious diversity in any country is the absolute number of *separate religious organisations* or faith traditions that are represented there. Indeed, Stark and Finke (2000: 198, [emphasis original]) regard this as the sole meaning of 'pluralism': 'To the degree that a religious economy is unregulated, it will tend to be very *pluralistic*... *Pluralistic* refers to the number of firms active in the economy; the more firms there are with significant market shares, the greater the degree of pluralism'. This is indeed a plausible idea, but it fails to take account of the possibility that some, or many, religious collectivities may be so small as to be insignificant for practical purposes. Another complication arises when some religious collectivities are confined to only one geographical location and are unknown in other places. In this situation it is not clear whether the entire country can be usefully described as 'religiously diverse' if its religious 'market' consists of only one or two massive faith communities and any number of tiny 'competitors', some of which are not easily accessible to the majority of the population. From the individual 'consumer's' point of view, choice may be extremely restricted.

(ii) An alternative approach is to concentrate not on the collectivities but on the *individuals* who associate with them. If a variety of religious groups can all attract significant numbers of people, perhaps this is a better basis on which to talk about religious diversity. But one difficulty lies in knowing what counts as a significant number. For example, members of the Greek Orthodox Church in Turkey who now number only a few thousands still insist, for political reasons, that their country has an honourable tradition of religious diversity. Another more practical difficulty lies in knowing whether to count the number of individuals who merely identify themselves with religious collectivities, those who are officially their members, or those who participate in their activities from time to time. The point at issue here is that individual and collective perceptions of diversity may be just as important as the numerical evidence.

(iii) An entirely different indicator of religious diversity is the number of *distinct faith traditions* or world religions represented in a particular country. For some purposes, this is a more useful indicator than the number of separate collectivities or individual members. It is useful because it may indicate significant differences in ideology and culture. Thus, any country in which two or more faith traditions have large followings could be described as 'religiously diverse'. In this respect, internal differences within each major tradition would not necessarily indicate diversity.

(iv) Another possibility, especially in countries where support for major religious organisations is relatively weak, is to assess the number of individuals who *combine different religious outlooks* in their own identity. This measure of diversity is difficult to calculate, of course, but it may throw useful light on the extent to which individuals embrace religious ideas and practices that come from different sources. Finer distinctions could be made between those people who (a) tinker with a variety of religious resources ('*bricolage*'), (b) those who meld these resources into a novel *syncretic* position, and (c) those who maintain the distinctiveness of the original inspirations in *hybrid* forms that merely coexist with each other. The most interesting feature of this type of 'internal' diversity is that it may be compatible with the formal or official dominance of a single faith tradition. Many Filipinos and Italians, for example, manage without difficulty to reconcile their personal interest in variegated religious and spiritual interests with the idea that their countries remain overwhelmingly Catholic.

(v) Finally, it is possible to conceive of religious diversity as a process whereby a formerly unitary religious tradition undergoes a process of *internal differentiation* into separate sects or schools. Divisions between the major currents of Islam in a country such as Turkey illustrate this point. There is clearly diversity, competition and occasionally conflict between different expressions of Islam, but the range of different positions is relatively limited. For certain purposes, then, it would be misleading to ignore the internal, factional diversity of faith traditions that approximate to monopolies – especially if the intensity or extent of such diversity increased.

In short, the notion of religious diversity is far from simple. It is complex and subtle. That is, assessments of the significance of these different indicators of diversity vary with political circumstances and scholarly purposes. There is no single, neutral, objective or all-purpose way of assessing the degree or type of religious diversity.

The fact that religious diversity can be conceptualised in many different ways has direct implications for the extent to which religions are publicly accepted and for the meaning that is attributed to 'religious pluralism'. I would like to show that a kind of 'grammar' governs the uses that are made of 'diversity' and 'acceptability' in different meanings of pluralism.

(b)   Public acceptance or recognition

Societies vary not only in respect of the extent to which they display religious diversity but also in respect of the extent to which different religions and religious groups are recognised as legitimate actors in the public sphere.[1] Again, this is a descriptive, if not objective, dimension of public religion. In trying to assess how far different religious groups enjoy public acceptance and legitimacy, I am describing, albeit with difficulty, a state of affairs. There is no normative or evaluative component in this second aspect of religion's public face. In other words, it concerns variations in the manner in which religious collectivities are permitted to operate and are regarded as part of the public sphere. The degree of acceptance and recognition ranges from arbitrary concessions, mere tolerance and warm approval, to legal entitlement. It is a barometer of relations among religions, as well as between different religious collectivities, the public and the State.

The admittedly vague terms 'acceptance' and 'recognition' have several dimensions. In the first place, *legal and constitutional provisions* determine how far religious groups vary in terms of what they are formally permitted, licensed and physically enabled to do. Relations between religion and the State fall into this category because it includes taxation arrangements and agreements with relevant authorities about such matters as the right or obligation of religious authorities to register births, marriages and deaths or to participate in the education of children in State-maintained schools. There can be even closer relations between the State and religions in countries with an established Church or some other constitutional basis for according priority to any particular faith tradition, as in Iran and Thailand. These legal and constitutional arrangements have emerged from widely different historical and ideological circumstances, as demonstrated by Françoise Champion's (1999) discussion of the right to the freedom of religion in various countries. She draws a contrast, for example, between the 'emancipatory pluralism' that emerged in France from the protracted conflict between the Roman Catholic Church and the post-1789 State and the 'identity-based pluralism' that is currently being pursued by some religious minorities in the UK. The former rests on notions of the individual citizen's right in law to hold religious beliefs in private, while the latter asserts the moral, and possibly the legal, right of faith communities to enjoy the same opportunities for public recognition and respect as the Christian majority. This contrast echoes other attempts to compare patterns of social integration in France and the UK (Lapeyronnie 1993) and is a helpful ideal-typical benchmark for comparison of the legal basis for religious activities in the two countries. This is an important aspect of the broader notion of 'acceptance' that I am advocating.

Second, a range of less formal and more subtle understandings, conventions and practices allow some religious groups to function as the 'normal', *taken for granted* point of reference when secular agencies require information and advice about religious matters. Another aspect of this informal type of acceptance concerns the selection of religious professionals or of leading figures in faith communities to represent the sphere of religion on occasions of civic and State ceremonies, commissions of inquiry, and public responses to major disasters and tragedies. Once again, the range of variation is wide, with some countries rejecting all forms of representation by religion, and others appointing 'recognised religions'.

A third dimension of public acceptance reflects the willingness of 'accepted' or 'recognised' religious groups *to accept others* as worthy partners or competitors in the public sphere. This is a particularly important consideration in societies where one organisation, or a small number of religious organisations, is already in a position of power or influence – as in the case of State churches in some Nordic countries, in the case of 'national' churches in England, Scotland and Sweden or in the case of 'territorial' churches in the Orthodox Christian tradition.

In other words, patterns of religious acceptance and recognition are varied and subject to change. Degrees of tolerance, accommodation, recognition, authorisation, empowerment, legitimation and respect can vary considerably over time, between different religious groups and between different societies. Some social scientists apply the term 'pluralism' to these widely differing degrees to which religions and religious groups are accepted, but for reasons of conceptual and terminological clarity I prefer to reserve this term for expressions that convey a positive evaluation of religious diversity.

(c)   Pluralism as a value

The term 'pluralism' is widely used in the sociology of religion but is less commonly explicated (but see Hamnett 1990; Riis 1999). Many authors seem to assume that the term's meaning is so clear and unproblematic that it does not require careful analysis. This probably has something to do with the fact that Peter Berger and Thomas Luckmann made extensive use of the concept in the highly formative stage of the sociology of religion's development in the 1960s. I'll return to this point later. Perhaps the renown of their writings persuaded other sociologists that it was no longer necessary to monitor the meaning of 'pluralism'. It could, they probably assumed, be taken for granted. In the current state of affairs in most late-modern societies it is also a term that carries a strongly positive ideological and emotional charge (but see Baumann 1999). Perhaps this helps to explain why so many sociologists are happy to use the term without specifying precisely what they mean by it. Indeed, there is a risk that sociologists of religion could be accused of bad faith or of unprogressive attitudes if they tried to examine 'pluralism' critically. But I want to suggest that such a critical examination is long overdue – not because I'm unsympathetic to pluralism as a value but, on the contrary, because I believe that the ethical and political force of the term would be even stronger if its meaning were made clearer. Its relationship with various notions of religious diversity is particularly in need of clarification.

I notice, in passing, that the apparent reluctance of sociologists of religion to scrutinise the term 'pluralism' is not characteristic of scholars in other fields of research. Political scientists and students of 'race' and ethnicity, for example, have subjected the term to searching scrutiny in recent years. The connection between pluralism and multiculturalism has been of special importance in the UK (Goulbourne 1991; Samad 1997; Baumann 1999; Parekh 2000).

The starting point for my analysis must be a distinction between the descriptive and normative usages of 'pluralism'. I am puzzled, for example, by Ole Riis's (1999) conflation of these two different meanings. He acknowledges that it would be a mistake 'to conclude from the empirical fact of plurality that such plurality should be embraced normatively' (1999: 2). In other words, he asserts no logical connection between the fact of religious diversity and moral approval of diversity in itself. Indeed, there are many people who regret the fact of religious diversity in their societies and who consequently object to the notion that pluralism is good. Normative statements cannot be derived solely from statements of fact, according to the Scottish philosopher David Hume and to many of his followers among moral philosophers. Yet, Ole Riis goes on to use the concept of pluralism 'in a descriptive and in an evaluative sense' in his article. This makes it difficult for the reader to know whether Riis is describing the extent of religious diversity or the extent of approval for diversity. In order to avoid confusion, then, it is preferable to associate 'pluralism' with ideological or normative positions. This is a case of elementary 'conceptual hygiene' in which I try to keep facts and evaluations separate for analytical purposes whilst I also recognise that in reality 'ought' and 'is' are often intimately interwoven (see Putnam 1981). Nevertheless, Mary Hesse's (1980: xxiii) point is the most important consideration: 'Evaluations may be constrained by facts, but cannot be determined by them'.

The second point is that, even in its normative or ideological meaning, 'pluralism' is far from simple. Let me try to identify a few distinct meanings that are relevant to my argument. I shall link each separate meaning of pluralism to different aspects of religious 'diversity'.

(i) Building on the notion of religious diversity as the co-existence of several distinct religious collectivities in a country, the first meaning of religious pluralism is the belief that such *diversity of collectivities* is good, especially if their interrelations are harmonious. Flanagan (1990: 83) makes this point admirably:

Pluralism is very much part of the heritage of the Enlightenment, representing a reasoned demand for tolerance before a diversity of cultural, ethnic, and political forms. The term contains an ideological imperative, a belief that the rationality of its proclamation will lead to a harmonization of difference and an ending of conflict and intolerance.

Some versions of pluralism in this sense assume that religious monopolies are bad and that orderly competition between religious organisations is good. This meaning of pluralism flourished in countries where varieties of the Christian faith managed to coexist, but the meaning has more recently been extended to include cases where different faith communities live side-by-side. At the same time, moral and theological opposition to the positive embrace of pluralism has not subsided (Surin 1990; Eddy 2002).

(ii) A second sense of religious pluralism welcomes the opportunity for *individual choice* between different religious outlooks and groups. The mere coexistence of religious organisations is only the starting point. More significantly, the opportunity for individuals to *choose* their religious affiliations and, if necessary, to change these affiliations is regarded as essential in a truly pluralist situation. From this point of view, the mere coexistence of religious collectivities is not enough in itself. Indeed, it may even be a secondary consideration. The freedom for individuals to make religious choices comes first, regardless of whether there is peace or hostility between religious groups.

(iii) A third, more radical, notion of religious pluralism places a positive value on the capacity of individuals to *combine elements from different religious groups or traditions*. The peaceful coexistence of religious collectivities and the opportunity for individuals to choose among them are normally pre-requisites for this further meaning, but it is significantly different from them because it implies that the separate collectivities may not necessarily be valued in themselves. Instead, they are valued for what they allow people to take out of them. In this sense, religious pluralism signifies a free flow of ideas, symbols and practices across the boundaries of traditions and organisations. The results may include 'bricolage', syncretism and hybridity. This is a state of affairs that might be appropriate in thoroughly 'mobile' social systems (Urry 2000) or 'postmodern' conditions (Lyon 2000).

These three evaluative meanings of religious pluralism are compatible with each other in principle but not necessarily easily combined in practice. In fact, there is a potential for sharp tensions between the first and second meaning. According to a long tradition of theorising about pluralism in political philosophy, the order and stability of pluralist societies depend on the stable identification of citizens with particular collectivities, categories or voluntary associations (Dahl 1967). The crosscutting ties between these 'intermediary associations' (Berger & Neuhaus 1977) supposedly provide the strength and flexibility of the social fabric. Pillarised societies or 'consociational democracies' such as the Netherlands and Belgium were said to exemplify this form of pluralism in the mid-twentieth century. But if individuals are in practice free to choose their religious group affiliations and are free to change them from time to time, in accordance with my second meaning of religious pluralism, the effect on the social fabric could be destructive. The outcome would be less like pillarisation and more like a patchwork or network of relatively weak affiliations on the basis of conscience or personal identity. Examples include single-issue political groupings, 'identity politics' and collective action campaigns (Melucci 1989, 1996; Castells 1997). The result would be a form of post-modern pluralism rather than liberal pluralism.

My third general point about religious pluralism as a positive value is that, in addition to having several different meanings, it does not occur in a vacuum or in the abstract. Instead, it is debated, contested, fought over, managed and asserted in various social and political circumstances. From a sociological point of view, therefore, it is important to take account of the forces that shape the forms that religious pluralism, as an ideological position, has actually taken in history. For example, discourses of tolerance towards responsible religious collectivities underpin some British ideologies of pluralism (Wilson 1985), whereas discourses of individual rights underpin some American and French ideologies of pluralism (Champion 1999).

This is especially important in the case of societies where the imbalance in the power exercised by different faith communities or religious organisations is great. For example, the fact that Protestant and Catholic communities exist side by side in the North of Ireland does not render the situation pluralist.[2] Similarly, the hostile relations between sections of the Buddhist and Hindu communities in Sri Lanka are no basis for pluralism in the normative sense of fruitful and mutually supportive relations between different religions. By contrast, a kind of 'consociational' pluralism existed in the Lebanon from 1943 to 1975. It ended when politico-religious power struggles and the de-stabilising effects of conflicts in other parts of the Middle East plunged the country into fifteen years of civil war. In short, religious diversity or the juxtaposition of faith communities does not mean that they are all necessarily regarded as equally acceptable or good. Processes of social construction select those that are regarded as acceptable and those that are not. This is why I have insisted on keeping the description of degrees of religious diversity and acceptance analytically separate from evaluative ideas about the merits of acceptance.

To sum up, my argument has been that religious 'pluralism' is best considered as a term denoting a normative or ideological view holding that the diversity of religious outlooks and collectivities is, within limits, beneficial and that peaceful coexistence between religious collectivities is desirable. But even as a positive value, pluralism is complex and variable. It can also be politically contentious, especially if the focus on diversity for its own sake distracts attention from the reality of gross imbalances between faith communities in power and access to justice. The 'cult controversies' that I shall examine in Chapter Five illustrate the struggles that take place in countries as different as France and China to determine the political limits of religious pluralism as an ideological position.

The legacy of the 1960s

As I indicated earlier, the quasi-canonical writings of Peter Berger and Thomas Luckmann heavily influenced the conceptual career of 'pluralism' in the sociology of religion. They placed the concept at the centre of their individual and joint interpretations of the direction in which religion in the Western world was developing. I want to show that their particular usage of 'pluralism' was in fact strongly coloured by the timing and location of their work and that it is questionable whether their views are reflected in today's religious realities. For the sake of simplicity I shall concentrate primarily on the work of Peter Berger here, with only passing reference to Thomas Luckmann.

Berger's starting point is the claim that 'Through most of human history religious establishments have existed as monopolies in society' (1969: 134). This is at best a debatable assertion and at worst patently wrong. But its truth value is less important to me than the fact that it helps to lay the foundation for Berger's more significant claim that the vicious struggles between Catholics and Protestants in sixteenth and seventeenth-century Europe created the potential for pluralism in three senses. The first is the fragmentation of Christianity and the rise of non-religious ideologies. The second is the development of market competition between the fragments. And the third is the progressive differentiation of religious institutions from the more powerful economic and political institutions of modern societies.

The main aim of Berger's analysis of pluralism in the modern world was to assist his original explanation of secularisation as a 'crisis of credibility in religion' or the 'widespread collapse of the plausibility of traditional religious definitions of reality' (1969: 126). According to Berger, modernisation, rationalisation and industrialisation are the driving forces of social structural changes that deter the State from enforcing particular forms of religion. Indeed, the State allegedly ceases to need religious legitimation and becomes an 'impartial guardian of order between independent and uncoerced competitors' (130). In these circumstances religion can no longer 'fulfill its classical task, that of constructing a common world within which all of social life receives ultimate meaning binding on everybody' (132–33). Instead, religion becomes, according to Berger, a matter of personal preference. As such, it 'can be abandoned as readily as it was first adopted' (133). It has to be 'marketed' and sold to a clientele, with the consequence that religious institutions become progressively bureaucratised and forced to enter into ecumenical cartels with their competitors in order to mitigate the worst effects of competition. The force of economic logic extends even to the content of religion, for, since most 'consumers' of religion live in a highly secularised world, Berger argues that 'they will prefer religious products that can be made consonant with secularised consciousness over those that cannot' (145). Moreover, the argument continues, they will prefer religious products that are relevant to their private life, since the public sphere has allegedly already lost most of its religious significance. Finally, Berger expected that, in conformity with the dynamics of economic markets, the content of religious products would become standardised within the limits imposed by the need for marginal differentiation. Yet, the plausibility of these secularised religious contents would supposedly be vulnerable to competition from other, different products. Even those people 'who continue to adhere to the world as defined by the religious traditions then find themselves in the position of cognitive minorities', according to Berger (1969: 152).

In many respects, Berger's analysis of the dynamics of religion, especially in the USA, has stood the test of time. In particular, his observations about ecumenism, standardisation and marginal differentiation still ring true. But he has subsequently recanted some of his claims about the inevitability of secularisation (Berger 1974, 1999, 2001).

My point is that the assumption that we live in a secularised world is false. The world today, with some exceptions to which I will come presently, is as furiously religious as it ever was, and in some places more so than ever ... There is no reason to think the world of the twenty-first century will be any less religious than the world is today. (Berger 1999: 2, 12)

Nevertheless, I want to show that his overall characterisation of the dynamics of Western religion as 'pluralistic' has turned out to be misleading. Admittedly, I have the benefit of writing with hindsight, but there are undoubtedly problems with the logic of Berger's thesis.

(i)   Responses to diversity

The first set of problems concern the notions of monopoly and diversity. It seems doubtful to me that religious monopoly has ever meant the *total* absence of religious diversity or the existence of indifference, cynicism, hypocrisy and so on. So, Berger's contrast between 'tradition' and 'modernity' is exaggerated. Consequently, the threat that the loss of monopoly allegedly presents to the credibility of all religious belief is a red herring. From a social scientific point of view it is misleading because it conveniently overlooks, first, the extent to which religious sentiments and beliefs have often been diverse and, second, the degree of force that has usually been required to maintain the fiction of a unitary world of religious truth. It is correct to say that early modern Europe witnessed competition and conflict between a growing number of philosophical and theological claims to truth. But, again, this reflects as much a decline in the capacity of power-holders to suppress dissent as a loss of faith in a single source of truth. The interesting sociological questions are not about the credibility of any kind of religious claim to truth but about the social conditions that enabled a variety of beliefs, practices and organisations to achieve acceptance, permission or legitimacy. The focus should be on power and violence rather than on the putative 'loss' or 'decline' of a monopoly over truth and the rise of philosophical relativism. In other words, the pluralism analysed by Berger is primarily philosophical and theological. It concerns the risk that competition between different notions of truth will lead to relativism, if not nihilism.

From my point of view, a more productive social scientific approach would be to study the ways in which religious (or secular) regimes that aspired to be monopolies have framed and tried to control putatively deviant religious currents. Examples could be taken from almost any time or place, but among the best known are the persecution of Jews in medieval and modern Europe, the Inquisition, the extermination of the Cathars, the squabbles among colonial missionary Orders in Africa, South Asia and Latin America, the extirpation of the fledgling Christian communities in Japan in the early seventeenth century, the suppression of virtually all religious activities in Communist Albania, the crushing of Protestants in early modern France and the present-day struggle against 'cults' in the same country. The other, neglected side of this particular coin would be studies of the ways in which victimised religious minorities have responded to the harsh treatment that they received at the hands of their persecutors.

A more important point is that Berger's reading of the socio-psychological responses to the removal of compulsion and to the perception of diversity in religion raises some unanswered questions. It is not clear to me why the removal of compulsion and the perception of religious variety should necessarily lead to a crisis of conscience. His interpretation omits the possibility that the responses could have included a greater degree of curiosity about religion[3] and/or a greater degree of determination to support the claims of the status quo. It seems unlikely that deviant or variant religious currents were perceived as equal in power or credibility with the would-be monopolistic competitors,[4] so why did their existence precipitate 'crisis'? In fact, it is common for religious majorities and minorities, even in situations of mutual tolerance and harmony, to regard each other with a range of attitudes including curiosity, indifference, amusement, derision, scorn and hatred. This was certainly true of the proto-pluralist *millet* system that imposed order on the various faith communities within the Ottoman Empire. The British *Raj* also kept the peace much of the time between the innumerable religions and religious factions in India. I find it hard to imagine a situation in which the mere co-existence of a variety of religious expressions would be likely to undermine religious faith in itself. On the contrary, the discourse of many religious groups contains rationalisations that seek to explain the existence of their competitors or enemies. The 'theology of religions' is just such a Christian account of other faiths. In short, relativism does not necessarily follow from the perception of diversity, although it clearly does so for a theological liberal such as John Hick.

Thomas Luckmann's position on this aspect of religious diversity is more cogent. Instead of speculating about the destructive effect of pluralistic competition on the plausibility of any and all claims to absolute truth, he concentrates on the implications of diversity for the standing of '"official" models of religion'. His view is that when there is competition between 'official' models of religion, they all risk losing their 'official' status – not their credibility (Luckmann 1967: 87). This is a significant point of difference from Berger's account. Pluralistic competition does not necessarily lead to chaos, according to Luckmann, but possibly to the weakening of religious forces relative to non-religious forces in society. At the same time, he argues that the declining authority of 'official' models of religion does not preclude the possibility that 'a new social form of religion' might replace them. Luckmann predicts that this new social form of religion will not be mediated by the major social institutions and that it will consist of more or less loose collections of themes arising from private life, such as autonomy, self-expression, sexuality and familism. His subsequent analyses of modern religion have specified the variable range of the experiences of transcendence occurring in everyday life (Luckmann 1990).

Another questionable aspect of Berger's interpretation of pluralistic competition is his assumption that voluntary subscription to religious beliefs, practices and groups is necessarily more precarious than is compulsory subscription. This interpretation elides two things that should be kept analytically separate. Berger confuses 'the traditional task of religion' with the actual practice of religion. His argument is that the advent of privatised religiosity obstructed religion's traditional task of establishing 'an integrated set of definitions of reality that could serve as a common universe of meaning for the members of a society' and that was binding on everybody (Berger 1969: 133). He considers that the plausibility of privatised religiosity, lacking the force of compulsion, must be weaker than that of traditional religion because its plausibility structure may, in some cases, be no broader than the nuclear family. 'Religion resting on this kind of plausibility structure is of necessity a tenuous construction. Put simply, a "religious preference" can be abandoned as readily as it was first adopted' (Berger 1969: 133). But, in my view, some of the most robust and intense forms of religion are cultivated by relatively small numbers of devotees constituting cognitive minorities. Examples that spring to mind include various sectarian minorities and isolated diasporic communities. Indeed, a case could be made for claiming that the intensity of a religion varies inversely with the size of its plausibility structure. Berger's error lies in failing to distinguish between the 'task of religion' and its effects. In reality, compulsion does not necessarily correlate positively with strong conviction, compliance or credibility. The thrust of Rational Choice forms of reasoning is in exactly the opposite direction (see Iannaccone 1994).

(ii)   Privatisation

A second set of problems concerns Berger's interpretation of 'privatisation'. In common with many other social scientists of the time Berger treated the 'private' as a relatively unproblematic category defined mainly by contrast to the 'public' world of economic activity, the State and politics. But this distinction reflects some questionable assumptions about the priority of the public over the private and about the relations between the two spheres. The thrust of much social critique of the 1970s and 1980s was to call into question the particular ways in which the public/private divide had been conceptualised in social science and to show that the two are interrelated in complex ways (Weintraub & Kumar 1997). To cite only one example, Jürgen Habermas exposed the so-called 'colonisation of the life-world by the system' in order to account for the interpenetration of public and private in the modern world. Many feminists have also argued that the conventional distinction carries the imprint of gendered interests (Gatens 1991; Marshall 1994).

The effect of Berger's particular way of operationalising the public/private distinction is to obscure the fact that much of religion is concerned precisely with either denying that such a distinction can be upheld or insisting that the boundary between them is not located in the place where it is widely supposed to lie. For example, many conservative Christians deny that questions of family life can be safely relegated to the realm of private choice but insist that they go to the heart of public policies and the well being of the entire society in which they live. We now know that many devout Muslims also refuse to accept the idea that conduct in what many Muslims regard as the private realm is separable from life in public.

Another questionable implication of Berger's distinction between public and private is that the State takes relatively little interest in trying to control religion when it has ceased to be a mechanism for integrating the whole of society under a 'sacred canopy'. The argument seems to be that religion is somehow 'relegated' to the private sphere because it is considered to have relatively little relevance to the distribution of power in society.

Thomas Luckmann's (1967) account of privatisation gives this argument a slightly different twist. In his view, the functional differentiation of a specifically religious institution in societies takes place alongside the expansion of secular spheres of life such as politics and the economy. Consequently, according to Luckmann (1967: 86), 'the individual... tends to restrict the relevance of specifically religious norms to domains that are not yet pre-empted by the jurisdictional claims of secular institutions. Thus religion becomes a "private affair"'. Now, this implies that individuals choose to preserve their religious convictions in the only sphere not yet invaded by secular norms, i.e. the private sphere. But, as with Berger's analysis, it is questionable whether the private sphere can be said to exist in any sense other than that imposed by the most powerful authorities in any society. In other words, 'the private' is defined as the sphere of life from which public authorities choose to exclude themselves in certain conditions. It is not, as implied by Luckmann, a kind of virgin territory previously untouched by collective influence. After all, powerful religious organisations in all the world's major religions had invariably sought to define and control the private life of individuals long before exclusively political or economic forces were able to attempt the same thing. In this sense, the private has always been a residual category for denoting the territory in which religious and secular authorities were willing to place restrictions on their own power. But it is important not to lose sight of the fact that religious authorities also cultivated complex ideals concerning personal spirituality as a form of self-imposed discipline (Séguy 1996). From this point of view, then, the so-called privatisation of religion was not the deliberate choice of individuals to restrict the applicability of their religious ideas and practices to the declining number of areas of life not yet dominated by secular authorities. Instead, privatisation makes better sense as the indirect result of decisions made by public authorities to limit the direct application of religious considerations to policies and practices concerning many areas of life. The boundary between the public and the private is, therefore, moveable in response to the shifting fortunes of contenders for power.

Yet, the highly public controversies that have grown up around so-called privatised religion in recent decades have provided clear indications that agencies of the State and other public bodies take a serious interest in aspects of religion that would have been the responsibility of religious organisations in the remote past. In other words, what appeared to be a process of privatisation in the 1960s is better understood as a process of 'massification'. This means that the role of intermediary organisations shielding individuals from the State has been eroded in favour of more direct involvement of the State in individuals' lives. As many individuals have loosened their bonds of attachment to religious collectivities and have begun to 'consume' religious products on the open market, so they find that agencies of the State are prepared to regulate both consumers and producers in the name of, for example, health and safety, anti-fraud measures, child protection and public order considerations.

In summary, I have two main criticisms of Berger's thesis on pluralism.

(a) The first is that he exaggerates the extent to which the removal of compulsion from religion and the growth of religious diversity in Europe precipitated a crisis about the credibility of all religious beliefs. This may have been how the situation looked in the USA in the 1960s in the eyes of relatively conservative thinkers. But we now know that Berger's account failed to take proper account of such things as the enthusiasm for relativism among some religious radicals, the resilience and powers of resistance displayed by strongly conservative forces of Christianity and Judaism, and the burgeoning market for sectarian forms of religion. These three developments provide no evidence of a religious legitimation crisis. It was only the middle ground of mildly conservative, socially conventional religious groups that experienced the decline of compulsion and the growth of competition as a crisis. Many of these groups have continued to decline in numerical strength and social influence over the past four decades, while more radical expressions of progressive and conservative religion have at least managed to maintain their position in the religious market.

(b) My second criticism is that Berger's use of 'private' and 'privatisation' assumes that the public/private distinction is unproblematic. In fact, the history of the last forty years has provided convincing evidence that the definition of 'private' is not a mechanical or accidental by-product of the differentiation of social institutions in advanced industrial societies but is intimately associated with ideological discourses, consumer culture, work practices, bureaucratic procedures and the interests of State organisations. The normative force of 'the private' emerges from all these different contexts in which distinctive notions of the normality of private individuals are constructed, made plausible and imposed.

In jargon terms, private individuals are 'interpellated' or called to account for themselves by the daily experience of being, for example, consumers of mass-media products and market goods, citizens of a State, employees of organisations, members of categories identified by age, ethnicity, gender, social class, 'life style', and so on. Moreover, individuals are capable of reflecting critically on their 'privatised' identity and therefore of choosing to flaunt it, to flout it, to flee from it or to fight it. The message of much interactionist and ethnomethodological investigation is that human beings are not necessarily dupes of their cultural and social surroundings. Yet, for Berger it seems as if privatisation is an objective process that is driven by the unstoppable forces of rationalisation, industrialisation and bureaucratisation – in short, modernity. The plausibility of his argument is weakened by the findings of research into the ideological underpinnings of the concept of modernity and into the bases of resistance to notions of privatisation.

Berger's use of 'pluralism' gives priority to images of the fragmentation of formerly unitary or monopolistic religious traditions. The crisis of religion is said to have its roots, therefore, in the perception that unity has been lost and in the vertiginous feelings of alarm triggered by the proliferation of alternative sacred world-views. In this sense Berger's work owes much to Durkheim's depiction of anomie as a social and psychological state of de-regulation or of unbridled appetites and loss of moral landmarks. Berger's proposals for responding to the problems of pluralism are also Durkheimian for involving 'intermediary associations' that can represent individuals with shared interests and can mediate between them and the State. The form of privatisation, according to this account, will be checked by the assertion of group-based interests and identities. Societal balance and harmony will be the product of the interplay between these 'intermediary associations', regardless of the inequalities between them in power and wealth.

A totally different version of pluralism emerges, however, if the starting point is not the belief that modern history represents first and foremost the loss of societal unity, the fragmentation of formerly monopolistic sacred canopies and the scattering of privatised individuals across rationalised wastelands. If, instead, priority is given to an entirely different set of processes, pluralism amounts to something very different from tolerant associationism. These processes include the continuous struggle through history between conflicting interest groups to impose control over collective life, the harnessing of religious ideologies to schemes for legitimating the exercise of power, and the subterranean persistence of robust superstitions, demonologies, heresies, and invisible or folk religions with the capacity to challenge and subvert 'official' versions of the sacred canopy. The emphasis of this alternative kind of pluralism, largely incompatible with Berger's, is not merely on tolerance or competition but on the search for justice, the eradication of discrimination and prejudice, and the moderation of gross inequalities.

Recent clarification of 'pluralism' in the sociology of religion

Although the legacy of 1960s thinking continues to pervade sociological ideas about religion in conditions of modernity or in advanced industrial societies, three sociologists of religion have recently helped to refine our understanding of 'pluralism'. Ole Riis, Jean Bauberot and Jacques Zylberberg have all identified social structural conditions that affect the way in which religious diversity is managed. They all show that the normative force of pluralism as an ideological concept can be channelled into a variety of policies, practices and structures. In short, they reinforce my general point that pluralism is a complex social construct that is in need of careful analysis these days.

(i)   Ole Riis

Riis begins his analysis of the different 'modes of religious pluralism' with the observation that processes of globalisation will not only intensify pluralism but will also generate a plurality of pluralisms. He shows that philosophers and political theorists have already used pluralism in many different ways but that social scientists tend to share the view that pluralism means 'a recognition of multiplicity in society' (Riis 1999: §1.4). The point of Riis's analysis is to show, however, that the principles of tolerance, free competition between religious groups, and the freedom of individual belief and practice can be combined and expressed in a number of different social forms. He argues that the American model, for example, favours minimal State intervention, competition and individual freedom, whereas pluralism in Western Europe has tended to lean in two different directions. The first is towards limited forms of pluralism based on individual freedom and public recognition of certain denominations and even State churches in some countries. The second is towards a structural segmentation into vertical 'pillars' based on Protestant, Catholic, Humanist and, possibly, Muslim identity, as in Belgium, the Netherlands and Northern Ireland. The latter cases rest predominantly on the ideal of tolerance and the notion of collective, rather than individual, rights to religious freedom.

Riis correctly points out that there are many varieties within the three main patterns that he has identified for the USA and Western Europe. More problematically, he also claims that there is a tension between two ideological positions. On the one hand, majorities defend pluralism on the basis of individual rights, whereas minorities deploy the notion of collective rights to justify their claims. In my opinion, this tension certainly exists; but I doubt whether it is simply a matter of majorities and minorities. For example, some members of minority faiths in Britain object very strongly to any policy that directly or indirectly reinforces the collective right of men to exercise patriarchal power over women in religious organisations (Anthias & Yuval-Davis 1992; Yuval-Davis 1994). Similarly, some members of the Christian majority in Britain try hard to influence educational curricula with the aim of strengthening the collective right of the majority to defend its cultural values (Beckford 1998).

The latter point was very clearly illustrated by conservative reactions to the well-publicised report on *The Future of Multi-Ethnic Britain* (Commission 2000). Against the report's recommendation that Britain should be considered as a loose federation of cultures held together by common interests and a sense of belonging, some commentators denounced what they saw as the threat to a cohesive sense of 'Britishness'. Their feelings of outrage were all the more intense because the report also suggested that the term 'British' and the Union Flag carried racial overtones and should be replaced by symbols that would be acceptable to all ethnic and religious categories of people. Their argument was that the new symbols would have to be free from association with Britain's imperial, racist history and heritage.

One of the merits of Riis's argument is that it emphasises the complexity and variability of 'pluralism' as an empirical description *and* as an ideological prescription. The precise balance between tolerance, competition and individual freedom is subtle, elusive and subject to change in each country. This is a valuable lesson. It goes a long way towards combating the assumption that pluralism is simply a matter of religious diversity, in the absence of compulsion, within an overarching framework of inclusiveness.

(ii) Jean Baubérot

The value of Riis's argument about cross-national differences in the conceptualisation and implementation of pluralism is confirmed by Jean Baubérot's historical and sociological analyses of the highly distinctive meanings attributable to 'pluralism' in France. With special emphasis on the formative events of the French Revolution of 1789 and its Napoleonic aftermath as well as on the legal separation of Church and State in the early twentieth century, Baubérot explains how Republican anti-clericalism forged the notion of laïcité as a set of principles designed to foster democracy, national integration and solidarity in the face of deep ideological and social divisions. The French school system has been the primary target *and* agent of laïcité for almost one hundred years, but all agencies and institutions of the French State are required to implement it. In this way, potentially divisive, if not destructive, ideological divisions between, say, French Catholics, communists, free thinkers, Jews and Protestants should be transcended by an overarching reference to the values of republicanism, parliamentary democracy, human rights and the State's disengagement from matters of religion. Baubérot (1990a, 1990b) has also argued that a new, critical phase of laïcité began in the 1980s. It marked the need to respond to the increasing involvement of France in European and other international agreements as well as the need to find a way of fully integrating a large population of Muslims into French society without abandoning the 'sacred' text of the Declaration of the Rights of Man and of the Citizen. The new 'moral settlement' must, according to Baubérot, enshrine universal values *and* particularisms in its respect of human rights. Baubérot admits that this is a major challenge but he clearly believes that laïcité is a dynamic force that can survive if it adapts to changing circumstances. There is even a hint (Baubérot 1990a: 225) that he considers a 'new settlement for laïcité' to be an attractive model for many other countries.

How do Baubérot's ideas about laïcité bear on the notion of pluralism? For my purposes, the main implication is that each of the two main phases of laïcité in France framed pluralism differently. Baubérot's speculations about the prospects for laïcité in the twenty-first century indicate that pluralism will take on yet another new significance. In the first phase of the Revolution and the Napoleonic reforms, pluralism means the retreat of the State from fulfilling religious functions, the annulment of Catholicism's virtual monopoly over freely practised religion in France and the specification that only a small number of recognised religions could legally continue to operate within the limits contained in the Concordat with the State. To some extent, then, Catholicism was 'de-institutionalised', but the State continued to intervene in its internal affairs and to acknowledge its social usefulness. This amounts to a very limited form of pluralism that left the Roman Catholic Church in a relatively privileged position *vis-à-vis* other religious organisations. It was not until the 1880s that anti-clericalism began to strip Catholicism of its remaining privileges.

The second main phase, from 1880 to about 1907, officially abandoned the idea of 'recognised religions' and installed a programme of strictly secular moral education in schools. In this context, pluralism meant the formal separation of churches from the State, practically and symbolically, and the implementation of legal controls over the official designation of religions as 'religious' and over their fiscal status. This represents a further stage in three respects: (a) the marginalisation of religious organisations, since they were no longer recognised for their social utility, (b) the State's attempts to distance itself from any religion by abandoning the idea of 'recognised religions', and (c) the formal recognition of each individual's freedom of conscience.

Baubérot expects the new phase of laïcité, beginning in the late twentieth century, to be more accommodating towards religious minorities and more flexible about the study of religion in school curricula and about the involvement of religious representatives in State-run commissions. This amounts to a recognition that it is one thing to separate church and State, but quite another, and much more difficult, to separate religion from public life. It suggests that the challenge to the laïcité of France in the twenty-first century is to find a way of balancing the following factors:

(a) the principle of State neutrality towards religions
(b) the right of individuals to the freedom of conscience and thought
(c) the acknowledgement that, within limits, religions can contribute many useful things towards social integration and the functioning of society
(d) the principle that religions should enjoy equal opportunities to contribute towards public life, especially in cases where State funding or co-operation is involved.

Meanwhile, Baubérot's observation (1999a: 319) about the paradox of laïcité at present is highly revealing about the practical significance of pluralism in France. On the one hand, the freedom of conscience is held in high regard in French ethical philosophy and law. On the other, French culture has not yet fully recovered from centuries of occasionally violent, monolithic religious power and over one hundred and fifty years of clashes with irreligion. As a result, the country is not fully acclimatised to the freedom of conscience. The result, according to Baubérot (1998; 1999), is a persistent tension between two principles that had previously worked in harmony in the first phase of laïcité. But nowadays the principle of 'freedom of conscience' can sometimes find itself in conflict with the principle of 'freedom of thought', especially when it seems to some observers that charlatans or authoritarian tyrants are abusing the freedom of conscience. 'Islamist', 'fundamentalist', 'integrist' are just some of the labels applied in France to the kind of uncompromising, ideologically exclusive, impatient and intolerant groups that are accused of abusing the freedom of conscience for their own profit. Many critics and opponents of such groups therefore invoke the principle of freedom of thought or 'freethinking' as the grounds for emancipating the 'victims' of supposedly ruthless exploitation or control. In different terms, the freedom of thought must logically precede the freedom of conscience. For, if individuals cannot exercise the power of independent thinking they are incapable of making a rational choice of beliefs.

There is direct support for Baubérot's reading of the paradox of laïcité in France in the findings of the 1998 International Social Science Programme survey in France (see Bréchon 2000). The results show that two thirds of French adults believe that religions bring conflict rather than peace and that strong religious beliefs make people intolerant. In Bréchon's opinion, French attitudes towards religion are mixed, but intolerance is considered to be a risk in religions that claim to have exclusive access to the truth. This suspicious attitude towards high-demand religious minorities was not a problem in the first two phases of laïcité because there were very few minorities large enough to cause problems and because the strength of anti-clericalism was strong enough to keep majorities and minorities under control. However, the situation in the third phase of laïcité has changed significantly. Religion is now much more diverse in France; religious minorities are much more visible and vocal; and the Catholic majority is more apathetic. These factors have given rise to the 'laïcisation of laïcité' according to Jean-Paul Willaime (1996). In these circumstances the State's apparently growing willingness to work with religions precipitates some problems of definition. How are the State's 'acceptable' religious partners to be chosen? By what criteria? Is greater intolerance towards unpopular religious minorities the price to be paid for the French State's greater readiness to co-operate with the religions that it recognises? In other words, the 'softer' form of laïcité could paradoxically give rise to greater degrees of religious intolerance towards minorities by making them appear to be more threatening than they used to be. This paradox is not yet reflected in the optimistic, eirenic notions of pluralism that tend to prevail in social scientific studies of religion.

(iii)   Jacques Zylberberg

Jacques Zylberberg's comparison of Germany, the UK, Canada and the USA (1995) does not seem to support Baubérot's view that laïcité could be exported from France to other countries. On the contrary, his argument is that each of these countries, in their very different ways, provides a framework of public law and understandings that shores up religion in its relations with the State. Moreover, critical reactions to modernity have, according to Zylberberg, given a new lease of life to religion and have obliged its detractors to recognise that religion remains, or has reverted to being, a legitimate force in public life. In fact, Zylberberg goes so far as to claim that religious organisations nowadays enjoy the advantage of being able to take either a left-wing position in defence of people left behind by progress or a right-wing position attacking modern, liberal, permissive society. This is why he believes that agencies of the State as well as political parties try to court religious organisations for tactical or strategic reasons. A not entirely dissimilar argument underlies José Casanova's

(1994) estimate of the potential that the Roman Catholic Church still has for making a contribution towards civil society and public politics.

For my purposes, the virtue of Zylberberg's (1995) approach is that it firmly situates the potential that religious organisations have for political mobilisation in the context of a framework of public law and administrative agreements. This is a much more precise and nuanced way of analysing changes in religion's potential for influencing public life than by attributing them to the unexamined notion of pluralism. Zylberberg's analysis shows that this potential varies widely among the four countries that he examines. This comes close to a 'political opportunity structure' or 'political process model' approach akin to that used by some analysts of social movements (see Kitschelt 1986; Kurzman 1996; McAdam 1982). It involves identifying factors such as the structure of political parties and trade unions, the nature of constitutional provisions, the ownership and role of the mass media, and the pattern of legal opportunities and constraints. It is clear that religious organisations, like social movements, can be helpfully analysed in terms of their responses to this kind of opportunity structure. Recourse to explanation in terms of an unexamined notion of pluralism would only obscure the factors that really affect the varied uses that are made of religion in public life.

A good example of the opportunity structure approach is Eric Morier-Genoud's (2000) analysis of the controversy that surrounded the approval in 1996 and subsequent annulment of a law in Mozambique that would have created two official holidays for Muslims in a State that was officially secular. The analysis emphasises the fact that the main political parties had been competing for the allegiance of Muslim voters for many years, that some politicians felt that it was desirable to compensate Muslims for the unfair discrimination that they had suffered under colonial and post-colonial rule, and that one of the law's objectives had been to establish equality between Muslims and Christians (who already enjoyed a Christmas holiday). Above all, Morier-Genoud argues that the removal of official restrictions on religious activity in Mozambique after 1989 created an unprecedented level of competition between many faith communities and induced the Mozambican State to try to mediate between them. As a result, tensions and rivalry between faith communities increased sharply. Against this background, the proposal for a law to create two Muslim holidays assumed heightened importance, especially because the State had not clarified the criteria governing its own involvement in religious matters.

Morier-Genoud (2000: 426) speculates that 'religious tensions and conflicts will probably carry on if the State maintains a "free religious

market" approach without adopting a clear position, or religious regulations or law'. His broader claim is that

'. . . a policy of religious "deregulation" (the creation of a free "religious market")
increases competition between organised faiths and that such increased competition does not merely bring greater religious freedom, pluralism and improved
religious "products", as neo-liberal sociologists would like us to believe. It also
brings tensions and conflict, especially it seems when deregulation goes too far
and/or when the State does not have a clear or secular position'. (Morier-Genoud
2000: 426–27)

This argument is a striking challenge to the prevalent understanding
of the secularising effects of competition. In effect, the Mozambican example shows not only that religious markets can certainly raise levels of
religious activity but also that they can be unruly and destructive as well
if they are not regulated. This strikes a double blow against much received wisdom in the sociology of religion: on the one hand it denies that
competition necessarily leads to secularisation; and on the other it denies
that 'de-regulation' of religion is necessarily a pre-condition of religious
vitality.

Finally, this example demonstrates the usefulness of placing religious
controversies clearly within a context of political opportunities and constraints. An equally instructive example relates to the experimental policy that Singapore adopted in the early 1980s to introduce the compulsory study of Religious Knowledge into the secondary school curriculum
(Tamney 1992; Hill & Lian 1995). The purpose was to harness religion to the task of educating citizens in morality and thereby helping to
strengthen national identity and international economic competitiveness.
In the event, however, the policy proved to be counter-productive for the
State because it inadvertently raised the profile of religion to unexpect-
edly high levels and exacerbated ethnic divisions. It also ironically led to
an upsurge of Christian evangelicalism. The government responded by
abandoning the Religious Knowledge curriculum in 1989 and by enact-
ing the Maintenance of Religious Harmony Act in the following year. A
'civics programme' that was intended to instil Confucian values was im-
plemented in schools at the same time. These sudden changes of policy
and practice are evidence of the Singaporean State's sensitivity about the
balance between different ethnic and religious communities. Its attempts
to engineer harmony in a religiously and ethnically divided country are
outstandingly clear examples of the concern shared by many late-modern
States with managing diversity by inculcating the value of pluralism as
an ideology of harmony. Consequently, the recent history of religion in
Singapore can only be properly understood in the context of the political

opportunities that were opened up and quickly closed down again within ten years.

Religious 'pluralism', policies and prison

The cases of Mozambique and Singapore may appear to be isolated accidents, but they are actually part of the much larger topic of the 'management of religious diversity' in societies where levels of religious diversity have placed strain on existing frameworks of law and politics.[5] The forces of globalisation have complicated the issues by accelerating the speed and reach of communications and population mobility and by transposing practices from their place of origin to other locations ('time-space distanciation' and 'disembedding' in Giddens' [1990] terms). In response to the challenges of religious diversity and globalisation, legislators, leading representatives of faith communities and agencies in civil society have been debating appropriate policies and practices in many advanced industrial societies. Various notions of pluralism and its closely associated term 'multiculturalism' are at the heart of the rationalisations given for policies for managing religious diversity. My interest here is in some of the dilemmas and paradoxes that have emerged from usually well-intentioned attempts to build pluralism into public policies in Britain. Broader discussions of this topic occur in Gilroy (1987), Baumann (1996, 1999) and Vertovec (1994) in connection mainly with ethnicity. Relatively few sociologists of religion have tackled the issue of policies regarding pluralism and religious diversity, but significant exceptions include Riis (1999), Champion (1999), Furseth (2000), Smith (2000) and Kühle (2002). My focus will be on the appropriateness of the term 'pluralism' in relation to policies regarding the provision of religious and pastoral care to prisoners in England and Wales.[6]

An observer of any one of the 140 prisons in England and Wales would notice that certain areas were reserved for religious activities. At least one Church of England chaplain would appear to take most of the responsibility for administering the chaplaincy premises and facilities, often meeting other prison staff to discuss individual prisoners or to organise religious festivals. Free Church Protestant chaplains and Roman Catholic chaplains would also be seen sharing some of these duties on a full-time or, more likely, a part-time basis. In addition, especially if it was Friday, a 'Visiting Minister' would probably be in the prison for two hours to conduct prayers with the Muslim inmates or to join them for religious festivals. Sightings of Visiting Ministers for Buddhist, Hindu and Sikh inmates or for Christian minorities and Pagans would be less frequent in most prisons. Very few of these Visiting Ministers are likely to attend meetings of chaplaincy committees; some of them would even require authorisation from the Church of England chaplain to be admitted to the prison; and only about one third of them would be allowed to draw keys at the gate-house. Perhaps the biggest surprise to the observer, however, would be the sight of one of the first ten full-time Muslim chaplains, all of whom were appointed in 2002 and 2003. Their appointment represents the most significant change in relations between the Christian chaplains and the representatives of what are often called 'other faiths' in the Prison Service.

The fact that the Prison Service of England and Wales enables inmates to practise their religion, within the normal constraints imposed by the need for order and security, may appear to be evidence of pluralism in the sense that there is no Christian monopoly and that different faith communities coexist side by side. This would be a reasonable inference for the casual observer to make, but it would fail to take account of the imbalances of power and the friction experienced by members of these faith communities. In other words, 'pluralist' is a superficial designation for a configuration of relations between faith communities that systematically favours mainstream Christians.

Recent changes at the highest level of the Prison Service Chaplaincy, including the appointment of a full-time Muslim Advisor and a Chaplain General committed to the ideal of multi-faith chaplaincy, have gone some way towards redressing long-standing imbalances in the distribution of power, influence and material resources between representatives of the different faith communities involved in prison chaplaincy. But it remains the case that Church of England chaplains still tend to be regarded by prison staff as 'the' chaplains and that they tend to control chaplaincy committees and the allocation of resources. They act as facilitators and brokers on behalf of 'other faiths'. Many of them are pleased to show 'tolerance' towards religious minorities. They have the right to talk to inmates from all faith communities, whereas Visiting Ministers are forbidden to talk to inmates who are not members of their particular community. As a result, inmates who are religious but not Christian undoubtedly benefit from the work that Christian chaplains do on their behalf. Indeed, leading representatives of some Muslim organisations in the UK have publicly argued that Muslims are better off living in a country where a Christian Church is 'established in law' than in a country where no religion or religious organisation enjoys a privileged position *vis-à-vis* the State. This is a rationalisation of lack of power and systemic inequality.

Furthermore, the legal and administrative framework within which prison chaplaincy takes place imposes systematic limitations on faith communities outside the Christian mainstream. First, the Prison Service officially allows each inmate to register as a member of only one of a list of 'recognised religions'. The three explicitly 'non-recognised religions' are the Church of Scientology, Rastafarianism and the Nation of Islam. Second, whereas the range of recognised categories of religious registration within the Christian grouping is wide, Muslims, Hindus, Buddhists, Sikhs and others do not have the option of choosing anything other than the 'one size fits all' category for their community. This creates friction in some cases between Visiting Ministers and inmates who do not share the former's particular theological or philosophical orientation. Third, Christian chaplains are eligible for various forms of training, induction and career development, but Visiting Ministers rarely have the opportunity for such integration into the Prison Service.

In short, the appearance of pluralism – in the sense of faith communities operating side by side in prison chaplaincy – is misleading. True, levels of co-operation, consultation and autonomy for Muslims have increased sharply since 2000. Yet, the discrepancies between mainstream Christianity and 'other faiths' remain sharp in terms of the latter's opportunities to act independently of Church of England chaplains, to have access to resources and to enjoy recognition as authentic religions on the same basis as Christian denominations. Other faiths are tolerated, within limits, in the Prison Service of England and Wales and are permitted to operate, but it is hard to avoid the impression that their presence is still a concession granted by the Christian majority to selected, relatively powerless minorities. So-called pluralism in this case does not reflect a plurality of faith communities with equal rights, equal opportunities or equal respect. On the contrary, it is a one-sided system of patronage and brokerage by concession, although the imbalance is slowly being redressed. This is why I believe it is unhelpful to describe such systematically unequal relations of power between faith communities as 'pluralism'. Instead, the task for sociologists of religion should be to map these power relations carefully and to describe their contours in detail, paying special attention to systematic variations in the relative access of different faith communities to opportunities for influencing the world around them.

This extended example of prison chaplaincy underlines the need for social scientists to be suspicious of simplistic notions of pluralism. Studies of relations between different faith communities and between them collectively and the State need to investigate, at the level of social interaction, precisely how power, recognition and resources are distributed. Moreover, some faith communities are excluded from participation in prison chaplaincy; and others are 'admitted' – but on disadvantageous terms. Finally, lest it be thought that my reservations about the uncritical use of 'pluralism' are a function of a uniquely British form of unfairness, I shall conclude by mentioning a legal dispute that developed in 2002 in a country that prides itself on being pluralistic – the USA. It concerns frictions among Christian chaplains in the US navy, who are officially categorised as Roman Catholics, 'liturgical Protestants' and 'nonliturgical Protestants'. Evangelical chaplains in the 'nonliturgical' category sued the relevant authorities for allegedly discriminating against them in favour of the other two types of chaplain. The alleged discrimination took two forms: not appointing a number of 'nonliturgical' chaplains in proportion to the number of navy personnel who identify with, for example, Baptist and Pentecostal styles of Christianity, and passing over well qualified 'nonliturgical' chaplains for promotion. The outcome is not known at this time of writing, but, regardless, this legal action is an interesting illustration of my point that the appearance of pluralism can conceal strong feelings of injustice and resentment in the face of perceived imbalances of power. There is no shortage of similar illustrations from the history of legal struggles conducted by, for example, Jehovah's Witnesses and the Nation of Islam against agencies of the US State.

Conclusions

I have tried to make three main points in this chapter. The first is that the tendency to conflate religious diversity, the degree of acceptance of certain religions in the public sphere, and the ideological commitment to the value of religious diversity and the increasing scope of religious acceptability is unhelpful. It is unhelpful because historically and in the present-day these three dimensions of religion can vary independently of each other. It is, therefore, confusing to lump them all together as expressions of a generic 'pluralism'. It is also misleading if the positive evaluation that many people attach to the term 'pluralism' obscures the reality of inequalities and power struggles that are just as much a feature of the religious life in late-modern societies as are the much more widely publicised phenomena of ecumenism and inter-faith co-operation.

Second, the influence of the early writings of Peter Berger and Thomas Luckmann can be seen in the assumption made by many sociologists of religion that pluralism is closely associated with privatisation and with the cognitive vulnerability of strong religious convictions in late modernity. Empirical investigations have begun to question whether this assumption is still sustainable at the beginning of the twenty-first century.

Third, recent work by Françoise Champion, Ole Riis, Jean Baubérot and Jacques Zylberberg has indicated that the meaning of 'pluralism' in terms of legal arrangements and less formal social patterns can vary across time and between societies. Consequently, pluralism can include such different scenarios as the American model of a supposedly open market in religion, the State churches of most Nordic countries, the system of laïcité in France, as well as the pillarised system of Belgium and the Netherlands. It is preferable, in my opinion, to abandon this generic sense of pluralism in favour of more precise ways of capturing the political opportunity structure for religion in late-modern societies.

My conclusion is that the bewildering variety of arrangements that qualify as 'pluralistic' is too wide to serve analytical purposes. So, instead of retaining 'pluralism' in a generic sense, I think it is better to make a clear distinction between the three separate phenomena that I have identified. In this way it is possible to show that the sociological issues that are allegedly at stake in 'pluralism' are not the same in all countries. In particular, the issues of religious diversity and the public acceptability of religions take on different meanings in different societies.

None of this implies that pluralism, as a social value, lacks legitimacy or credibility. Support for the view that diversity in religions, and diversity of religions, is in itself preferable to religious monopolies is widespread but far from universal in late-modern societies. Notions of balance, harmony, mutual support and equality of opportunity between faith communities usually meet with approval in abstract terms. Pluralism represents a popular ideological ideal, especially for academic researchers and political liberals. It is important, therefore, for social scientists to examine the forms that pluralism takes in various discourses. The affinity with uses of 'tolerance', for example, is strong[7] but much weaker with uses of 'equality' or 'justice'. It is no less interesting to investigate the uses to which the value of pluralism in religion is put in political life. It would be a mistake, however, to confuse this ideological or evaluative meaning of pluralism with the empirical realities of diversity and relations between faith communities.

Finally, let me explain that my reason for being cautious in the preceding paragraph about the degree of popular and political approval of religious diversity and equal opportunities for all religions is that 'pluralism' comes in for strong criticism from three sources. Racism and intolerance of difference are the first source. Second, some feminists oppose all religions that allegedly discriminate against, and oppress, women. Consequently, these opponents of the value of pluralism do not support religious diversity or equal respect for religions that are deemed to be anti-women. The third source of opposition to pluralism as a value arises from philosophical and political grounds for suspecting that doctrines of pluralism and multiculturalism have the effect of reifying and essentialising ethnic and religious categories that should be better conceptualised as vague, flexible and shifting. According to Bhatt (1997), these doctrines have also worked to the advantage of conservative factions that claim particularist rights for themselves but deny the rights of other minorities. There is also some evidence of this in Hindu and Sikh nationalist movements (van der Veer 1994, 2000). On the other hand, these arguments about the problems associated with naïve uses of pluralism and multiculturalism as values have been challenged, mainly in the name of pragmatic compromises (Modood 1998). It is unlikely that the findings of empirical research will bring closure to these debates that go to the heart of questions about social solidarity, justice and identity in late-modernity. Religion, as Lemert (1999) has argued, is integral to these questions.

4   Globalisation and religion

Introduction

Ulrich Beck's *What is Globalization?* (2000) concludes with a chapter entitled 'Decline à la carte: the Brazilianization of Europe'. It is a thoroughly dystopic depiction of the future as a slide into factional disputes, polarisation, lawlessness and protection rackets. The nightmare scenarios of post-modernity and of neo-liberal globalism would have come true: States would be weak, whereas select transnational corporations would be gigantic.

This is one possible reading of some of the tendencies already discernible in an increasingly globalised world. But it is far from being the only interpretation: it is merely the most shocking. What is most surprising about Beck's notion of 'Brazilianization' is that it makes only one passing reference to religion in the guise of 'salvation armies'.[1] Yet, one of the most fascinating aspects of Brazil's history in the twentieth century was the proliferation of a mesmerising variety of syncretistic religious movements. Brazil also experienced a steady growth in the popularity of Protestant, especially Pentecostal, churches (Martin 1990; Freston 1994, 1995; Lehmann 1996, 2001; Aubrée 2001; Martin 2002). In the last three decades of the twentieth century Brazil generated a number of hybrid religious organisations that have spread to other countries and are now part of global religious networks.

I am not suggesting that these developments in Brazilian religion have anything to do with Beck's dystopic vision of globalisation. I mention them only for two different reasons. The first is that very few of the social theorists and social scientists who write about globalisation ever make more than a passing reference to religion. Significant exceptions include Peter Beyer, Roland Robertson, Frank Lechner and David Lehmann. The second reason is that religious developments in Brazil may be a forerunner of things to come. In other words, there is much to be gained from considering the relations between religion and globalisation; and the case of Brazil indicates how religion may develop in other areas of a globalising world.

My argument in this chapter will be that globalisation, in all its various meanings, represents more continuity than discontinuity with processes originating in earlier phases of modernisation. Nevertheless, if globalisation in relation to religion is sensitively analysed it throws into sharp relief some new aspects of religious changes and some new challenges to more conventional perspectives in the sociology of religion. In this sense, it is unquestionably helpful to 'think with' the notion of globalisation, provided that the concept's limitations are kept in mind. I see no reason, however, to try to reduce all explanation to a matter of globalisation – just as I previously saw no reason to regard 'post-modernity' as the key to understanding religious change (Beckford 1992, 1996).

The way forward, in my opinion, is to analyse carefully the widely differing meanings attributed to 'globalisation' and, in the light of these differences, to assess their relevance to explanations of religious change. This means paying attention to the findings of empirical research as well as to conceptual and theoretical discussion. Above all, it means exposing the failure of many social theorists either to recognise or to account for the distinctiveness of religion in conditions of globalisation. My strategy runs the risk of making me appear simply to be complaining that social theorists tend to ignore the work of sociologists of religion. I am prepared to take the risk of being seen to engage in special pleading on behalf of the sociology of religion, but my motivation is actually different. My aim is to suggest ways of improving the social scientific understanding of what is meant by 'globalisation' and, by implication, how we understand the character of religion in conditions of globality. Since the theorists of globalisation have tended to paint a misleading picture of religion or to omit religion altogether from their pictures, it is difficult for me to avoid giving the impression of special pleading.

'Religion is good to think with'

Some preliminary remarks are necessary about the advantages and disadvantages of focusing discussion of globalisation on religion. Many commentaries on globalisation, as well as empirical studies that utilise the concept, are exclusively concerned with its economic and political dimensions. Even the relatively few studies of the cultural dimension of globalisation tend to have little to say about religion beyond a few banalities. The primary concern is usually with the evolution of popular culture and the spread of American cultural products throughout the world. Careful consideration of religion, from the viewpoint of globalisation, is rare. Integration of the findings of empirical research about religion into high-level theorising about globalisation is rarer still. Regardless of whether this is a function of ignorance, laziness, indifference or implicit acceptance of the idea that religion is irrelevant, the result is that, outside the confines of the sociology of religion, the religious dimensions of globalisation have received relatively little attention from social scientists.

On the rare occasions when theorists of globalisation do take religion into account they tend to make highly *selective use* of empirical findings. That is, they seize upon findings that confirm or support their views of globalisation. It seems that the more exotic or sensational the findings about religion, the better. For extreme cases seem to leave little room for debate. They simply clinch the argument. As a result, there is apparently no necessity to inspect the representative quality, the validity or the reliability of the chosen examples. They are merely assumed to exemplify the phenomenon of globalisation in relation to religion. Yet, as I shall try to show, religion is far too subtle and complex to fit so easily into simplistic scenarios of globalisation, especially those that reduce globalised religion to fundamentalism.

One of the reasons why the topic of religion is a challenge for simplistic versions of globalisation is that, by definition, religion is *self-reflexive*. Religions are not simply the effects of external forces; they are also agents, observers and critics of their own development. In fact, there is evidence to suggest that religious organisations can be sensitive and pro-active agencies for processing information about the changing circumstances in which they operate. They are like filters that detect and analyse evidence of change in the atmosphere. Of course, the filtering is neither neutral nor objective by scientific standards. It reflects each religious group's values and beliefs. Consequently, their recipes for responding to change draw on ideological resources, including theology and sacred jurisprudence. Religious organisations reflect on globalisation by filtering its perceived impact on their activities and place in the world; and they respond to the challenges and opportunities that they detect in globalisation.

Another problem with religion, from the viewpoint of simplistic concepts of globalisation, is that it does not conform to a single model of the process. Indeed, the sheer variety of religious ideas about globalisation and the bewildering diversity of religious responses to globalisation present obstacles to any attempt to impose a unitary schema on the process. Religion is not entirely constrained by the logic of economic markets. Nor is it limited by the international treaties, agreements and organisations that apply to nation States. The forces allegedly leading to the standardisation or homogenisation of economic and political organisations do not necessarily apply with the same weight to religious phenomena.

In short, religion is 'good to think with' in relation to globalisation for three main reasons. First, it challenges simplistic theorising based on highly selective examples. Second, it forces attention on religion's capacity for self-reflexive critical thinking about globalisation. Third, religion resists any single model of globalisation by demonstrating a kaleidoscopic range of responses.

An additional reason for thinking that religion presents peculiar problems for notions of globalisation is that, unlike economics and politics, it is not affected to the same degree by '*de*nationalisation' (Beck 2000: 14). This concept refers to a process whereby global forces are said to erode the sovereignty of nation States and possibly transform them into transnational States. The growing power of multi-national corporations lies, according to this concept, beyond the regulatory reach of any particular States. These corporations' pursuit of profit and competitive advantage on a global scale is believed to put national tax revenues at risk and to erode the investment in national infrastructures and welfare programmes that supposedly undergird capitalist development and growth. In other words, the interests of multi-national corporations and nation States may be not only at odds but also in conflict. There are indications that this argument applies to religion in countries such as Russia, Greece, Saudi Arabia and China where resistance is being mounted against the unfettered incursion of religious influences from other parts of the world. But this is far from being a recent phenomenon. It is merely the present-day expression of conflicts and tensions that have often surrounded the international diffusion of the so-called world religions. And it is not clear how far the global spread of religions in the twenty-first century actually threatens to undermine the sovereign identity of States. In some cases we are witnessing the emergence of international efforts to protect the freedom of individuals to practise the religion of their choice without interference from States. In other cases, international efforts are being made to establish codes of practice and regulatory regimes with the aim of protecting States against 'alien' religions. In this sense, religion does not always fit conveniently into the category of a 'de-nationalising' factor. There are good reasons for arguing that, in some instances, the re-sacralisation of national identity is taking place as a defensive reaction against threats perceived to arise from global forces. It may even be the case that religion represents a major resource in some anti-globalisation campaigns.

These considerations amount to an argument for showing much more than the normally perfunctory interest in the relevance of religion to debates about globalisation. Studies of religion not only 'flesh out' accounts of globalisation with detail that is usually overlooked but they also challenge some taken-for-granted assumptions about the process. Roland Robertson (1987: 36) has even gone so far as to claim that religion is 'a critical ingredient of globalisation'. And, in extreme cases, such studies call into question the usefulness of even deploying notions of globalisation. For all these reasons, then, there is much to be said for closely examining the relationship between religion and globalisation.

Discourse about globalisation is, in roughly equal measures, exciting and frustrating. The excitement arises from the fact that globalisation is a fashionable term that offers the prospect of characterising the development of human societies and cultures at the highest level of generality. It works like a trump card in so far as it promises to supersede all previous explanations. Another aspect of the excitement is associated with the dizzying speed with which fresh explanations of the term emerge in journalism as well as in social science. Nobody knows precisely where the proliferation of meanings and implications will end, but many writers are keen to 'ride the tiger'. Lively debates about globalisation as a concept and a reality also feed the excitement.

On the other hand, all the excitement about globalisation is frustrating because the term can appear to be out of control. It is used in a bewildering variety of ways and contexts. The range of meanings extends from the casual implication that 'global' means 'extremely widely distributed around the world' to the technical claim that only phenomena that are not based unambiguously in at least one geo-political location can be considered 'global'. Most uses of the term fall somewhere between these two extremes. It is irksome to have to scrutinise each usage in order to determine how far 'globalisation' is intended as a casual or a technical term. The scope for misunderstanding and for talking at cross-purposes is therefore extensive.

How should we respond to this combination of excitement and frustration? For my purposes, it is important to keep firmly in mind the broad range of meanings carried by 'globalisation'. Nothing is to be gained from arbitrary exclusion of any particular meanings. This is because my aim is to explore the opportunities and challenges that the concept, in *all* its various forms, presents to the sociology of religion. It would be counterproductive, then, to restrict my interest to a limited range of meanings. Instead, I shall consider the implications that a variety of approaches to the understanding of globalisation have for social scientific studies of religion. This is in keeping with the pluralistic tenor of this book. And it exemplifies my belief that social sciences thrive on controlled comparisons and collisions between different perspectives. I make no claims for 'progress' or 'advancement', however, since these terms imply the existence of undisputed landmarks along the route from ignorance and error to knowledge and truth. My concern is only with perceptions of effectiveness in understanding.

Although my intention is not to legislate for the meaning of terms, it is nevertheless helpful to seek clarity about them. This is why I shall begin by considering the uses to which 'globalisation' and some of its cognates have been put in religious contexts – with particular concern for their relevance to the study of religion. I shall make some conceptual distinctions that, in my view, help to explain the variety of ways in which religion and globalisation are mutually implicated. After discussing the religious uses of 'globality' and 'globalisation' I shall turn the tables and discuss the ways in which social scientists tend to interpret religion in global circumstances.

The uses of 'globality' and 'globalisation' for religious purposes

The starting point has to be the social *and* religious construction of '*globality*'. This is the term that Roland Robertson applies to a consciousness of the growing connectivity and integration not only between countries and regions of the world but also between all manner of economic, political and cultural spheres and processes. In this sense, globality is the idea that so many aspects of life have attained such an elevated degree of inter-connectedness that it has become customary, if not obligatory, for people to sense an overarching oneness. As a result, everyday experiences are increasingly relativised by reference to the global whole of which they are perceived to be a part. In everyday parlance 'the world has become a smaller place'. This is a facet of social theorising about globalisation that social scientists have sometimes ignored in their eagerness to study the supposedly hard, objective evidence of globalising tendencies in political, economic and cultural activities. Religion is an ideal medium for focusing attention on ideas of globality[2] because religious ideologists are active in constructing its meanings.

Given the concern that many religious ways of thinking and feeling demonstrate with the 'perceived whole' or the 'ultimate significance of things', it is not surprising that consciousness of globality assumes great significance for sociologists of religion. The 'global-human condition' (Robertson and Chirico 1985) lends itself to construction and interpretation in religious terms. Indeed, globality is an idea to which countless religious leaders have warmed, recognising that they have a claim to stake or to defend in this area. But globality is more than a form of consciousness or an idea. In criticism of the cognitive bias that he detected in many sociological analyses of religion in a global context Simon Coleman (2000) focused much of his study of the Word of Life charismatic movement on the aesthetic, experiential and bodily dimensions of its followers' lives. He could see that they acquired characteristic dispositions, patterns of physical activity and forms of social interaction that embodied the movement's globalising ideology and aspirations. This is why Coleman used the inclusive term 'orientation', rather than 'consciousness', to capture the variety of ways in which Word of Life embraces globality and in which members embody a global orientation in their styles of language and physical deportment.

The fact that competing accounts of the essential oneness of the world and of its inhabitants have existed side by side throughout human history has been no deterrent to belief in any particular account. In truth, the competition has often taken the form of internecine warfare between the protagonists of different ideas about the oneness of the world. This continues to be the case today, but at the same time there is also a growing familiarity, at least among intellectual elites in some places, with a wide range of such all-embracing world-views. World-wide flows of information through the means of international travel, education and the mass media have helped to document the sheer diversity of world-views and to sharpen the focus on the structural similarities cutting across them. Juxtaposition of differences does not dissolve them or resolve conflicts between them. But in a world where awareness of differences is highly developed, the search for common ground recommends itself increasingly as an alternative to head-on collisions and conflicts. The refinement of differences can go hand-in-hand with the identification of points of agreement at higher levels of generality and abstraction (Wieviorka 2001).

For example, familiarity with the world-views and practices of more than one major world religious tradition was rare at the time of the first World's Parliament of Religions in Chicago in 1893. But by the time of the second such event one century later in 1993 the world's press and religious studies specialists were much better placed to understand its significance. Admittedly, the spectacular conflicts, abstentions, exhibitionism and walkouts attracted a lot of publicity, but there was also interest in the possibility of inter-faith dialogue and the emergence of a 'global spirituality' (Roberts 1995). The emergent form of spirituality in the Parliament's debates was rooted in a productive tension between the universal and the particular: diversity and commonality. The celebration of diversity was a pre-condition for the appreciation of a common humanity facing shared problems and threats. Thus, globality was at stake in the very structure of the Parliament's programme; and it was quite explicit in many of the discussions of environmental problems, human rights issues, gender equality and poverty. In the words of Richard Roberts (2002: 264), 'The peculiar and distinctive ways in which religion represents the global condition acknowledges the relativity of all validity claims, yet it does not abandon them; it cannot, because tensions between universal and particular are endemic and acknowledged in religion'. Dissent from the view that the Parliament represented a 'global religious event' (Roberts 2002: 257) was largely confined to conservative religious leaders who were unwilling to accept that their particular faiths could be relativised in the search for points of global agreement. These dissenters would probably take no consolation from Peter Beyer's (1994: 227) prediction that different visions of global religion are likely to clash with one another 'since the appeal to holism is itself partisan'. Indeed, among the ironic outcomes of the 1893 Parliament were the early stirrings of interest in highly particularistic Hindu nationalism. But this is not incompatible with my point that notions of globality have long been a feature of many faith traditions and that current tendencies in world-wide communications are only enabling or forcing them to confront each other more directly. Indeed, as the world appears to shrink, local and regional conflicts can assume potentially catastrophic significance. As religious discourses are among the few cultural resources capable of expressing such significance, it could be argued that globalisation stimulates religious or spiritual outlooks.

While notions of globality are far from novel in religions,[3] notions of *globalisation* have few roots in religious traditions. Moreover, the diversity of ways in which 'globalisation' is understood in the social sciences, journalism and popular parlance makes it unlikely that the term will be easily assimilated into religious discourses. Instead, religious leaders tend to borrow the term from non-religious sources in forms that suit their purposes. Their purposes may include warning their followers against the moral and spiritual dangers attributable to the allegedly homogenising effects of globalisation. Alternatively, they may intend to argue that their particular religious tradition can contribute valuable cultural resources towards the elucidation and control of the emerging global circumstance. But in both of these cases warrant for the depiction of globalisation as a process will probably come from sources outside religious institutions, although a distinctively religious gloss will usually be put on the significance of the process.

Religious discourses that regard globalisation as a positive achievement or an opportunity to exercise beneficial influence on the world place selective emphasis on the emergence of global consciousness, the intensification of world-wide communication and the possibilities for concerted action to deal effectively with transnational problems of, for example, crime, environmental pollution, sickness, malnutrition or poverty. This version of globalisation is mainly about the establishment and co-ordination of transnational activities modelled on prevalent notions of representative democracy in advanced industrial societies. Certain non-governmental organisations (NGOs) figure prominently in this discourse as exemplars of disinterested global consciousness and action.

Religious discourses that depict globalisation, by contrast, as a con-spiracy to impose homogeneous standards on all areas of life as a con-sequence of the marketisation and the Americanisation of everything are equally selective. But this time the emphasis is placed on the capacity of globalisation to destroy particular cultures and identities, to undermine differences, to insist on uniformity and to reduce the idea of value to a calculation of instrumental advantage.

Between these two extremes there is a wide spectrum of intermediary viewpoints, many of which combine a scepticism and caution towards globalisation with a recognition that, properly understood and controlled, the process might produce some beneficial effects.

A good case in point concerns Jehovah's Witnesses. Until the closing decades of the twentieth century the Witnesses had shown little interest in things global and had, under the leadership of 'Judge' Rutherford in the 1920s and 1930s, excoriated schemes to create global institutions such as the League of Nations. It has recently come to light, however, that the Watch Tower Society secretly held the status of an NGO at the United Nations from 1992 to 2001. Moreover, articles in the Watch Tower Society's magazines have begun to deploy the word 'global' in a vari-ety of positive senses. Yet, in each case, the Watch Tower writers are careful to locate the term in an ideological framework that is indisputably separate from that of most social scientists and journalists. They do so by recognising that world-wide communications have increased significantly in rapidity and intensity and that human beings are now obliged to take account of transnational phenomena. This approach appears to be thor-oughly conventional and in line with that of many other commentaries on globalisation, but Watch Tower writers then re-frame their arguments in such a way as to insist that the benefits of global thinking and co-operation will necessarily remain elusive until a 'truly' global order is established. At this point, Watch Tower writings depart sharply from the direction taken by secular accounts of globalisation in order to emphasise the in-disputability of 'superhuman' solutions to human problems at the global level.

For example, a series of articles about human rights that appeared in the Jehovah's Witnesses' magazine, *Awake!*, in November 1998 begin with copious details about the history of the UN Declaration of Human Rights and the International Bill of Human Rights. In addition to explicating the meaning of the Declaration's major clauses, the articles supply brief academic commentary and examples of human rights problems. But they abruptly conclude that 'Despite the mammoth efforts of human rights organisations and despite the dedication of thousands of activists who literally risk their lives to improve the lot of men, women and children worldwide, human rights for all remains just a dream' (*Awake!* 22 November 1998: 11). The final article in the series explains that a change of individuals' outlooks and a change in the form of government must occur before the dream of 'human rights for all' can become a reality. The article insists that there must be an acknowledgement that human beings have rights only because God gave them their faculties of reason and conscience when He created them in His own image. And there must be a world government inspired by God and based on biblical principles if a truly global and lasting human rights culture is to be created. The combination of these two conditions would supposedly be the 'superhuman solution' to human rights problems.

The articles in *Awake!* give a brief insight into the ideological work that a world-wide religious movement such as the Jehovah's Witnesses is prepared to invest in appropriating selected parts of the discourse about human rights in order to defend and promote its own highly distinctive view of globalisation. In this way, the Watch Tower Society can portray itself as an informed participant in debates about matters of public interest, even using much of the same vocabulary as that used by secular writers. But the specific meanings attributed by the Society to 'global' and 'globalisation' derive from its apocalyptic frame of reference – not from the ways in which social scientists and journalists use them. In other words, the Watch Tower Society has incorporated popular words referring to globality into its time-honoured and unchanging message about the allegedly impending millennial upheaval that is expected to transform human societies into a single theocracy. This represents an extremely distinctive notion of the global but it serves to illustrate my point about the great diversity of religious appropriations and refractions of 'globalisation'. The Watch Tower Society has been purveying its particular version of the global future for more than one hundred years. But, strictly speaking, its orientation is transnational rather than global. Control over the Watch Tower Society has centred on Brooklyn since the early twentieth century, and branch offices around the world are nothing more than local outlets for the standardised products authorised by the leaders in the USA. The gap between the ideological attention that the movement has recently given to themes of globality and the reality of its resolutely transnational form of operation reinforces my point about the need for social scientists to study critically the social construction of religious phenomena.

Soka Gakkai International (SGI), the Japanese lay Buddhist 'value creation' movement with origins in the 1930s, has fashioned a contrasting version of globality and globalisation. Instead of following the Witnesses' example of waiting for Jehovah to unleash the destructive forces of Armageddon and the Great Tribulation that is prophesied to follow, the SGI has been training its eleven million followers since the 1970s to ferment a 'human revolution' on a world scale by transforming their inner selves through meditation and chanting and, thereby, laying the foundations for a new global civilisation based on ideals of peace, unity and respect for difference. The aim is to create 'world citizens', dedicated to the promotion of prosperity, peace and happiness, by means of global programmes of education, cultural activities and peace advocacy. The self-image of the SGI is modelled on the global character of the UN and is inscribed in its organisational structure. It is a movement that aspires not only to take advantage of globalisation but also to stimulate and strengthen tendencies towards global consciousness and global forms of action.[4] As with the case of the Watch Tower Society, however, it seems more appropriate to characterise SGI as a transnational movement in the sense that control has always rested in Japan, although national branches enjoy limited autonomy in some matters.

Yet another, different way of appropriating notions of globality is found in the ideology, organisation and practices of the Baha'i faith (Warburg 1999; McMullen 2000). This is probably the most enthusiastic religious embrace of global ideals, based as it is on a vision of a 'world federal system' that would supposedly liberate all people from misery and injustice. Moreover, the patterns of life chosen by many individual Baha'is, at least in Western countries, reflect their cosmopolitan values and global networks of communication. Yet, Baha'is depart from most forms of 'one-worldism' by holding that representative democracy is not an appropriate model for the politics of a global civilisation. The world order envisaged by Baha'is would rest, instead, on a deliberate conflation of religion, politics and law – all governed by what they claim to be universal principles of ethics. This amounts to a form of globalism that seems to owe less to diversity than to an imposed form of unity.

These examples of the religious uses of 'globality' and 'globalisation' illustrate one of the challenges facing researchers on globalisation: terms such as 'globality' and its cognates are not exclusively tools of sociological analysis. They are also central to the ideologies and the activities of some religious organisations. Moreover, to make matters more complicated, these terms have become the stock-in-trade of journalists,

programme makers, commentators on current affairs and, to a lower degree, the person-in-the-street. This is an indication of the extent to which
the discourse of social sciences has penetrated everyday life and has enabled the current stage of modernity to be characterised as 'self-reflexive'
(Giddens 1991). It means that individuals and organisations have acquired not only the language with which to analyse their identity and
performance but also, and more importantly, the sense that such methodical self-scrutiny is morally and/or practically desirable. A less well
explored aspect of self-reflexive modernity is the possibility that it also
increases the likelihood of self-fulfilling prophecies, leading to a form of
collective hypochondria. Thus, anxiety about the feared effects of globalisation is not uncommon in religious discourses.

Good sociological research into globalisation needs to take account of
the fact that usage of the concept is more highly developed than is understanding of the reality to which it supposedly refers. This is an important,
if relatively neglected, aspect of the relations between religion and globalisation, for the theological and moral implications of globalisation are
already being elaborated in religious organisations and built into hom-
ilies for practical action. Even if some religious organisations strive to
combat what they regard as the harmful effects of globalisation they are
nevertheless obliged to accept, in doing so, that the process is real. This,
in turn, lends further credence to the concept. Indeed, it is unusual for
religious leaders to try to deconstruct a concept such as globalisation or
to assess the evidence for and against its usefulness and credibility. They
are much more likely to respond in their writings and sermons to journalistic and other popular treatments of globalisation, most of which simply
take its existence for granted. In this way, the concept of globalisation has
become part of the reality of religious phenomena through the medium
of sermons, topics for meditation, the study of sacred texts, discussion
of inter-faith relations, and so on. 'Globalisation' therefore operates in a
host of different ways in religious ideologies and their practical applications in missionary strategies and schemes for seeking to exercise political
influence.

Sociological studies of religion explore the fact that notions of globality and globalisation have been absorbed into many different religious
discourses, ideologies and theologies. It does not follow, however, that
the process of absorption is the same in every case. The manner in which
globality and globalisation are appropriated or constructed varies in accordance with pre-existing frameworks of religious ideas and values as
well as with political, economic and social circumstances. Thus, in areas
such as Greece and Eastern Europe where Orthodox Christianity is the

dominant religion, globalisation is likely to be constructed as an external force that threatens to undermine the claims made about a primordial link between territory and the sacred. At the other extreme, globalisation can be welcomed as a valuable opportunity for evangelism in those Protestant traditions that accord primacy to each individual believer's personal relationship with Jesus Christ regardless of ethnicity or nationality. Hindu nationalist movements and Islamist movements have also turned global communications technologies to their advantage (Bhatt 1997: 252–53; van der Veer 2000). But the case of Singapore, as discussed in Chapter Three, demonstrates the ambivalence felt by the island's government in the 1980s towards the growth of religious diversity associated with globalisation. The decision to make Religious Knowledge compulsory in the Singapore school curriculum and the rapid reversal of this decision ten years later indicate the difficulty of trying to engineer a suitable balance between local circumstances and global influences.

For different reasons, some new religious movements that aspire to extend their coverage to every part of the world also seek to ride on the coat tails of globalisation understood as the intensification of networks for communication. Indeed, the very idea of globality exerts pressure on religious groups and entire faith communities to identify and clarify their particular place in the world. This is not necessarily tackled at a high level of abstraction or sophistication but is, rather, 'worked out' in the process of devising appropriate responses to practical challenges and problems. The latter include such diverse things as calls for humanitarian responses to natural or human-made disasters, epidemics, the rulings of international courts of law, movements of transnational trade or finance, and militarised hostilities inside and across national borders. None of these phenomena is new, but the readiness to identify them as having global causes or consequences that, in turn, can be explained within religious frames of reference is largely unprecedented. In this respect, religions are helping to establish reasons not only for regarding globality as a real condition and globalisation as a real process but also for putting a distinctive gloss on them.

There is nothing surprising in the readiness of religious leaders to adopt and adapt discourses of globality and globalisation. In fact, it is in their interest to raise the public profile of global issues for either positive or negative reasons. This is clearly true for the leaders of religious organisations seeking to extend their outreach to all parts of the world. The Roman Catholic Church, along with Soka Gakkai International, the Baha'is, the Word of Life and the Church of Scientology, for example, fall into this category. Notions of universality and globality figure prominently in their doctrinal principles, their rhetoric and their activities, although each of them has an entirely unique way of using these notions. They provide what Coleman (2000: 114) describes as 'a form of ideological resource through which discourses of globalising influence and interconnection can be accessed without necessitating submission to a strictly defined and constraining set of social relations'.

Ironically, it is also in the interest of the leaders of religious groups *opposed to* notions of globality to keep the discussion of globalisation high on their agenda. This is because their fears and misgivings about the allegedly corrosive and corruptive effects of globalisation can be turned to their advantage. They do this by representing their own religious tradition as being under threat from external alien forces – often implicitly associated with the unwelcome influence of American mass culture and economic might. The sharp contrast that such leaders draw between the integrity, purity and primordial quality of their own tradition and the upstart, mongrel consumerism attributed to the alien forces of globalisation is integral to their claims to legitimacy and authority. This paradox is a feature of the way in which the Iranian Revolution of 1979 began by asserting the primacy of Shia Islamic principles over the allegedly corrupt values of Western liberalism, capitalism and consumerism but has evolved into a more pragmatic movement for equality and progress within a Muslim framework. Thus, according to Peter Beyer (1994: 161), 'the consummately anti-global revolution has almost paradoxically demonstrated itself to be part and parcel of the furthering of globalisation. Conservative religious responses are part of the process of globalisation as much as liberal ones'.

This is an especially important consideration in places where the authority of religious leaders and the significance of their organisations are felt to be increasingly under threat. Russia and Greece, for example, are countries where relatively high levels of religious belief and practice among the laity are not matched by a correspondingly high impact of the Orthodox Church on public life. In both cases, the advocates of a greater role for the Church in public affairs blame their lack of success on the pernicious influence of globalisation. Evidence of globalisation, as seen from their point of view, includes the spread of American sectarian movements and the Roman Catholic Church, and, in the case of Greece, the EU's opposition to the inclusion of religious identification on national identity cards.

In summary, globality and globalisation lend themselves to a variety of quite contradictory uses by religious leaders.[5] Regardless of whether their attitudes are positive, negative or mixed, leaders are unlikely simply to ignore the debates about globalisation. In fact, these debates present interesting opportunities for the deployment of metaphysical and theological arguments, the scope for which has long been considered to be negligible in the rationalised, modern world. It is as if the development of purely economic and political factors has generated an unanticipated set of issues of a broadly religious nature. They are an emergent property of modernity but they are also assimilable into pre-existing frameworks of religious ideas. This is one of the ways in which religion can be deployed as a 'cultural resource' (Beckford 1989: 171) in attempts to understand and to respond practically to the economic, political, social, ecological, medical, scientific and ethical problems thrown up by developments in a globalising world. In other words, religious ways of thinking, feeling and acting are not extinguished or excluded by globalisation. In some respects, they even enjoy new forms of appeal in global conditions. For example, the appeal of neo-Hindu movements to relatively well educated young professionals in countries such as France and the UK (Altglas 2001) depends on a heightened awareness of a spiritual oneness, or a 'vibratory awareness' (Coney 2000), that participants can apparently detach from specific features of Indian ways of life. A similar process takes place – albeit for entirely different ideological reasons – in Christian charismatic movements where belief is strong in the unifying power of 'the Spirit' to transcend all national, social and cultural boundaries and therefore to create global communities of believers. According to Coleman (2000: 60), new communications technologies allow the Word of Life movement to sustain both a virtual form of global community and local forms of physical community which permit expression of neo-tribalism. In the words of David Lyon (2000: 118), 'religious flows and sacred landscapes originate in or at least connect with some place or places. And however far they travel, they are still experienced in particular places, where people live'.

Having reviewed the challenges and the opportunities that the study of religion presents to social theorists, who wish to explore notions of globality and globalisation, I now want to shift the focus of my discussion to the approaches that some authoritative theorists of the global circumstance have taken to the study of religion. For, although analyses of religion are relatively uncommon in works on globalisation, a pattern has, nevertheless, begun to emerge. That is to say, social theorists tend to make certain assumptions and inferences about religion that are, in my opinion, in need of serious assessment and critical comment. My intention is not to dismiss this work but, rather, to offer judgements about the aspects that appear to be well founded and those that fail to be convincing. The more general aim is to encourage the kind of research and theorising about the global that is well adapted to what is reliably known about changes in the social construction of religions in the early twenty-first century.

Social theorists of globalisation: a selection

The most general starting point is my belief that, notwithstanding the preceding discussion of the uses that religious leaders make of 'globality' and 'globalisation', these terms are subject to widely differing conceptualisations in the social sciences. Their implications for the study of religion are equally diverse. More importantly, I have reservations about the extent to which 'global' and its cognates are appropriate ways of designating many of the religious phenomena to which some commentators apply them. In fact, the omens are not at all good, to judge by Jan Aart Scholte's (2000: 39) claim that 'the only consensus about globalization is that it is contested . . . Moreover, the level of globalization debates is often disappointing. Much discussion is couched in soundbite. Many claims take extreme and overgeneralised forms'. And so on, in a sorry litany of the weaknesses and failures of theorising about globalisation.

I shall begin by analysing 'globalisation' as it functions in social scientific arguments, always acknowledging that the term is heavily contested. Then I shall review some authoritative writings on globalisation in order to establish just how broad is the spectrum of conceptualisations. My selection will deliberately include authoritative theorists who tend not to place religion at the forefront of their concerns. It would be all too easy to concentrate, instead, on the work of sociologists such as Roland Robertson, Peter Beyer, David Lyon or Frank Lechner, each of whom has tried to make interesting sense of religion in conditions of globality. But my aim here is to take an even-handed approach to a wider range of theorising about globalisation in order to bring to light some general tendencies in today's social theory to constitute religion as a particular kind of phenomenon. It seems to me that, with very few exceptions, specialist studies of globalised religion or of religion in a globalising world have not yet exercised much influence over these broader tendencies. Yet, there are good reasons for a re-consideration of both globalisation and of its relations with religion.

There is no shortage of lists of the defining characteristics commonly imputed to globalisation – either as a descriptive or an analytical concept. They usually include the following:

- the growing frequency, volume and interconnectedness of movements of ideas, materials, goods, information, pollution, money and people across national boundaries and between regions of the world
- the growing capacity of information technologies to shorten or even abolish the distance in time and space between events and places in the world

- the diffusion of increasingly standardised practices and protocols for processing global flows of information, goods, money and people
- the emergence of organisations, institutions and social movements for promoting, monitoring or counteracting global forces, with or without the support of individual nation states.

(Beckford 2000: 170)

This list amounts to nothing more than a lowest common denominator among conceptualisations of globalisation. It serves only to mark out the territory in a crude fashion. The variety of more specific attempts to map the outlines of globalisation that fall within this general framework is much more interesting. I shall review four particular conceptualisations of globalisation in order to demonstrate their differences and similarities. I shall also indicate their respective ways of framing religion as a more or a less significant feature of a globalising world.

(i)   Ulrich Beck

Among the most authoritative conceptualisations is the following:

Globality means that *we have been living for a long time in a world society*, in the sense that the notion of closed spaces has become illusory. No country or group can shut itself off from others. Various economic, cultural and political forms therefore collide with one another, and things that used to be taken for granted (including in the Western model) will have to be justified anew.

Globalization . . . denotes the *processes* through which sovereign national states are criss-crossed and undermined by transnational actors with varying prospects of power, orientations, identities and networks. (Beck 2000: 10, 11, emphasis original)

Ulrich Beck's approach accentuates the corrosive effect of globalisation on the capacity of nation States to retain their autonomy, thereby begging the question of how far States ever have enjoyed untrammelled sovereignty. There is a distinct possibility that this approach, by definition, exaggerates the novelty of globalisation and its strictly political implications. It is not surprising, then, that questions about religion or spirituality hardly arise in Beck's writings.

(ii)   Malcolm Waters

Malcolm Waters (2001) adopts a different, less political, approach to defining globalisation. He defines it as a process that began in the fifteenth century AD in which the constraints of geography on economic, political, social and cultural arrangements recede, in which people become increasingly aware that they are receding and in which people act accordingly. (Waters 2001: 5)

One of the merits of this approach is that it not only permits an analytic distinction between three domains of social life (economy, polity and culture), but it also recognises that the effects of globalisation may be different for each of them. Thus, 'material exchanges localize; political exchanges internationalise; and symbolic exchanges globalize' (Waters 2001: 20). These distinctions hold out the promise that the specificity of religion, located in the cultural region, according to Waters, will be respected and that due recognition will be accorded to religious changes and continuity. Indeed, Waters acknowledges the universalising thrust of the so-called world religions and the particular boost that Pentecostalism has given to individualism and thereby to universalism. Yet, his perception of religion under conditions of globality is limited to the growth of fundamentalism and (in a single paragraph) ecumenism. Ignoring the precise and complex historical roots of fundamentalism in early twentieth-century squabbles among American Protestants, Waters identifies fundamentalism as a reaction to the 'hyperdifferentiating tendencies of postmodernization' (2001: 188). The only three examples that he provides of this category are 'genuine fundamentalist Protestants', the 'fundamentalist revival in Islam' that began in the 1970s and Sun Myung Moon's Unification Church.[6] The conclusion is that:

In each of the dimensions of culture, globalization is highly advanced. Religious ideas must now be understood and often reinforced by fundamentalism in relation to the religions and the secularisms of all others. The commodification and marketing of religious ideas as a set of lifestyle choices is highly advanced and thus highly de-territorialized. (Waters 2001: 209)

This is a predominantly negative assessment of the character of religion in a globalising world. It emphasises the oppositional and marginal stance of religion towards global developments. On the other hand, the cryptic comments about the commodification and marketing of religious ideas hold out the promise of a different interpretation of religion's global future. But Waters does not expand on this point.

(iii)   Jan Aart Scholte

By way of a more spatially inclined approach to globalisation, Jan Aart Scholte (2000) goes to considerable lengths to distinguish his sense of the term from that of closely related terms such as internationalisation, liberalisation, universalisation and Westernisation. What is entirely unprecedented, in his reading of globalisation, is that

Place is not territorially fixed, territorial distance is covered in effectively no time, and territorial boundaries present no particular impediment...Globality (as supraterritoriality) describes circumstances where territorial space is substantially transcended. (Scholte 2000: 49)

It follows from Scholte's analysis that communities, markets, production processes, organisations and consciousness have been globalised. He adds that the research strategies, questions and methods deployed by social scientists should also lose their territorial focus and become global and therefore 'post-territorialist'. But, since the world is only partially globalised, he concedes that research methods cannot afford to ignore territoriality completely. Instead, they should examine the *interplay* of globality and territoriality, according to Scholte. This compromise proposal is characteristic of his entire approach to globalisation. It promises to determine the distinctiveness of globalisation, but every boundary marker that he plants is immediately qualified by reservations, notes of caution and counter-examples (Rosenberg 2000). Yet, as I shall argue below, Scholte's account of globalisation at least has the merit of including numerous references to religion.

(iv)   Anthony Giddens

Finally, an approach that gives more attention than the others to questions of ontology and identity surely deserves to be taken seriously in the context of reflections on religion. There is, of course, much more than this in Anthony Giddens' wide ranging writings about modernity, late modernity and reflexive modernisation, but I shall extract only those ideas that mark out his understanding of globalisation. I shall also make inferences about the implications of these ideas for the sociological interpretation of religion in a globalising world. The results will lend further support to my argument that the pay-off from ambitious theories of globalisation, in terms of explaining religion, is meagre.

In a deliberate departure from most of the sociological perspectives prevalent in the 1980s, Giddens' highly influential work on *The Consequences of Modernity* aspires towards re-focusing social theory on how social systems '"bind" time and space' (Giddens 1990: 14). This is part of a broader strategy to provide a 'fresh characterization of modernity' that will supersede the accounts given of an earlier stage of modernity by Karl Marx, Max Weber and Emile Durkheim. He insists, however, that the unfolding of globalisation is part of the *intensification* of forces that were already inherent in earlier stages of modernity. It does not represent a post-modern rupture. According to Giddens, 'modernity is inherently globalising' (1990: 63), and globalising processes are of central importance to modernity's dynamism. The globalising scope of modern social systems, in his view, derives from (a) the *separation of space from time*, (b) the process of *disembedding* (removing aspects of social life from their original local settings and transferring them to other times or places) and (c) the *reflexive ordering* and reordering of social relations in the light of continuous increase in knowledge. Globalisation is also facilitated by the free circulation of '*symbolic tokens*' (such as money) and by the pervasiveness of '*expert systems*' (specialised knowledge applied by professionals and bureaucrats in the control of ever widening swaths of everyday life). Globalisation, defined as 'the intensification of worldwide social relations which link distant localities in such a way that local happenings are shaped by events occurring many miles away and vice versa' (Giddens 1990: 64) is said to weaken the basic *trust* on which human societies depend for continuity, stability and predictability. The damage is allegedly mitigated, however, by the 'reembedding' of social relations in local conditions by means of encounters with abstract systems at 'access points' where disembodied relations of trust can be created and monitored.

The four dimensions of Giddens' schema of globalisation include: the world capitalist economy; the nation-State system; the world military order; and industrial development. In contrast to Robertson (1992b), for example, he excludes culture and religion from this schema. In fact, Giddens falls back on a social psychological constant, which appears to be somehow immune from globalisation, in order to explain why most people are not permanently racked by existential insecurities: '"Normal" individuals...receive a basic "dosage" of trust in early life that deadens or blunts these existential susceptibilities' (Giddens 1990: 94). More particularly, the trust that is instilled during early childhood is said to derive from the experience of noticing that caretakers are sometimes absent, but that they nevertheless reappear and become present again. 'Trust thus brackets distance in time and space and so blocks off existential anxieties' (Giddens 1990: 97). There is no attempt to connect this psychological, if not psychoanalytical, mechanism to, say, Georg Simmel's (1905) account of the origins of religious sentiments in everyday experiences of faith and trust in the reliability of *other* people.

Giddens regards religion as one of the four localised contexts of trust in *pre-modern* societies (alongside kinship, local community and tradition) because it 'generates a sense of the reliability of social and natural events, and thus contributes to the bracketing of time-space' (1990: 103–4).

Nevertheless, he adds that religion can also create its own terrors and can mediate anxieties about nature. Still, the processes of disembedding and time-space distanciation in late modernity supposedly disable religion's purchase on existential questions. 'Religious cosmology is supplanted by reflexively organised knowledge, governed by empirical observation and logical thought, and focused upon material technology and socially applied codes' (Giddens 1990: 109). Tradition in modern conditions is said to be equally doomed to irrelevance because 'A world structured mainly by humanly created risks has little place for divine influences' (Giddens 1990: 111). As we shall see in the next paragraph, however, Giddens acknowledges that 'the return of the repressed' in modern conditions opens the door to religion.

The main implication of Giddens' account of life in modern, globalised societies *seems* to be that religion has little or no role to play because the sources of ontological insecurity, as well as the proffered re-assurances, have changed into forms permeated by abstract, expert systems of self-reflexive knowledge. 'Apocalypse has become banal, a set of risk parameters to everyone's existence' (Giddens 1991: 183). Nevertheless, he retreats to some extent from this position in order to admit that 'religion not only refuses to disappear but undergoes a resurgence' (Giddens 1991: 195) in late modernity, albeit in the relatively diminished form of one authority among others. His explanation for the resurgence of religious belief and conviction rests on a reprise of his argument about existential anxieties:

What was due to become a social and physical universe subject to increasingly certain knowledge and control instead creates a system in which areas of relative security interlace with radical doubt and with disquieting scenarios of risk. Religion in some part generates the conviction which adherence to the tenets of modernity must necessarily suspend: in this regard it is easy to see why religious fundamentalism has a special appeal. But this is not all. New forms of religion and spirituality represent in a most basic sense a return of the repressed, since they directly address issues of the moral meaning of existence which modern institutions so thoroughly tend to dissolve. (Giddens 1991: 207)

Thus, moralised institutions may be under threat from abstract systems, according to Giddens. But opportunities (or pressures) still exist for a form of re-moralisation of human life at the level of individual self-reflexivity.

'The ethos of self-growth', in the opinion of Giddens (1991: 209), is at the centre of the new forms of religion and spirituality which, in turn, are one small part of 'life politics'. The politics of lifestyle are supposed to foster a sense of personal authenticity and continuous self-identity against a backdrop of rapid change. Since 'The more we reflexively "make ourselves" as persons, the more the very category of what a "person" or "human being" is comes to the fore' (Giddens 1991: 217), questions about spirituality and morality are supposedly unavoidable. This is because 'life politics brings back to prominence precisely those moral and existential questions repressed by the core institutions of modernity' (Giddens 1991: 223). Globalisation is said to ensure that issues of self-identity are articulated with issues that simultaneously affect the individual and the world. Personal and intimate aspects of everyday life are thus intertwined with time-space distanciation.

Sociologists of religion have explored many facets of this particular configuration of personal and global concerns enshrined in, for example, New Age world-views and holistic therapies (Beckford 1984, 1985c; Heelas 1996a, 1996b; York 1995; Hedges & Beckford 1999). Giddens refrains, however, from adequately investigating the tensions between reliance on *expertise* as a basis for notions of self-reflexive spiritual growth and, on the other hand, *tradition* as a source of feelings of ontological security. He offers only the highly questionable claim that, in a globalised world,

Tradition becomes *fundamentalism*. There is nothing mysterious about the appearance of fundamentalism in the late modern world. 'Fundamentalism' only assumes the sense it does against a background of the prevalence of radical doubt; it is nothing more or less than 'tradition in its traditional sense', although today embattled rather than in the ascendant. Fundamentalism may be understood as an assertion of formulaic truth without regard to consequences. (Giddens 1994: 100, emphasis original)

I believe that this is a misguided view of fundamentalism, as will become clear below, but I can also see clearly how it fits into Giddens' theoretical framework of globalisation and late modernity.

I find it paradoxical that, despite the evident differences between these four influential approaches to globalisation, their accounts of religion in globalised circumstances tend towards a small number of more or less similar points. Moreover, some of their points of similarity tend to frame religion in ways that receive relatively little support from good quality empirical research. The result is a curiously flat or one-dimensional image that does not do justice to the richness, subtlety and variety of expressions of religion – not to mention their contradictory character. This is partly because the writers do not appear to be familiar with enough of the relevant studies[7] and partly because they have an interest in 'selling' a theoretical idea, the scope of which is sufficiently general to cover all kinds of phenomena. Religion is thereby squeezed into a mould that is not tolerant of its kaleidoscopic diversity and fluidity.

Problems and opportunities

There are two striking features of studies of globalisation. On the one hand, the varied conceptualisations of globalisation have not engaged adequately with questions about religion. But, on the other hand, suitably amended notions of globalisation are capable of throwing fresh light on the sociological aspects of religion. I shall develop both of these points below before concluding that debates about globalisation are a valuable opportunity for forging productive links between social theory and the social scientific study of religion.

(a)   Confusion

One of the recurring difficulties with writings about globalisation is confusion about the logical status of the central concepts. In some contexts, 'global' refers to the untrammelled movement of social and cultural phenomena around the world leading to their world-wide *distribution*. A good example of this usage of the term is Karla Poewe's (1994: xi) stipulation that, for the purposes of her edited collection, 'The term *global* refers to the unbound spatial, temporal, institutional, and linguistic reach of charismatic Christianity'. In other contexts, 'global' implies an unprecedentedly high level of *integration* among social and cultural phenomena tending towards the crystallisation of a single world-wide system or market. This includes assumptions about the high density of underlying networks of communication. In still other contexts, 'global' emphasises the idea that unfettered circulation of phenomena leads to unprecedentedly high levels of *standardisation* or homogenisation of the circulating products in all parts of the world.

By contrast, some of the most interesting research conducted on religion accentuates the local refraction and re-appropriation of religious currents circulating around the world. Robertson's concept of 'glocalisation' is the best-known attempt to capture the relativising dynamic between the global and the local. A markedly different understanding of the global/local interchange is Hexham and Poewe's (1997) notion of new religions as 'global cultures'. According to them, 'a global culture is a tradition that travels the world and takes on local colour. It has both a global, or metacultural, and a local, or situationally distinct, cultural dimension' (Hexham & Poewe 1997: 41). Thus, 'new religions, despite their globality, must fragment existing traditions, recombine them with others in new ways, and yet remain true to a very old and very local folk religion' (Hexham & Poewe 1997: 42). It seems to me that this approach has more to do with global visions than with global realities.

It is worth mentioning in passing that the meaning given by Martin Albrow (1996) to 'globality' is distinctly different from, and more radical than, the sense in which other writers use the term. Whereas Robertson, for example, regards globality as awareness of the interrelatedness and mutual constitution of phenomena that are simultaneously local and global, Albrow uses 'globality' in the sense of an objective state of affairs. Indeed, globality in his schema is a hallmark of the 'Global Age' which, in turn, signifies a distinct epoch that has already displaced much of the 'Modern Age'. Albrow even claims that phenomenological investigation can collect experiential evidence that the Global Age has arrived, along with its own ideological register in the form of 'globalism'.[8] In addition, he insists that globalisation is an inherently indeterminable and ambiguous process that is not just an intensification of modernity but is also without an end-point and is always relative to perceptions of the past. It signifies social and cultural transformation of a type that is not law-like and is not commensurable with processes of modernisation because its driving forces are not identifiable. It is not a project like that of modernity. Albrow uses globalisation, then, to describe an aggregate of myriad changes that seem to be mutually implicated without necessarily displaying an inner logic. I shall return to Albrow's understanding of religion in the Global Age a little later.

There are, no doubt, other implications of 'global', but for my purposes these particular uses of the term are sufficiently different and specific to substantiate my general point about the wide scope for confusion. An even more serious problem arises, however, from the different uses to which the term is put in theoretical and explanatory arguments. I am referring to the difficulty of knowing whether writers regard 'global' as part of an explanation (*explanans*) or as part of the thing to be explained (*explanandum*).[9] In some cases, making a distinction between causes and effects is not part of the exercise: the aim is, rather, to identify a syndrome or a constellation of interrelated elements without any clear assignment of causal priority. There is also uncertainty about whether 'global' functions as a single-stranded explanation (i.e. as the sole cause) or whether it is merely one among several causes in a multi-stranded explanation. This is not a criticism of researchers who do not choose to separate independent and dependent variables. It is merely a criticism of those who fail to be clear about the nature of the interpretations or explanations that they offer.

Uncertainty about the *time frame* within which notions of 'globalisation' are believed to operate is a further source of confusion. Some writers locate the origins of the phenomenon in the remote past, finding examples in the emergence of universalising concepts in so-called World Religions.

Other writers claim that processes of globalisation had their beginnings in the early modern period. Still others insist that, despite evidence of much earlier instances of global thinking, the last quarter of the twentieth century was the period when the intensification and acceleration of globalisation processes reached a point where they acquired real significance for the first time in the sense of shaping changes in most spheres of life.

(b)   The fixation with fundamentalism

It has become a truism to observe that social scientific studies of religion tend to emphasise marginal, deviant or sensational aspects of religion and to show relatively little interest in the 'normal' range of religious beliefs, actions and organisations. In this respect, the sociology of religion comes close to being a 'sociology of error', to borrow Ian Hamnett's (1973) disapproving phrase. Controversies and scandals in religious groups are particularly likely to awaken the interest of social scientists who, otherwise, regard religion as a side show in comparison with the three-ring circus of economy, polity and social class. This is indeed what has happened since the 1970s when social scientists and journalists began to note that some forms of religion could be destructive, violent, criminal and 'uncivil'. 'Cult controversies' (Beckford 1985a), the religious roots of violent opposition to abortion (Baird-Windle & Bader 2001), the rise of Christian Patriotism (Aho 1990, 1996), the long-running association between religions and bloody struggles for national sovereignty or political power in South Asia (Juergensmeyer 1993), the Islamic Revolution in Iran (Arjomand 1988), and the rising profile of Islamist movements in North Africa, South East Asia and the Middle East (Antoun & Hegland 1987; Halliday 1996; Juergensmeyer 2000) have all helped to persuade some social theorists that it might be premature to see the fate of religion as either secularisation or privatisation. As a result, theories of postmodernity, late modernity and globalisation have been adapted to take account of these relatively spectacular outbreaks of religious fervour and deviance. Other theorists remain unmoved, however. Organised religion is still a force for authoritarianism, according to Alain Touraine (Touraine & Khosrokhavar 2000), or for conservatism, according to Jürgen Habermas (1987).

At the same time, the well-publicised entry of conservative evangelical Christians into political campaigns in the USA in the 1970s aroused scholarly interest in the possibility that the 'public square' was an arena in which non-sensational, non-deviant forms of religion could still exercise some influence. Rising levels of support for conservative evangelical and pentecostal/charismatic churches in East Asia, Latin America and

Sub-Saharan Africa were a further reason to take the public expression of religion seriously. And the election of a conservative Pope in 1985, to be followed soon afterwards by the coming to power of neo-liberal leaders in the USA and the UK, Ronald Reagan and Margaret Thatcher, symbolised a growth of confidence in conservative ideologies in dominant regions of the Western world. But it was the 1979 Islamic Revolution in Iran, the growing militancy of various ultra-conservative Jewish organisations in Israel and the spread of movements for the re-Islamisation of countries in Asia and the Middle East that popularised the idea that religious *fundamentalism* was the common denominator in all these developments. A diversion will be necessary at this point in order to show how the topic of fundamentalism has become virtually inseparable from theorising about globalisation and globality.

'Fundamentalism' has always been a heavily contested term. Conceptualisations of fundamentalism are notoriously varied, but the term is usually associated with a rejection of relativism and secularism and an unreserved application of 'true' beliefs and sacred law to all aspects of personal and public life in the context of exclusive communities, many of which are structured by patriarchalism. Objections to crude use of the concept in social scientific discourse are based on several interrelated arguments:

- strictly speaking, 'fundamentalism' refers only to doctrinal disputes in certain American denominations in the early twentieth century (Barr 1977)
- the differences between religious traditions and organisations labelled 'fundamentalist' are greater than the points that they have in common[10]
- the label 'fundamentalism' conceals important differences between radically conservative religious world-views
- 'fundamentalism' has become a blanket term for thinly disguised scorn for any conservative ideology, especially if it is also anti-western.

Misgivings about the term 'fundamentalism' are therefore extensive, but van der Veer's (2000) claim that a 'global discourse of fundamentalism' has gripped the imagination of journalists, the public and social scientists is undoubtedly correct.

By contrast those scholars who use 'fundamentalism' for analytical purposes argue that it faithfully captures a distinctive and relatively stable configuration of characteristics that are:

- united in their opposition to secularism and relativism
- unique to the late twentieth and early twenty-first centuries
- discernible across the boundaries of States and religious communities
- associated with important changes in social, political, economic and cultural life.

Nevertheless, agreement on the precise denotation and connotation of 'fundamentalism' has proved to be elusive despite the many admirable attempts to specify the concept carefully within the framework of the massive 'Fundamentalism Project' sponsored by the American Academy of Arts and Sciences and published in five volumes edited by Martin Marty and Scott Appleby (1991, 1993a, 1993b, 1994, 1995). Not surprisingly, Marty and Appleby (1991: 835) opt for a lengthy statement of family resemblances in their attempt to capture the concept of fundamentalism as it emerged from their first edited volume:

In these pages, then, fundamentalism has appeared as a tendency, a habit of mind, found within religious communities and paradigmatically embodied in certain representative individuals and movements, which manifests itself as a strategy, or set of strategies, by which beleagured believers attempt to preserve their distinctive identity as a people or group. Feeling this identity to be at risk in the contemporary era, they fortify it by a selective retrieval of doctrines, beliefs, and practices from a sacred past. These retrieved 'fundamentals' are refined, modified, and sanctioned in a spirit of shrewd pragmatism: they are to serve as a bulwark against the encroachment of outsiders who threaten to draw the believers into a syncretistic, areligious, or irreligious cultural milieu. Moreover, these fundamentals are accompanied in the new religious portfolio by unprecedented claims and doctrinal innovations. By the strength of these innovations and the new supporting doctrines, the retrieved and updated fundamentals are meant to regain the same charismatic intensity today by which they originally forged communal identity from the formative revelatory religious experiences long ago.

Two particular points of uncertainty that arise in this conceptualisation and in many other conceptualisations of fundamentalism have a direct bearing on my discussion of religion in social theory. The first is whether fundamentalism is a modern or an anti-modern phenomenon. The second is whether fundamentalism is traditionalist or anti-traditionalist in orientation. I want to suggest that the struggles to resolve these uncertainties throw interesting light on the wider debates within social theory about modernity and tradition.

A representative statement of the view that fundamentalism is a *modern* phenomenon, albeit expressed through anti-modernist world-views, is given by Frank Lechner:

As I and others have argued over the years, fundamentalism is a quintessentially modern phenomenon. It actively strives to reorder society; it reasserts the validity of tradition and uses it in new ways; it operates in a context that sets non-traditional standards; where it does not take decisive control, it reproduces the dilemmas it sets out to resolve; as one active force among others, it affirms the depth of modern pluralism; it takes on the tensions produced by the clash between a universalizing global culture and particular local conditions; it expresses fundamental uncertainty in a crisis setting, not traditional confidence about taken-for-granted truths; by defending God, who formerly needed no defense, it creates and recreates difference as part of a global cultural struggle. So compromised, fundamentalism becomes part of the fabric of modernity. (Lechner 2000: 340)

But Lechner and others are quick to add that the prospects for fundamentalism in late modernity are not bright because circumstances are not conducive to the restoration of a single, sacred canopy or tradition over increasingly differentiated social institutions. This is not the opinion of all writers on this topic. Indeed, Bryan Turner (2001) characterises fundamentalism as a form of modernisation in itself. David Lehmann (1998) goes even further by claiming that 'far from being a flight from modernity, fundamentalist movements are a quintessentially modern phenomenon – not because they constitute a reaction against modernity but, on the contrary, because they are bearers *of* modernity' (Lehmann 1998: 630, emphasis original). And Peter van der Veer (2000) regards Hindu nationalism as part of a modernising drive towards a distinctly modern State of India, with a religiously homogeneous population subject to a single system of law within clear geographical boundaries. This nationalist vision, with fundamentalist overtones, has a strong appeal for Hindus in diasporic communities, thereby further complicating the meaning of globalisation.

Other observers are more circumspect. For example, an important distinction between modernity and modernism is central to Bruce Lawrence's (1989) book on fundamentalism. In fact, he characterises fundamentalists as 'at once the consequence of modernity and the antithesis of modernism' (Lawrence 1989: 2). His argument is that they accept and exploit the practical advantages of modernity without subscribing to modernist values such as individual autonomy, relativism, liberalism or pluralism. This is why, according to Lawrence, there could never have been pre-modern fundamentalists. But he regards the complex interaction between fundamentalism and modernism as a 'battle' that began in the eighteenth century in Western Europe and North America but which now affects all parts of the world as a struggle between two incompatible universalisms and absolutes. This means that fundamentalists are not a marginal, reactive presence on the sidelines of modernity but are an integral development within modernity of world-views and ways of life that aim to place all knowledge and practice on a new footing. The stakes could hardly be higher, in Lawrence's opinion. Consequently, fundamentalism presents challenges to social theory that are rarely taken up because theorists are too eager to pigeon-hole it as nothing more than an exotic form of religious deviance.

Specialised studies of fundamentalism have therefore highlighted the uncertainty within notions of modernity about the grounds on which claims to universal truth might themselves be partial. They have also called into question the links between modernity and modernism, showing how it is possible to be anti-modernist in a thoroughly modern fashion. This disjunction between modernity and modernism also enables fundamentalists to embrace the instrumental benefits of globalisation without subscribing to any implications of relativism or pluralism. The only global religion that fundamentalists could accept is their own religion 'writ large'. The next question is whether the anti-modernism of fundamentalists implies that they are also traditionalists. Again, the answers given by specialists are nuanced in ways that many social theorists of globalisation tend to ignore.

Many commentators emphasise the *traditional*, 'traditionalist' (Riesebrodt 1993) or 'neo-traditional' character of fundamentalist beliefs and practices. Terms such as 'return', 'revival' and 'resurgence' also help to convey the idea that fundamentalism involves a return to a way of practising religion that is somehow authentic and traditional. It also implies a degree of frustration with social and cultural conditions that prevent religious traditions from reproducing themselves. In a slightly different vein Sharot (1992) prefers to apply the term 'neo-traditional' to

religious movements that self-consciously attempt to represent or reassert what they regard as their authentic religious tradition against what they perceive as threats in modern developments. A past society is believed to have embodied the authentic tradition, and this provides a model to be reconstituted or emulated. (Sharot 1992: 25)

Sharot's cogent arguments against adopting 'fundamentalism' as the basis for comparative studies lead him to prefer, instead, a focus on the opposition of 'neo-traditional' movements to selected components of cultural modernism. Religious movements that are unhelpfully labelled 'fundamentalist', in his view, tend to accept the scientific and technological components of modernity whilst rejecting such cultural components of modernity as secular ideologies, permissive morality, liberal individualism, pluralism and ethical relativism (Sharot 1992: 44). This high level of sensitivity to differences between the movements in terms of their historical development, basic beliefs, forms of organisation and collective relations with the societies in which they operate is rarely reflected in the caricatures of fundamentalism to be found in the writings of some social theorists.

Let me take the example of Manuel Castells' characterisation of fundamentalist religious movements as 'defensive reactions' against globalisation and as attempts to construct a 'communal heaven'. His assumption is that fundamentalists are somehow 'excluded from or resisting the individualisation of identity attached to life in the global networks of power or wealth' and that their 'cultural communes . . . appear as reactions to prevailing social trends' (Castells 1997: 65). This way of portraying conservative Christian movements as well as Islamic radicalism is not completely misguided: but it is one-sided and historically short-sighted. It overlooks the cautious welcome that fundamentalists extend towards modernity and their rejection of modernism. What Castells fails to capture is, first, a point repeatedly made by empirical investigators, namely, that many leading members of conservative religious movements move in thoroughly modern milieus as a result of their technical, scientific, medical or commercial training. Second, Castells fails to take sufficient account of the active involvement of conservative religionists in a wide variety of political and moral campaigns. Far from living in self-imposed exile in 'communal heavens', they insist on taking their religious convictions out of the private sphere and into the public realm in the attempt to exercise influence and power. It is characteristic of the movements that he labels 'fundamentalist' to want to transform the world around them by engaging in selected political struggles – to 'fight back', in Marty and Appleby's (1991) terms.

In short, 'fundamentalist' religious movements draw upon many modern resources such as new communications technologies (Bhatt 1997: 251–54), a positivistic view of science (Bruce 1984) and an instrumental model of politics in their efforts to control the direction of social and cultural change. They certainly reject such aspects of modern culture or modernism as moral relativism and liberal attitudes towards sexual behaviour and intimate relationships, but they thrive on other aspects of modern life such as the importance of taking individual responsibility for one's life course, working hard, and having a positive attitude towards education preferably in the technical, non-discursive disciplines. The stance of conservative religionists towards modernity and globalisation is therefore subtle and deeply ambivalent in ways that are only tangentially related to a 'defensive reaction'. No less interesting is the fact that conservative religion highlights the ambiguities inherent in the very notion of modernity. It calls into question the value of the dualities that have conventionally served to distinguish modernity from its predecessor social formations: tradition vs. novelty; community vs. individuality; universal vs. particular; and compulsion vs. voluntarism. The continuing popularity and influence of conservative religion in many parts of the world calls for analysis in terms that cut across such rigid dualities, thereby indicating some subtleties and uncertainties to which theories of modernity that do not take religion seriously are unresponsive.

The argument against Castells can be taken further. Margaret Poloma (1998), for example, depicts Pentecostal and Charismatic Christianity as a distinctly late-modern or post-modern phenomenon. Her view is that this buoyant form of religion, far from being a defensive reaction against modernity, is successful precisely because it is in keeping with the spirit of the times. Thus, time-space distanciation and time-space compression are regarded as normal in Pentecostalism's account of supernatural occurrences. The Holy Spirit illustrates a fluid notion of free will. Belief in prophecy requires a high degree of self-reflexivity because of the need for constant interpretation and discernment. The charismatic gifts of the spirit and strongly embodied experiences of the sacred illustrate the priority that Pentecostalism places on direct, immediate experience. Pentecostalism transcends all boundaries of age, gender, class, ethnicity, language and nationality. Charismatic fellowships are structured in decentralised networks and are not strongly attached to particular locations or buildings. In all these respects, then, Poloma claims that Pentecostal and Charismatic Christianity qualifies as a decidedly late-modern or post-modern phenomenon.

Just as Castells seems to present the fate of religion as either fundamentalism or secularisation, so Zygmunt Bauman (1998) also offers a choice between two restrictive options in conditions of globalisation:

Thrown into a vast open sea with no navigation charts and all the marker buoys sunk and barely visible, we have only two choices left: we may rejoice in the breathtaking vistas of new discoveries – or we may tremble out of fear of drowning. One option not really realistic is to claim sanctuary in a safe harbour. (Bauman 1998: 85)

At a stroke Bauman's scenario airbrushes out of existence the hundreds of millions of active participants in not only Pentecostal and Charismatic forms of Christianity but also sectarian movements such as the Jehovah's Witnesses, Mormons and Seventh-Day Adventists – to say nothing of the myriad conservative activists in Islamic, Hindu and Buddhist organisations. The fact is that, from the viewpoint of all these religionists, Bauman's existentialist scenario is virtually meaningless because they believe that they have already reached the uniquely 'safe harbour'. Their concern is to repel attacks and to persuade other 'right minded people' to join forces with them. Military and militaristic figures of speech come readily to people with strong religious convictions who see themselves as 'beleagured' or 'embattled' – but 'unbloodied'.

Contrary to the view that fundamentalism is oriented in any simple way towards tradition I believe that the situation is more complicated. 'Tradition' in the literal sense of things that are 'handed down' is an ambiguous term. It leaves open the question of whether 'tradition' refers to the earliest known written or oral sources of a religion or to the beliefs and practices that, over the course of history, become accretions to the original forms.

Another source of ambiguity lies in the fact that 'traditions' are, at some point in their history, inventions, selections or elaborations of inventions (Anderson 1991; Hobsbawm & Ranger 1992). It is therefore difficult to accept that fundamentalist movements simply hark back to tradition. Traditions are socially constructed and contested. Indeed, as Giddens (1994) and others have pointed out, the deliberate attempt by religious groups to return to traditions is itself a non-traditional strategy that smacks of a self-reflexive, late modern attitude to knowledge. Even if the activists in religious groups categorised as 'fundamentalists' are committed to the restoration of what they regard as traditions, it does not follow that social scientific observers must use the same ambiguous language in order to interpret their actions.

Furthermore, fundamentalists rarely content themselves with mere repetition of sacred texts, even when the texts are considered inerrant. Instead, they practise what Bhikhu Parekh (1992: 24) terms a 'double abstraction'. This means that, first, the sacred text is abstracted from its tradition and, second, a set of 'fundamentals' is abstracted from the text. The process is a dynamic form of interpretation, especially when the fundamentals have to be related to perceptions of rapidly changing realities in the outside world. A social constructionist approach is indispensable for the investigation of these processes.

In fact, the most sensitive and nuanced studies of fundamentalism or conservative evangelicalism stress its complex understanding of, and relation to, tradition (Ammerman 1987; Poloma 1989; Marty & Appleby 1991; Smith 1998; Harding 2000). The diversity of evangelical and fundamentalist outlooks is well-documented in sociological studies of religion but curiously neglected by social theorists intent on cramming conservative religion into a single, narrow mould.

In spite of all the qualifications, misgivings and objections that surround the use of 'fundamentalism' in the social scientific study of religions,[11] the term is currently enjoying a vogue among theorists of postmodernity and globalisation. They show relatively little awareness of the difficulties attached to use of the term or of the subtle distinctions in its denotation that students of religion have introduced.[12] Their concern is to find a convenient way of integrating selective evidence about religious change into their broad-brush landscapes of late modernity, post-modernity, the mobile society or the network society. For the most part, it suits their purposes to argue that those concepts of modernity that took the process of secularisation for granted must have been wrong or out-dated because some forms of religion are clearly thriving in the early twenty-first century. 'Fundamentalism' is, according to these theorists, the label to be placed on this eye-catching resurgence of religion.

It is significant that Martin Albrow's (1996) account of the Global Age is not fixated on fundamentalism. In accordance with his belief that 'old modern theory' is incapable of grasping global phenomena adequately, he does not deploy notions such as 'the return of the repressed' or 'the re-moralisation of social relations' in order to explain religion in the Global Age. In fact, he draws attention to the danger of focusing exclusively on 'extreme' phenomena that are unrepresentative of the range of religious developments. His own strategy is to emphasise the importance of the fact that individuals inhabit multiple worlds and can therefore construct various self-identities that are not constrained by categories of nationhood, social class, gender or age. Identity 'enclaves' or 'milieus', according to Albrow, support new bonds of identity and loyalty. They may be totalising, in the way of many sects and religious movements. Alternatively, they may permit participation in different cross-cutting networks or enclaves, as in the case of progressive social movements.

For example, Albrow interprets the spread of the charismatic experience that began in the Airport Vineyard Church in Toronto as the kind of ecstatic emotionalism that has always transcended social boundaries but that, in the Global Age, is able to benefit from the power of global communications. Thus, a local phenomenon rapidly becomes global. He could have taken this argument further by exploring the universalising potential of a religious practice that centres on the embodied experience of laughter and tears. Lyon (2000) suggests that the origins of the 'Toronto blessing' at an international airport are also significant for the movement's global outreach. Such airports are simultaneously local and global – 'non-places' in Marc Augé's (1992) terms. Another reason for the universal appeal of Pentecostalism, according to Corten (1995), may be the fact that the movement does not portray the Holy Spirit in anthropomorphic terms.

Albrow, like Robertson (1987, 1992b) before him, also identifies the Unification Church of Sun Myung Moon as a religious movement that responds directly to globality by promulgating globalist values. It is noteworthy that, unlike many other theorists of globalisation, however, Albrow does not seek to explain the success of the Unification Church's campaigns to achieve world-wide outreach in terms of ('old modern') concepts such as ontological insecurity or re-moralisation.

In short, ideas about fundamentalism tend to exercise a disproportionately heavy influence over theoretical writings about religion and globalisation. Evidence is used in a highly selective manner to confirm, rather than to test, pre-existing assumptions about the single-stranded significance of one unrepresentative, complex expression of religion. Moreover, a misleading impression is given that fundamentalism represents a unitary, homogeneous phenomenon. As we shall see next, the exaggerated claims made about fundamentalism in theories of globalisation achieve some of their effects partly by ignoring evidence of other forms of religion.

(c)   The neglect of non-fundamentalist religion

The other side of social theorists' fixation with fundamentalism is their neglect of virtually every other form of religious expression in an increasingly globalised world. Regardless of their particular, and widely differing perspectives, on globality and globalisation, social theorists have contributed very little to the social scientific understanding of religious change and continuity. In fact, references to 'religion' and 'spirituality' are commonly absent from their writings. But my claim that social theory tends to neglect non-fundamentalist forms of religion will be meaningful only if I can show that this neglect is damaging to our understanding of the globalising world. In other words, the onus is on me to demonstrate that globalisation, however it is understood, is still associated with interesting aspects of religion other than fundamentalisms.

My first point about the narrowness of the perspectives that theorists of globalisation tend to adopt on religion concerns the lack of attention to two important phenomena for which conceptions of modernity offer confident, if contested, accounts. On the one hand, globalisation theorists rarely acknowledge, let alone comment on, the persistence of relatively high levels of religious beliefs in many parts of the world. I am not thinking here of fundamentalist beliefs but, rather, of the more or less conventional, more or less clear and more or less orthodox beliefs that are routinely reported in the findings of questionnaire surveys. The link between the character of these beliefs and the frequency with which they are reported is subject to extensive debate. There is an even more intense debate about the link between individuals' reported beliefs and the strength of their association with religious collectivities. Yet, no echoes of these topics occur in analyses of globalisation. And globalisation theorists make very few attempts to explain the persistence of these 'normal', non-spectacular religious beliefs in a Global Age or a Network Society that is supposedly incommensurable with (old) modernity. Such theorists are more likely to highlight the extremes of fundamentalism or non-religious rationalism. The following quotations from Scholte (2000) illustrate this tendency with a degree of clarity that borders on caricature:

[G]lobal flows have in some ways made room for nonrationalist knowledges such as religious revivalism, ecocentrism and postmodernist thought. However, most knowledge that has circulated in global spaces to date has continued to exhibit the core rationalist attributes of secularism, anthropocentrism, scientism and instrumentalism...In these ways contemporary globalization can be associated with a further ascendance of rationalism to unprecedented strength. Indeed, religious practices have declined across much of the planet during the period of accelerated globalization, particularly in the OECD countries where supraterritoriality has become most widespread...[C]yberspace, transworld publications and global conferences have served rationalist academics far more than holy persons and other nonrationalist teachers...These circumstances of the globalising world have made it harder for nonrational knowledges to survive. (Scholte 2000: 185, 187, 230)

It is difficult to see how Scholte's account of religious decline under conditions of globalisation differs in any significant respect from that of thoroughly modernist accounts. Variants on the theme of secularisation are, as I showed in Chapter Two, central to notions of modernity. Even those theorists who are suspicious of simply equating modernity with secularisation nevertheless accept the challenge of explaining change and continuity in patterns of religious believing and belonging. This is not a challenge, however, that often finds a place in theorising about globalisation. It is as if the fixation with fundamentalism has blinded the theorists to questions about other expressions of religion that are, as it happens, much more widely and frequently distributed around the world.

A second point about the narrow scope of much theoretical work on globalisation is that it either neglects evidence of persisting interest in liberal forms of religion or reduces them to indications of self-reflexivity under conditions of globality. The effect is, of course, to reinforce the impression that fundamentalist forms of religion are uniquely compatible with, or somehow required by, life in a globalising world.

It is as if the only recourse for mainstream religious organisations is to fall back on to a defence of cultural identity in the face of global forces sapping their legitimacy. Yet, evidence of other, more liberal responses is plentiful (Davie 2000: 22). For example, the principal Christian Churches in Western Europe have not abandoned their earlier experiments in ecumenism. Indeed, ecumenical initiatives at the European level have proliferated in recent decades as globalisation has had the effect of relativising each Church's position in relation to others

(Willaime 1996). Thus, Bizeul (2001: 198) cites as evidence of ecumenism the signing in 1999 of a joint declaration by the Lutheran World Federation and the Vatican and the signing in April 2001 of a 'Charta Oecumenica' between the Conference of European Churches and the Council of European Bishops' Conferences.[13] A host of bilateral dialogues between Christian Churches has also been taking place for many years – largely unnoticed by the mass media and, therefore, by the social theorists who sketch quick caricatures of religion in post-modern globality. The steady growth and consolidation of inter-faith networks has also gone mainly unremarked. And numerous organisations have come into existence to co-ordinate social action among different, but increasingly interrelated, religious agencies such as the International Prison Chaplains' Association, Christians united against torture and the death penalty, and networks of Church agencies in the field of social welfare and economic development. These developments have benefited from the technological and cultural advances of globalisation as well as from the rise in the importance of the European Union as an actor in global affairs. But Wydmusch (2000: 258, trans J.A.B.) insists that European Protestant Churches still feel 'caught between the global and the local' and are therefore divided between their attachment to particular territories and their ideal of being universal.

Research has also documented the growing popularity, especially but not exclusively in countries with the most advanced investments in education, technology and business, of various New Age spiritualities (Heelas 1996a; York 1995), 'self religions' (Heelas 1992) and human potential movements (Wallis 1984). Among the characteristics that these highly diverse religious and spiritual phenomena have in common is a concern with ways of liberating the self from social and cultural constraints that are considered to be inimical to authentic selfhood and/or freeing the potential of individuals to realise their capacity for spiritual growth. Variants on ideas of spiritual and religious liberation have seeped into sundry spheres of life to the point where, for example, management training programmes, therapeutic practices, new social movements and 'human resource management' schemes have appropriated them. They deserve therefore to be examined carefully in theorising about globalisation.

These liberal expressions of religion presented little or no problem to theorists of modernity who found in them evidence of such things as the 'colonisation of the lifeworld' by elements of the economic system (Habermas 1987), responses to the moral confusion of the 1960s (Tipton 1984), the 'triumph of the therapeutic' (Rieff 1966) or narcissism (Lasch 1981). So, if the global age has really transformed social relations, how can the continuing influence of liberal spiritualities and religions be explained? What effect, if any, do global conditions have on receptivity to liberal religion? One proposed answer is that the consumption of commodities has become a duty or ritual endowed with sacred significance (Featherstone 1991). As a result, the integration of late-modern society could be dependent on consumer culture and, in particular, on the readiness to consume images, identities and goods carrying a positive symbolic charge. The odd thing about this type of argument, however, is its reliance on Durkheimian, modernist theorising for the purpose of explaining a supposedly post-modern, global phenomenon.

My third point about the inadequate consideration of religion in social theories about the globalising world is that the category of ethnicity is often allowed to mask the phenomenon of religion. That is to say, leaving aside the work of specialists in the sociological and anthropological studies of religion and ethnicity,[14] the tendency has been for social theorists who situate the study of migration, settlement, refugees and asylum seekers in a globalisation framework to lose sight of, or to suppress, the specifically religious dimension of cross-national mobility. They give priority, instead, to ethnicity as the primary marker of identity, thereby blurring the lines between culture, politics and religion.

An important exception is the work of Yasemin Soysal (1994, 1997) on the mobilisation of Muslim migrants and settlers in Western Europe. She is careful to avoid the trap of equating the political mobilisation of Muslims with 'Islamic extremism'. Instead, she emphasises the somewhat paradoxical fact that Muslim organisations tend to stake claims for a wide range of entitlements using the discourse of universal rights. In some cases they even claim particularistic benefits, such as State support for Muslim schools or the freedom to wear clothing considered appropriate or mandatory for Muslims alone, on the basis of universalist principles enshrining the rights of individuals. She summarises the paradox as follows: 'The particular and the universal are not categorically opposed – rather the particular is interpreted by the universal' (Soysal 1997: 518).[15] This observation parallels Roland Robertson's argument that globalisation helps to precipitate a heightened consciousness of the category of 'humanity'. Religions can draw on extensive theological and philosophical resources in conceptualising humanity. It goes without saying that Muslims in Europe are far from universally agreed on the kind of claims-making in which they should be engaged and that the religious basis for this activity is not categorically separate from its ethnic and national dimensions (Nielsen 1992). But Soysal's main point about the *religious* basis for Muslim mobilisation is entirely clear and valid. Her work on Muslims in Europe is a sophisticated reproach to social theorists who find it hard to think beyond the equation of Muslims with Islamic extremism, fundamentalism or ethnicity. Modood (1994, 1998) has presented similar arguments outside the framework of ideas about globalisation.

In the case of Hindu and Sikh nationalist movements in India and in diasporic Indian communities around the world Peter van der Veer (2000) traces the roots of the religious basis for their mobilisation back to British colonial policies and practices. The imposition of clear boundaries between religious categories was an administrative expedient for the colonists that seemed to offer the prospect of more effective control over a hugely diverse sub-continent. But van der Veer's argument is that these imported ideas took root in the popular consciousness and imagination to such a degree that the previously vague, shifting and overlapping categories of Hindus and Sikhs hardened into political ideals as the basis for exclusive sacred territories and national status. Achieving clarity about their nature as religious entities was therefore a way of becoming modern and, incidentally, of embracing the instrumental advantages of globalisation. The opening up of India to global markets and global products, especially Westernised popular culture, has only sharpened the sense of a distinctive religious identity among Hindu and Sikh nationalists. At the same time, Hindu nationalists use friction and conflict with Muslims in order to confirm their conviction that India should ideally be a Hindu – not a secular – State. The strength of these religious convictions indicates the need for social theories of modernisation and globalisation to give due consideration to the religious basis of movements for ethnic and national liberation. The social construction or enhancement of religious identities is proceeding apace in many spheres of Indian life – and is generating criticisms and opposition.

Fourth, the claim that the autonomy and sovereignty of nation States is under threat lies close to the centre of many theoretical ideas about globalisation. According to Jan Aart Scholte, for example,

In the face of unprecedented globalisation since the 1960s, States can no longer be sovereign in the traditional sense of the word. For both physical and ideational reasons, a State cannot in contemporary globalising circumstances exercise ultimate, comprehensive, absolute and singular rule over a country and its foreign relations. (Scholte 2000: 136)

Indeed, evidence has been accumulating for many years in support of the view that nation States are in the process of being 'de-centred', marginalised or superseded in a globalising world. The increasing strength of transnational profit-seeking corporations, the force of global markets, the weight of international treaties, codes and conventions and the budding authority of a few transnational social movements have all contributed to a relative diminution of the capacity of individual nation States to act in a sovereign fashion. Admittedly, there are counter-arguments and more subtle assessments of the precise scope for sovereignty that nation States still have in the Global Age. But these qualifications make no difference to the point that I wish to develop here, which is that both the proponents and the opponents of arguments about the demise of nation State sovereignty have tended to ignore the issue of the *regulation* of religion in a globalising world.

Research on globalisation has been dominated to such a large extent by notions of marketisation, commodification and consumption in a world with apparently fewer and fewer official boundaries that relatively little attention has been paid to issues of regulation and control (but see Drahos & Braithwaite 2001). The ethos of globalisation, at least as reflected in discussions of economics and popular culture, appears to favour *laissez-faire* principles. Yet, I shall argue that many countries that are supposedly 'globalised' still confront quite serious difficulties when it comes to controlling religion. There are many different reasons for the persistence of problems in relations between States and religions, and some of them are associated with aspects of globalisation. Social theorists of globalisation, however, have missed the opportunity to examine this intriguing field of tension and conflict.

Agreement is virtually universal on the point that globalisation processes have had a major impact on communication. The speed, volume, intensity and reach of communication within and between countries have all increased dramatically as a consequence of the introduction of new information technologies. Communication of, and about, religion is no exception. Thus, the condition of globality has made it easier, quicker and cheaper for religious ideas to circulate around the world. The personnel of religious organisations and, indeed, the 'ordinary' members of faith communities have also come to enjoy higher rates of transnational communication and travel. Some theorists are even prepared to argue that these global conditions may facilitate the emergence of one or more global religions. The development of a substantial religious component in a potentially global civil society is also conceivable (Beyer 1994).

What is much less frequently discussed in connection with the enhancement of global communication of religion is the attempt by public authorities to monitor and, on occasion, to regulate the flows of religious ideas, practices, resources and personnel. Again, religion is no different in this respect from other increasingly globalised phenomena. 'Markets' for religion are in operation within and across national boundaries, but, unlike economic markets, international institutions for the control of religious market behaviour have not (yet) materialised. True, there are clauses in various declarations and codes of human rights, as well as many State constitutions, that are intended to protect the freedom of individuals to hold, to change or not to hold religious beliefs. Many constitutions also contain provisions designed to buffer the State against attempts to impose a religious monopoly or, in some cases, to prohibit any kind of collusion between States and religions. The growing number of scholarly studies of religion-State relations suggests that globalisation has aggravated or accentuated some issues in this area.[16] The regulation of minority religions gives rise to particularly important questions (Baubérot 1994; Modood 1997; Galembert 2001; Ferrari & Bradney 2000; König 2001), but the globalised world has not yet produced universally recognised instruments for monitoring, regulating and protecting the operations of religious markets. Instead, a variety of initiatives have been taken to put in place the rudiments of a regime for monitoring the rights of individuals to religious freedom.

The framers of Article 18 of the Universal Declaration of Human Rights[17] in 1948 struggled to find an appropriate way of dealing with issues of religious freedom (Evans 2000), as did the designers of Article 9 of the European Convention on Human Rights in 1950.[18] Moreover, the heated debates that have taken place at the UN World Conferences on Women in Mexico City (1975), Copenhagen (1980), Nairobi (1985) and Beijing (1995), as well as the International Conference on Population and Development in Cairo (1994), about the religion-related subjects of birth control, abortion and sexuality have demonstrated that the discourse of human rights is important but far from capable of resolving all extremely deep-seated disagreements about the ideal balance between notions of individual rights and collective, religiously warranted values (Witte & van der Vyver 1996). The appointment by the UN's Commission on Human Rights in 1986 of a Special Rapporteur to examine issues of religious freedom marked a further stage in the recognition that, in a globalising world, issues of religious freedom remain acute or have become more acute in some places.[19] Following the Treaty of Amsterdam, which came into effect on 1st May 1999, there is now also a clause in the Treaty of the European Union authorising action 'to combat discrimination based on sex, racial or ethnic origin, religion or belief, disability, age or sexual orientation' (Moon and Allen 2000: 583).

The reason why globalisation has brought some of the issues about religious freedom to a head is partly to do with the growing size of Christian and non-Christian religious and ethnic minorities in many Western countries. Economic migrants, settlers, refugees and asylum seekers, as well as their descendants born in the West, now constitute large enough components of the population to command attention. Religion is one of the vehicles for the expression of their identity and of their demands for improved conditions of life. At the same time, the notion of 'collective rights' has gained some support in political philosophy (Kymlicka 1995) and in policy-making circles. It is also integral to debates about multi-culturalism (Parekh 2000) and changing notions of citizenship (Soysal 1994). Furthermore, international agreements such as the UN's 'Declaration on the Rights of People Belonging to National or Ethnic, Religious or Linguistic Minorities' (1992) and documents such as the Council of Europe's report on 'Religion and the integration of immigrants' (Council of Europe 1999) embody the idea that minorities have collective rights. In a globalising world, States are therefore expected to respect these rights and to avoid discriminating against minorities unnecessarily. Thus, the effects of globalisation are nudging States towards a new understanding of their place in the globalising world, especially in relation to religious 'communities' that previously had a choice between being merged with the majority or marginalised. Several agencies of the US government have recently taken a leading role in making religious freedom a matter of global concern.

The decision of the US Congress in 1998 to create a Commission on International Religious Freedom (CIRF) as a means of monitoring the state of 'international religious freedom' around the world[20] only reinforces my point that heightened concern with regulation in matters of religion has accompanied globalisation. An Ambassador at Large delivers an annual, country-by-country report that identifies general trends as well as noteworthy incidents or cases. In cases of particularly severe violations of religious freedom, the reports may trigger action by the US Government. American embassies and consulates have increased their 'advocacy, monitoring and reporting on this issue' (Parmly 2001: 2). At least one of the countries heavily criticised in successive reports, France, has responded vigorously through the organ of its Inter-Ministerial Mission to Combat Cults (MILS). It has not only tried to refute the charge of acting unfairly towards so-called dangerous cults but it has also questioned the right of the US Congress to take actions that are deemed to amount to interference in France's internal affairs. This is a clear instance of a negative response at local level to a procedure that claims to have a global mandate. This is 'glocalisation' (Robertson 1992b) in the unusual sense of a mutual rebuff between the local and the global. It is important to stress that, in this case, glocalisation has not resulted in a compromise or a hybrid solution. It has merely sharpened some mutually inimical opinions in the USA and France.

In yet another exercise of monitoring the constitutional and legal provisions for the protection of religious freedom, the US Congress's Commission on Security and Cooperation in Europe prepared a

350-page report on 'Religious liberty: the legal framework in selected OSCE countries' in 2000. The report not only described the legal structures and processes in twelve countries but also identified current issues concerning religious liberty, as interpreted by American observers. Finally, the US State Department's 'Country Reports on Human Rights Practices', prepared by the Bureau of Democracy, Human Rights, and Labor, also contain sections on the freedom of religion and on religious minorities.

It is interesting to note, by way of comparison, that a Council of Europe (2002) report on 'Religion and Change in Central and Eastern Europe', prepared by the Parliamentary Assembly's Committee on Culture, Science and Education, was much more concerned than the American reports to strike a balance between protecting the rights of individuals and protecting national, cultural, ethnic and religious identity. The report acknowledged that Churches in Central and Eastern Europe, after decades of enforced weakness, must confront religious differences in a context of unprecedented pluralism. Its recommendations therefore include provisions to guarantee the freedom of religious minorities and to protect them against discrimination by religious majorities. The thrust of the report is towards the legal protection of *collective* rights and heritage – not simply towards the freedom of individuals to choose their own religion.

It is characteristic of the global circumstance *and* ironic that the arguments marshalled by public authorities in modern democracies to justify their controls over religion necessarily draw upon the presumably positive aspects of globalisation. That is, controls are justified in terms of the threats that are perceived to the 'truly' free circulation and consumption of religion on a global scale. They do not call into question the right of individuals to choose what to believe. In all these respects, a global market in religion does not appear to create a problem in itself. In fact, State controls over religion correspond to the logic of consumerism (Beckford 2003) as well as to each State's history of relations with religion (König 2001). By this I mean that they usually claim to protect the unwary, unwise or vulnerable 'consumer' of religion against the presumed risks of fraud and harm. It is only in relatively closed countries such as Iran, Saudi Arabia and Nepal that the authorities still base their attempts to exclude the influence of religions other than the one that is approved in law on the grounds that only one religion is authentic and acceptable. The justification for attempts to control religion in countries that are more unreservedly immersed in global networks rests, by comparison, on the need for *consumer protection* (Beckford 1993). Religion is therefore no different from any other marketised phenomenon in so far as limitations on its free circulation and consumption rest on assumptions about the conditions in which the freedom of individual consumers can be sustained without condoning fraud or exploitation. I shall argue in Chapter Five that the controversies surrounding new religious movements that are accused of brainwashing and deceiving their would-be, current or former members are only the tip of a much larger iceberg concerned with the consumer protection role of States in a globalising world. These complications are virtually invisible in social theorising about globalisation.

(d)   Nuanced studies of religion and globalisation

Having explored a number of the problems that arise when social theorists speculate about religion and globalisation without paying sufficiently careful attention to the findings of empirical research, let me bring the chapter to a conclusion with some indications of the productive uses to which notions of globalisation have been put in studies of religion. These findings are considerably more interesting and challenging than the jejune asides about 'fundamentalism' that one finds in some theoretical works about globalisation.

Writers in the French language seem more circumspect than many of their Anglophone counterparts about unqualified use of 'globalisation', in some cases insisting on their own term 'mondialisation'. Their studies of religion in particular tend to make important distinctions between the concepts of international, transnational and global, reserving the last one for phenomena that are truly global in the sense of not being controlled from any single geographical location and of being guided by 'new logics' (Bastian, Champion & Rousselet 2001: 10). The 'de-territorialisation' of religion is particularly evident in formerly colonised parts of the world. It can result in a process of 'confessionalisation', that is, the clarification and formalisation of religious sentiments, beliefs and practices that had previously been weakly defined and easily combined with others. This is happening in India among Muslims (Gaborieau 2001) and in Brazil where Candomblé is emerging as a local movement with global ambition (Motta 2001). The local/global dynamic in these cases is complex and open-ended.

Indeed, research published in the French language is distinctive for the emphasis placed on the differentiating effects of globalisation. Admittedly, an increasingly global market for religion is emerging, but at the same time this market is deeply segmented along lines of ethnicity and other dimensions of inequality. Nowhere is this clearer than in Brazil where Marion Aubrée (2001) has documented not only the acceleration of Pentecostal expansion since the mid-1970s but also the apparently limitless capacity for schisms among the many different expressions of Pentecostalism. It is as if each layer of Brazilian society has fashioned its own form of Pentecostalism in keeping with its own particular sub-culture. Aubrée (2001:12) captures the kaleidoscopic quality of these developments by borrowing a pun from André Mary (1994): 'bricolage' (do-it-yourself handiwork) has given way to 'bris-collage' (breaking up the collage or picture). The conclusion is that globalisation permits and encourages a radical break with old patterns of belief whilst also subsuming them under a new, overarching framework structured around the Holy Spirit. The fact that the Holy Spirit is not conceived in anthropomorphic terms facilitates the global spread of Pentecostalism (Corten 1995) and its malleability to local circumstances. A similar observation by Hurbon (1992, 2001) about the subsumption of beliefs about the devil and other spirits under the banner of Pentecostalism in various Caribbean societies reinforces the argument of Aubrée and Mary about the capacity of globalisation to provide a high-level framework of belief and practices which, nevertheless, retains local connections and colour.

In a further development of these ideas about the global/local dynamic in religions, David Lehmann (2001) probes an interesting paradox. He notes that some of the charismatic Christian movements that are expanding rapidly in South America and Sub-Saharan Africa rail against paganism whilst appropriating some of its symbols and rituals. Thus, charismatic healing is close to evangelical healing; and the idea of spirit possession is not so different from that of possession by the devil or exorcism and deliverance, as practised by evangelical Christians. These ideas clearly derive their original meaning from very different 'theologies', but processes of globalisation have enabled and accelerated the emergence of complex syntheses and borrowings between them. This is especially evident in Sub-Saharan Africa where competition is intense between Pentecostal Churches originating in North America or Western Europe and a wide variety of prophetic and neo-Pentecostal movements originating in Brazil and the Republic of Korea. According to André Mary (1999, 2001), there is little scope for cosmopolitanism, tolerant multiculturalism or ecumenism in Southern Africa. Instead, robust competition leads individual Churches to accentuate their distinctive features without entirely abandoning the cultures that they share in common with their competitors and enemies.

The growth of the Celestial Church of Christ (CCC) and of the Universal Church of the Kingdom of God (UCKG) in various parts of the world illustrates different ways of achieving a balance between the old and the new. The former tries to maintain symbolic links with its original heartland in Nigeria, whilst nevertheless seeking the status of a global Church within the evangelical field and condemning paganism, syncretism and fetishism. By contrast, the UCKG moves its pastors around and makes little attempt to draw attention to its Brazilian origins. Yet, it also mimics some of the religions that it criticises. For example, its hierarchical and centralised structure of authority relations echoes those of the Roman Catholic Church; its rituals of deliverance from evil spirits form a bridge between Brazilian possession cults and African witchcraft beliefs (Birman 1998); and its celebration of material wealth and generosity to the Church evokes the high esteem that traditional cults have for 'strong men' and 'winners'. There is a close, but paradoxical, relation, then, between the UCKG and the religious organisations and practices that it regards as demonic. Mary (2001: 167) concludes that globalisation is directing the CCC towards higher levels of formalisation and codification of beliefs, whereas the UCKG's trajectory is towards further syncretism rooted in its Brazilian past. Careful empirical investigation of the kind practised by the scholars whose research has been reported above is helpful in identifying the subtle, complex and paradoxical aspects of globalisation.

Scholars working in the English language have also corroborated the importance of the local/global dynamic. Mark Mullins (1994), for example, argues that Pentecostalism's spectacular growth in the Republic of Korea from the 1960s onwards owed much to its capacity for melding with elements of the local cultures:

All-night prayer meetings, exorcisms, prayer mountains, and healing services did not just appear in Korean churches by accident. Although Pentecostal church leaders would deny the influence of 'pagan religion', most scholars agree that shamanism has been the central force shaping the development of Korean Pentecostalism. In both Korea and Japan, shamanistic folk religion constitutes the native culture to which organized religions have been forced to adapt. (Mullins 1994: 91–2)

In fact, Mullins (1994: 98) also argues that Pentecostal leaders in Japan preach a message that 'is often indistinguishable from that of the modern shamans of many new religions who advocate new and old ways of controlling the spirit world and its powers for personal protection, happiness, and success in this world'. In this way, Pentecostalism was grafted on to traditional Korean shamanism and, subsequently, on to new and old expressions of religion in Japan as well.

The idea that globalisation lends a new lease of life to popular, informal or indigenous expressions of religion is central to Karla Poewe's (1994) claim that charismatic Christianity has become a 'global culture'. The same idea is also at the heart of David Lehmann's (2002) argument that globalisation promotes much more diversity than homogeneity

in religions. For, although intellectual elites and the wielders of eccle-
siastical power have often sought to impose a 'cosmopolitan' form of
globalisation in the shape of would-be universal, standardised religious
beliefs and practices, the truth is that 'local' forces invariably refract and
appropriate them in decidedly non-standard forms. Lehmann's argument
applies with even greater force to the less cosmopolitan and more local
or grassroots attempts to cultivate new religious sensibilities and enthusi-
asms on a global scale. Charismatic Christian movements, for example,
are able to '"plug in" to local cultural practices and to incorporate them
into their ritual and symbolic procedures, but without "theorizing" them
(in the manner of cosmopolitan forms of globalisation)' (Lehmann 2002:
306). Thus, a prominent feature of the global circumstance, according
to Lehmann, is a relatively high degree of tension and conflict between
popular and erudite forms of globalised religion.

Another aspect of the differentiating effects of globalisation is illustrated in Gerrie ter Haar's (1998) subtle categorisation of Christian
Churches among African migrants and settlers in The Netherlands.
She found that broad notions of 'black' or 'black-led' Churches did
not do justice to the complex processes of fission that have so far produced African-independent, African-initiated, African-institutionalised,
African-indigenous and African-international Churches. My earlier remarks about the growing salience of issues concerning the public regulation of supposedly de-regulated religions are congruent with Lehmann's
and ter Haar's strictures against sociological accounts of globalisation
that exaggerate the importance of standardisation and pluralism. Bryan
Turner's (2001: 143) assertion that 'A global age does not automatically
result in "McDonaldization", because there can be equally powerful pressures towards localism and hybridity' is well founded.

Although the fate of a globalising world may amount to more than
McDonaldisation, there seems little doubt that the long-term effect of the
implementation of international agreements and conventions on human
rights will be a degree of standardisation in the legal status of individual human beings. The rapidly expanding sector of international courts
of law, NGOs and cross-national social movements and voluntary associations also suggests the possibility of a global civil society. Given the
experience of religious organisations in thematising 'humanity', it is not
unlikely that they will play a formative role in any form of civil society that
might emerge at a global level. In any case, as George Thomas (2001) has
argued, it is important to find ways of preventing conflicts between faith
traditions from seeking to destroy each other in a world where they can
hardly avoid mutual contact. In short, globalisation creates challenges
to which a global civil society may be an appropriate response (Deakin

2001). If so, then religion is likely to generate particular problems and, perhaps, workable solutions as well (Casanova 2002). By comparison, the prospects for a rigidly *secular* global civil society seem less promising, especially as ethno-religious traditions tend to base their claims for recognition more on notions of collective, rather than individual, rights. But in my view the prospects for a 'global civil religion' (*pace* Beyer 1994 and Davie 2001a) are even weaker.

Conclusion

This chapter has shown that some religious organisations use notions of globality and globalisation in their teachings and other activities. These terms are not simply analytical tools in the hands of social scientists but are also theological and ideological constructs. Yet, social theorists have paid very little attention to the religious uses that are made of ideas about the global. Instead, theorists of globalisation, in their different ways, have tended either to ignore religion altogether or to accommodate it in one or more unsatisfactory ways. The dominant practice is to conflate fundamentalism with religious reactions against globalisation. This carries the disadvantage of concealing the importance of other religious phenomena related to globalisation which have little or nothing to do with fundamentalism. Yet, careful empirical research on religion in conditions of globality has generated some interesting findings that corroborate the analytical usefulness of properly understood and nuanced concepts of globalisation.

I am sceptical about the wisdom of attributing causal powers to globalisation,[21] but there are excellent reasons for investigating the complex ways in which religions are simultaneously constructing their own images of the global *and* refracting the influences from global forces that they detect. Notions of globality are a resource that is put to widely different uses in religious collectivities. For, in addition to facilitating the world-wide circulation of ideas, people and material goods globalisation is 'good to think with' – critically. This means, first, that leaders of religious organisations, as well as ordinary participants, have much to gain from orienting themselves towards global conditions as both challenge and opportunity. Second, it means that social theorists have much to learn from studies of the ambivalence that many religious organisations and individuals display towards globality. The findings of research on religion in a globalising context provide a valuable counter-balance to the ungrounded and unbalanced claims made about the alleged realities of globalisation that permeate social theory.

5   Social theory and religious movements

Social and political contexts

Social scientists aspire to explain or interpret the patterns that they detect in social relations, social processes, cultural meanings and social structures. The results of their work are often contentious but sometimes persuasive. By contrast, their attempts to predict the future are rarely successful. The development of religious movements is a good case in point. Even those scholars who were familiar with earlier generations of religious movements had not foreseen that a wide range of new religious movements (NRMs) would quickly emerge in the 1960s, attract new members and achieve public notoriety in many advanced industrial societies. Only in Japan where the production of new religions, or at least new combinations of religious beliefs and practices, had been accelerating over the course of the twentieth century (and particularly after 1945) had researchers and commentators detected signs of a 'Rush Hour of the Gods' (McFarland 1967). The possibility of an upsurge of interest in movements such as the Church of Scientology, the Unification Church (now the Family Federation for World Peace and Unification [also known as the Unificationist Movement]), the Children of God (now The Family), the International Society for Krishna Consciousness (ISKCON) and Transcendental Meditation (TM) was not only unexpected but also improbable from the point of view of the dominant strands of social theory at that time. The resurgence of Hindu nationalist movements in India and elsewhere was not widely anticipated. Nor was the growth of interest in radical movements in Islam. Charismatic, Pentecostal and Liberation Theology movements were only just beginning to attract the attention of social scientists in the 1960s. This chapter will chart the ways in which theoretical thinking has either succeeded or failed to come to terms with the variety and complexity of religious movements.

Social scientific studies of religious movements or 'cults' (as many of them are labelled by journalists, by the person-in-the-street and by their opponents) have proliferated since the 1960s in many parts of the world.[1] Most of these studies have appeared in North America, Western Europe and the Nordic countries, but a significant amount of research has also taken place in Japan, Latin America and Australasia. Sociologists have been in the forefront of research on religious movements, although anthropologists, political scientists, historians and students of Religious Studies have also made their own distinctive contributions. Publications about religious movements were predominantly in the English language in the 1960s and 1970s, but the number of publications in French, Italian, Portuguese and Spanish has increased steadily since then. The literature in Japanese is extensive, and works written in English by Japanese scholars have appeared in a growing number of English-language journals and edited collections.

My argument will be that the challenge of explaining religious movements in social scientific terms has produced some paradoxical results. On the one hand, a vibrant field of research has come into being with its own networks of scholars, scholarly journals, doctoral theses, conferences, research centres and books. Discussions have been particularly lively about the meaning of basic terms, ways of classifying religious movements, their institutional trajectories, mass media portrayals of the controversial movements, the growth of anti-cultism and the ethical dilemmas that arise in studying religious movements that are variously described as vulnerable, contentious and threatening. On the other hand, however, the linkage between this burgeoning field of research and broader currents of social theory has tended to be relatively weak. I mean this in two senses. First, exponents of social theory have shown little interest in religious movements. Second, studies of religious movements have failed to exercise significant influence on social theory.

At this point in the chapter I can only sketch my claims in rather stark terms. As the argument unfolds, however, I shall try to nuance them in various ways and, eventually, to show how a more productive relationship between studies of religious movements and social theory could develop. My main aim is not to complain that religious movement studies have been unjustly neglected but to provide reasons for thinking that their significance could be enhanced and that social theory would also benefit from taking better account of phenomena, such as religious movements, that present interesting challenges.

The chapter's structure is chronological. It begins with an account of how social theorists categorised and interpreted religious movements in the mid-twentieth century as predominantly marginal and deviant phenomena. The growth of theoretical interest in the 1960s in religion as a form of cognition drew attention to religious movements as crucibles of alternative meaning systems. At the same time, Marxist ideas, which had previously served to explain social class-based movements of religious rebellion, offered few insights into the proliferation of modern religious movements. There was also the possibility in the 1980s and 1990s of including religious movements in the category of new social movements, but the leading theorists, reproducing a widespread practice among social movement scholars, offered several reasons for keeping religious movements separate from other social movements. The second half of the chapter scans the range of current theoretical ideas about religious movements, beginning with rational choice theory. The findings of empirical research are reviewed in order to assess the value of theoretical ideas about 'free space' in late modern societies, the political and moral controversies concerning new religious movements, and the salience of issues about identity and culture in post-modern conditions. The conclusion is that the low degree of mutual awareness demonstrated in the work of social theorists and social movement scholars alike is regrettable but is far from being an insuperable obstacle to fruitful co-operation.

Before I can open the discussion I need to place the study of religious movements in their broadly political context. For, while social scientific research on religious movements has been unfolding, a closely related debate about them has also been taking place in the mass media and among participants in various types of anti-cult activity. I am referring to both the informal and the formal campaigns that have been conducted in many countries as well as at the level of the European Union to criticise religious movements deemed 'dangerous' or 'destructive'. Some of these attempts are inspired by religious motives for *countering* the allegedly baneful influence of religious movements. Massimo Introvigne (1995) coined the term 'counter-cult' to designate this form of opposition to religious movements. The designation of 'anti-cult' is more appropriate for predominantly secular ideas, organisations and activities that aspire to *combat* and, ideally, to defeat religious movements by preventing them from operating. The clearest example of anti-cultism is the French State's aggressively secularist apparatus for a 'struggle against cults' at all levels of the country's civil administration (Beckford 2003; Hervieu-Léger 2001b; Bauberot 2001; Richardson & Introvigne 2001). It includes three things: a law aimed at controlling cultic 'excess'; an Inter-Ministerial Mission to Combat Cults; and a co-ordinated strategy for eliminating the influence of cults in the public sphere.

Counter-cultism and anti-cultism are inseparable from the mass media – another dimension of the context in which social scientists study religious movements. Portrayals of religious movements in the print media and the broadcast media are overwhelmingly critical, focusing mainly on alleged and real scandals, atrocities and other abuses reportedly wrought on their members, ex-members or their close relatives (Beckford 1999a). Social scientific research on religious movements has therefore had to take special account of the ways in which the mass media depict them.

In combination, then, counter-cultism, anti-cultism and the mass media have exercised an important influence over the image of religious movements as a topic of social scientific research. Not only have they succeeded in pushing the issue of religious movements higher up the list of problems requiring public regulation but they have also helped to generate and to popularise lay, psychological ideas about the movements' *modus operandi*. In other words, there is a large amount of what I shall call 'lay theorising' about religious movements. This is not a problem in itself. Indeed, it makes studying religious movements from a social scientific perspective even more interesting and challenging, for the lay theories are an integral component of the topic. The fact that lay theories of religious movements are not just sets of abstract ideas but are actually at work in counter-cult, anti-cult and journalistic discourses and activities only increases their importance. This is particularly true in countries where State-sponsored investigations and official reports have led to the implementation of policies for the monitoring and control of religious movements, as in France and Belgium. The analysis of social theoretical ideas about religious movements must therefore take proper account of this particular aspect of the context in which the movements operate and in which social scientists conduct their investigations.

Finally, the context for social scientific studies of religious movements also includes the movements' own investment in such studies. Some religious movements have established their own institutions of higher education where research is conducted not only for the purposes of refining the movements' beliefs, teachings and forms of organisation but also for undertaking historical and social scientific studies of, for example, the movements' social composition or relations with the State. The Unificationist movement's seminary at Barrytown in New York State is among the best known institutions run by an NRM, while the investment in its own universities in Japan and the USA by the Soka Gakkai movement is on an even larger scale. The movements' 'organic intellectuals' often discuss their research with 'outside' researchers, in some cases even collaborating with them. This is particularly true of the ISKCON movement's creation of the *ISKCON Communications Journal*, the establishment of the Oxford Centre for Hindu and Vaishnava Studies, and the involvement of academic researchers in studies of its history and problems (Rochford 1997, 2000). Other religious movements, notably the Unificationist movement and Soka Gakkai International have also tried to stimulate and/or to control research on them by organising academic symposia and conferences, by establishing academic journals, web sites and e-mail user groups, and by publishing edited collections about themselves and other religious movements.

These in-house institutions for research are not entirely without precedent among older religious movements; and they still have a long way to go to match the long-standing investment of mainstream Christian Churches in higher education and academic research. But what is distinctive about the energetic involvement in research by some of the controversial NRMs of the post-war period is the relatively high degree of investment in studies of their own 'performance' and treatment at the hands of the mass media, agents of the State and opponents. These developments reflect the rising salience of social scientific perspectives in virtually all spheres of life. They may also indicate awareness among the leaders of today's religious movements that secrecy and seclusion are hard to achieve in a world where techniques of surveillance and monitoring are all-pervasive. No doubt, these leaders are also intent on using the findings of social scientific research to improve their own performance and to control the image of them portrayed by the mass media. For these reasons, then, the movements' relatively high levels of self-reflexivity and investment in social scientific research have complicated the study of religious movements.

In short, the context in which social scientists study religious movements is significantly different from that in which investigations of an earlier generation of sectarian movements took place. It no longer makes sense to regard religious movements as 'tribes' that could be studied in isolation from their surrounding society and cultures. They are certainly not passive objects to be investigated as if they take no interest in the process. Moreover, society's responses to them have become the primary focus for much of the recent research on religious movements. All these considerations of context and reflexivity suggest – misleadingly – that religious movements would be of considerable interest to social theorists.

The neglect of religious movements in social theory

The inescapable starting point is the fact that social theorists who are not also specialists in the study of religion have paid little attention to religious movements. True, there are passing references to them in discussions of, for example, deviance and collective behaviour. Herbert Blumer (1963), for example, categorised 'cults' as expressive phenomena that represented the chaotic stage of 'elementary' collective behaviour, out of which might emerge a new social order. Similarly, Neil Smelser (1962) included cults among the value-oriented responses to excessive strain in the social system. Indeed, the tradition of collective behaviour theorising has usually coupled 'cults' with 'crisis'. A comparable pattern emerges from anthropological studies of religion in non-Western societies with relatively simple technology (Aberle 1970; Thrupp 1970; La Barre 1972; Wilson, B. 1973; Lewis 1986) as well as from disadvantaged sections of Western societies (Fauset 1944; Hutten 1950). Yet, as Wuthnow (1982: 49) argued, efforts to match types of social strain to types of religious movement 'run into trouble when confronted with historical reality'.

In fact, it is rare for the topic of religious movements to figure nowadays in high-level or medium-range theorising about modernity and its development or supersession. It is mainly in theories of secularisation, as I showed in Chapter Two, that theorists have tried to account for the unexpected persistence, re-invigoration or generation of religious movements. It has to be added, however, that debates about secularisation are not often integrated these days into more general social theorising. For the most part, social theorists act as if the social and cultural significance of religion has sunk to such a low level that it no longer 'appears on their radar screens' unless, as in some cases, religion is associated with ethnic or nationalist identity. For example, influential studies of the Civil Rights movement in the USA highlighted the crucial role played by African-American religious networks (McAdam 1982; Morris 1984); and the religious underpinnings of the Solidarity movement in Poland were well documented in Alain Touraine's 'interventionist' study (Touraine, Dubet, Wieviorka & Strzelecki 1983).

My sweeping claim about social theory's neglect of religion in recent decades can easily be justified by consulting the index of virtually any book published in the last few decades on social theory. Remarkably few of them contain an entry for 'religion' or any cognate terms, with the occasional exception of 'secularisation'. The exception only underlines the fact that, in sharp contrast to the practice of the founding generations of sociology as an academic discipline (O'Toole 1984; Vidich & Lyman 1985; Beckford 1989), it is mainly the decline or absence of religion that is of interest to social theory these days. This was not always the case. And, as I shall argue below, it is not a defensible position to hold at the beginning of the twenty-first century.

The situation in scholarly journals specialising in social theory is even bleaker. For example, I could find only five articles about religion in issues of *Theory and Society* from its beginning in 1974 to the end of 2000. Similarly, *Theory, Culture and Society* carried only two articles about religion between the journal's foundation in 1983 and 2000. Admittedly, religion may have been referred to in passing in other articles in these two journals, but it did not warrant a mention in their titles.

Yet, as recently as the 1950s many social theorists, especially those operating within a normative functionalist framework, found good reasons for analysing the 'functions' fulfilled by religious institutions for the social system, the role of religion as a mechanism for transmitting values and integrating individuals into society, and the affinities between religious values and democracy, work ethics and the stability of nuclear families. This approach to social theory had no difficulty in accommodating a wide variety of new religious phenomena. Sectarian and cultic groups such as Jehovah's Witnesses or Christian Science could be explained in terms of the social system's internal re-adjustments to anomie, tension and conflict. This could take the form of 'safety valves' that vented excessive pressure or frustration by means of ecstatic religious rituals, trance states or immersion in tight-knit religious communities. An alternative interpretation of old and new religious movements within the same theoretical framework was that they helped to re-socialise marginal or excluded groups into mainstream ways of life (Johnson 1961). Some early, influential accounts of the NRMs that became controversial in the 1970s were also based on similar assumptions. For example, Robbins and Anthony (1972) argued that the rehabilitation of drug abusers among the followers of Meher Baba was facilitated by the movement's mysticism. Another of their arguments (Anthony and Robbins 1974) was that the same movement helped young adults to come to terms with their feelings of alienation from American society. Meanwhile, other commentators such as Tipton (1984) and Foss and Larkin (1976, 1979) detected a tendency for post-countercultural religious movements such as Erhard Seminars Training (now the Landmark Forum) to re-combine instrumentalism and expressivism in ways that could help their participants to fit into the routines of mainstream social life.

Cognition, consciousness and consistency

A successor generation of social theorists, without totally abandoning functionalist assumptions, found it more interesting to analyse the mechanisms and processes whereby religious world-views were said to supply meaning and stave off despair. The scope of this more phenomenologically oriented approach included, at one extreme, claims about the anthropological necessity for symbols of the sacred and, at the other, arguments about the marginal differentiation of religious world-views in an increasingly marketised world. The focus on such topics as the social construction of reality, multiple levels of reality and signals of transcendence kept religion near the centre of social theory in the 1970s. It also helped to inspire numerous investigations into the cognitive and symbolic dimensions of religious movements. A primary concern was with ways in which 'cognitive minorities' such as religious movements managed to sustain faith in their supposedly fragile belief systems (Snow & Machalek 1982). This was closely connected with a continuing stream of interest in the notion of religious conversion and religious identity.

The confluence of phenomenological sociology with symbolic interactionism generated further interest in the processes whereby new outlooks and identities were negotiated and symbolised. Religious instances of radical changes in world-views and identity loomed large in the work of social theorists as diverse as Kai Erikson, Peter Berger, Thomas Luckmann and Robert Bellah. In fact, Bellah was central to an ambitious programme of pioneering research that culminated in the publication of the co-edited volume on *The New Religious Consciousness* (Glock & Bellah 1976). (It might not be an exaggeration to see the much better known volume entitled *Habits of the Heart* [Bellah *et al.* 1985] as at least in part a late-maturing fruit of the same theoretical curiosity about changes in religion, spirituality, identity and morality).

The central questions of *The New Religious Consciousness* were how far the erosion of the legitimacy of American institutions had proceeded in the 1960s and to what extent new forms of religion and spirituality in the early 1970s, such as the Healthy-Happy-Holy Organization or the Church of Satan, had abandoned the USA's foundations in biblical religion and utilitarian individualism. Indeed, Bellah (1976: 339) went so far as to claim that the 'deepest cause' of the legitimacy crisis in the USA was 'the inability of utilitarian individualism to provide a meaningful pattern of personal and social existence, especially when its alliance with biblical religion began to sag because biblical religion itself had been gutted in the process'. The study of religious movements was central, then, to theoretical inquiry into the dynamics of American society in general and into the threats allegedly posed by 'cynical privatism' in particular.

Relatively few scholars have subsequently speculated at such a high level of generality about the significance of religious movements as potential sources of either the fragmentation or the re-integration of American society. But Robbins, Doucas & Curtis (1976) approached these issues from the combined perspectives of mass society theory, normative functionalism and the theory of civil religion. Their reasoning was that, while structural differentiation and atomisation had undermined the American civil religion, some religious movements could provide the kind of legitimation required to support young people's engagement with wider society. The Unification Church in particular was said to function as a 'civil religious sect' in so far as it combined patriotism and theism within an authoritarian, totalising organisation.

These functionalist interpretations of the surge of NRMs in the 1970s did not meet with universal acceptance, however (Beckford 1978b, 1981). For example, there were historical grounds for arguing that the production of religious movements had been a constant feature of American society since the seventeenth century (Moore 1986) and was not, therefore, a feature unique to the 1960s and 1970s. According to the American church historian, John F. Wilson (1973: 596), 'myriad religious sects, cults and movements have populated American society throughout its history'. Doubts were also expressed about the extent to which the NRMs were actually new in terms of their religious ideas. It seemed as if 'alternative' religious beliefs, which had in some cases been circulating for centuries on the fringes of mainstream religion merely 'moved out of the narrow cultural and ethnic niches to which they were largely confined' (Melton 1987: 47). The so-called new religious consciousness (Wuthnow 1976, 1978) was allegedly re-cycling distinctly old ideas with roots in Christian and Asian traditions. These historical arguments seemed to cast doubt on the claim that the alleged crisis of American civil religion or a broader crisis of legitimation had generated crisis cults in the form of NRMs. This was not to deny, however, that the wars in South East Asia and the student movements of the 1960s had given a conjunctural boost to the long-running interest in alternative forms of spirituality and religion.

Not all theorising about religious movements followed the contours of normative functionalism, however. There was also a distinctly Weberian way of constituting religious movements as an interesting object for sociological study. In fact, it was the mismatch between the authoritarian forms of organisation adopted by some of the most controversial NRMs and their self-proclaimed ambition of freeing their followers from the constraints of a corrupt or controlling society that helped Roland Robertson (1979) to detect a shift in the reasons for studying religious movements. In his view, the theoretical significance of religious movements did not simply lie in their capacity to re-integrate Western societies or to re-socialise marginal youth. Robertson's argument was that, unlike the early modern sects that Max Weber had labelled 'consistent' because of their commitment to the freedom of religion in society *and* to the freedom for their individual members to pursue their own spiritual development, the NRMs of the 1970s tended towards inconsistency. As such, their implication for modernity was different from that of their nineteenth-century predecessors.

Robertson's thesis was that late twentieth-century NRMs signified a new stage in the relationship between individuals and society, especially 'new modes of individual existence', either as critiques of, or as alternatives to, society. In particular, so the argument went, theoretical interest was growing in the 'compatibility of major societal trends, on the one hand, and religious, mystically flavoured concern with self, on the other hand' (Robertson 1979: 306). In turn, this sociological aspect of NRMs gave rise to issues concerning the very definition of religion and the extent to which individuals might legitimately devote themselves to its practice. A similar idea was also central to Richard Fenn's (1978, 1981) understanding of a secular society as one in which decisions about what counts as 'real' religion would increasingly be taken in courts of law. As I indicated at the end of Chapter Two, the sociological debate about secularisation has begun to investigate fruitful questions about the processes whereby boundaries are socially constructed and contested between religion and non-religion as well as between authentic and inauthentic religion. Religious movements are an interesting site for theorising about the changing 'location' of religion. I shall return to this point later because it opens up a potentially rewarding area for social theorists interested in transformations of selfhood.

Further reasons for regarding religious movements, old and new, as important phenomena throughout the world since the sixteenth century have been proposed by Robert Wuthnow (1982) in an interesting extrapolation from theorising about the world-system. Following Immanuel Wallerstein's (1974) lead, Wuthnow argued that the conflictual dynamic between core and peripheral nations in the expanding world economy had elicited and shaped distinctive types of religious responses. He claimed that six forms of religious movements, each of which reflected the differential impact of major changes in world order on particular populations, could be identified: revitalisation, reformation, religious militancy, counter-reform, religious accommodation and sectarianism. For my purposes, the most rewarding aspect of Wuthnow's analysis is its capacity to transcend both the collective behaviour perspective and the normative functionalist perspective by linking religious movements not to social strain or anomie at the national level but to perceptions of fundamental shifts and crises in the world order. There are some echoes of this approach in attempts to theorise relations between globalisation and religion, but few scholars have tried to consolidate or to refine Wuthnow's analysis.

Marxist theory and religious movements

Marxist theoretical ideas also continued in the 1970s to offer interpretations of religion's appeal to various social categories, formations and conjunctures. By means of weakly articulated arguments that religion was, for example, 'the self-consciousness and self-awareness of man who either has not yet attained to himself or has already lost himself again' or 'the sigh of the oppressed creature, the feeling of a heartless world, and the soul of soulless circumstances. It is the opium of the people' (Marx 1977: 62). Some Marxists tried to maintain that religion had a revolutionary potential.

Other Marxists kept alive the idea that a theoretical understanding of religion remained an important pre-requisite for understanding the evolution of capitalist social formations. But, as Bryan Turner (1991: 85) observed, there is an uncomfortable tension between the claim that each social class cultivates its own class-consciousness and the claim that a dominant ideology representing the interests of the ruling class alone somehow trumps working-class consciousness. If an attempt is made to resolve the tension by arguing that religion represents a false consciousness of class, then it becomes difficult to sustain the view that 'primitive rebels' and 'labour sects' could have been religiously motivated expressions of class conflict. Turner's own preference for regarding the religion of dominant classes as a legitimation of systems of property transfer by primogeniture helps to avoid excessive reliance on arguments about (a) the effectiveness of ideological transmission and (b) the susceptibility of the working class to ideological mystification. But it remains to be seen how well Turner's argument applies to societies lacking a system of primogeniture. Nor is it clear how he could account for the continuing vitality of religious movements in Western societies where the principle of primogeniture is no longer dominant – except by abandoning his commitment to materialism and resorting to a form of functionalism. Indeed, Turner (1991: 200), following Robbins, reasoned that 'Such religious cults as the Divine Light Mission and Meher Baba serve to resocialise and integrate marginal adolescents, "drop outs" and drug addicts back into the conventional routines of employment, monogamous family life and education'. Is this reasoning not also in the spirit of the 'dominant ideology' thesis that Turner was at such pains to dismiss?

Religious Marxists have also sought ways of demonstrating the emancipatory potential of religion in certain circumstances. On the one hand, the example of early modern movements of popular protest and resistance against the exploitative power of emerging nation-States in Europe and, on the other, the prospects for 'liberation theology' and 'theologies of struggle' on the periphery of the capitalist world-system in the late twentieth century also continued to enliven the more humanistic strands of Marxist social theory. Yet, the NRMs of the late twentieth century in the Western world, Japan and Australasia failed to attract the theoretical interests of Marxists. This was partly because NRMs did not appear to reflect the interests of the working class or, indeed, of any obviously oppressed or exploited categories of people. NRMs did not have the potential to bring about revolutionary change in social relations between the holders of power and the relatively powerless. But Marxists also tended to consider NRMs as inward looking, non-progressive, controlling communities with weak concerns for people who were neither their members nor their potential members. In short, NRMs were at best an irrelevance from most Marxist viewpoints or at worst a symptom of the problematic aspects of capitalist societies that called for a revolutionary, rather than a religious, solution.

'New social movement' theory

There is strong continuity between the Marxist theorisation of religious movements as either irrelevant or obstructive to progress and the way in which theories of *new social movements* (NSMs) also refuse to regard religious movements as 'new' in their terms. There are many different reasons for claiming that the 'old' labour movement has lost the capacity to respond effectively to the supposedly new fault lines, cleavages and contradictions of late capitalist or post-industrial society. But theorists as different as Alain Touraine (1981, 1985), Jürgen Habermas (1981, 1987), Klaus Eder (1985) and Alberto Melucci (1989, 1995, 1996) are all agreed that religious movements do not represent a serious challenge to the prevailing social order. Whilst acknowledging that a wide range of supposedly new social movements or 'collective actions' either emerged or were relaunched in the 1960s in pursuit of collective goods such as sex equality, world peace, environmental protection and human rights, these theorists, along with many others,[2] exclude or omit from the NSM category the spiritual and religious movements that also emerged in the 1960s. Their reasons for this exclusion echo the reluctance of most Marxist scholars to regard any form of religion as liberating.

Habermas's (1987) reasoning is particularly clear on this point. He argues that novel forms of conflict arose in the sphere of culture in the 1960s. The conflicts centred on the defence and restoration of endangered ways of life and not on the economic and distributive problems of the 'old' politics. 'The new problems have to do with quality of life, equal rights, individual self-realization, participation and human rights' (Habermas 1987: 392). The reservoir of potentials for protest was wide and deep, according to Habermas, including such disparate causes as the antinuclear movement, feminism, the peace movement, the squatters movement, gay groups, 'youth sects' and 'religious fundamentalism'. The last two, belonging firmly in the category that Habermas labelled 'resistance and withdrawal', were not concerned with 'conquering new territory' and were not therefore considered to have 'emancipatory potential'. Rather, they resisted 'the colonization of the lifeworld' by experimenting with new ways of co-operating and living together. The significance of resistance and withdrawal movements merely lay, according to Habermas, in their capacity to generate polemics and to highlight the harmful consequences of capitalism's headlong rush for growth. Since he clearly does not believe that they are rational enough to make the social system more just or humane he does not regard them as progressive. In fact, Habermas seems to regard religion as 'a monolithic and reified phenomenon', which is the antithesis of rationality (Dillon 1999: 291).

A more nuanced and better-informed interpretation of what he nevertheless misleadingly terms 'religious revivalism' is Alberto Melucci's (1996) analysis of the new bases for collective action to challenge the cultural codes of 'the information age'. But it is clear from the context and from the scholars whose work he cites that Melucci is referring to NRMs. Unlike Habermas, he acknowledges that NRMs do actually form part of the movement of antagonism towards the complex systems of information, symbols and social relations that control economic production and the exercise of power in 'post-modern' society. NRMs resemble other 'antagonist' mobilisations in many different ways, including the following: their goals are not negotiable, they are not interested in seizing political power, they challenge the separation between the public and the private, they are accused of being deviant, they place a premium on solidarity, and they require participation and direct action from their supporters. Moreover, Melucci's (1996: 104) argument is that the 'regressive Utopianism' of these movements, which is shared by some other movements, can in some cases still form the basis of a genuine challenge to the 'instrumental rationality of dominant apparatuses'. Melucci accepts that the sacred can serve as the basis for an appeal to a different, alternative social order. In other words, he does not categorically distinguish between NRMs and NSMs. But, in common with Habermas and Touraine, he does claim that NRMs run the risk of generating a 'totalizing myth' or a 'totalizing monism' that reduces 'reality to the unity of one all-embracing principle' (Melucci 1996: 104). Such movements are also vulnerable to the risks of being manipulated by political forces, marginalised as sects or transformed into marketable fashions. In this way, 'Contestation dissolves into individual flight and a mythical quest for the Lost Paradise, or it crystallizes into fanatic fundamentalism' (Melucci 1996: 105). Religious movements that withdraw from society completely give rise to a 'communitarian integralism' that, in Melucci's opinion, forfeits any chance to effect social transformation.

Alain Touraine, the doyen of French studies of social movements, also tends to exclude religious movements from 'the' social movement of 'new modernity'. This is his way of labelling life in societies where the main problem is no longer about relations between capital and labour, or about citizenship and inclusion, but is, rather, about the cultural struggle against fragmentation and manipulation at the hands of those who control the all-important information and theoretical knowledge (Touraine & Khosrokhavar 2000). Touraine's highly distinctive view is that the solution to this problem no longer lies with social actors such as political parties or social movements but with the mobilisation of 'the Subject'. This refers to the capacity within individuals to reject the current social order and to fight back by insisting on changes that would protect personal and collective values and human rights.

Like Habermas and Melucci, Touraine is well aware of the risk that religious movements might turn inwards and establish 'nostalgic' communities that would cancel out the Subject's power of resistance. But, unlike many other theorists of social movements, he does not regard this as a necessary outcome. Religion, in Touraine's sense of a reference to the transcendental Other or the divine, has the capacity to inspire Subjects to reject the established order. He firmly denies that religious institutions or organised religions are capable of fomenting cultural resistance; but he admires the heroism and the single-mindedness of individuals who base their refusal to comply with what he regards as indefensible norms on their conviction that the transcendent provides an ideal model of subjective conduct. The 'success' of religion as a source of inspiration for the Subject's principled struggle against co-optation and control by external forces depends on keeping its distance from organisational roles and power. In effect, then, Touraine has no time for religion as a social institution or organisation; but he acknowledges that ideas of the divine can inspire the search for subjective autonomy.

Touraine has no doubt that the power of religious institutions and organisations to integrate societies in new modernity has declined but he also recognises that transcendental ideals are still capable of lending meaning to life: 'Neither religion nor politics gives meaning to life today. But the divine, as an exteriorised form of the subject, is still present in personal and collective life, and the religious vision of human rights is stronger than before' (Touraine & Khosrokhavar 2000: 215, trans. J.A.B.). Touraine is careful to make it clear, however, that the kind of individualisation cultivated by Pentecostal and charismatic Protestant movements, particularly in Latin America, is radically different from that of the Subject. This form of the 'individualisation of religion' in Latin America is, in his opinion, compatible with conservative and authoritarian attitudes. In addition, despite his admiration for certain heroic exponents of Liberation Theology within Roman Catholicism, Touraine regards it as a mistake for people with left-wing sympathies to try to recreate social and political communities to resist oppression. He also argues that it is not enough for sociologists of religion to interpret the growing popularity of Protestant groups in Latin America as a reaction against the loss of traditional community or the harshness of urban living. Perhaps surprisingly, Touraine favours a 'religious explanation of religion', emphasising spiritual considerations, compared to what he considers to be the 'mediocre' explanations offered by sociologists.

To sum up, the first reason for the reluctance of Marxists and theorists of NSMs to regard NRMs as theoretically interesting is that such movements are not self-evidently a critical or alternative response to structural tensions or contradictions in capitalist societies. Their followers allegedly have no consciousness of themselves as engaged in a collective struggle to liberate themselves and all other oppressed people from systematic exploitation. The second reason is that NRMs do not offer a new set of values or cultural codes that would transform the 'grammar of the forms of life' (Habermas 1987), 'break the codes' (Melucci 1996) or 'deprogramme' society (Touraine 1985). The third reason for refusing to regard NRMs as NSMs is that the former supposedly tend to encourage their followers to huddle together in conservative havens instead of campaigning to transform the society around them. Fourth, the basis on which many NRMs are organised is considered by the theorists of NSMs to be authoritarian and anti-democratic. NSMs, by contrast, are supposed to work best when they amount to nothing more than local groups of activists loosely articulated in networks at regional, national or international levels. Imbrication or overlap between mutually sympathetic networks is also highly prized in NSMs but not in NRMs. Finally, NRMs' ideologies are categorised as irrational and therefore not conducive to progressive enhancement over time.

For all these reasons, then, theorists rarely consider NRMs alongside NSMs. In fact, there are grounds for suspecting that religious movements represent many of the features of late modern or post-modern society that NSMs are intended to challenge and to supersede. Even so, theorists of NSMs seem to have little appetite for exploring the meaning of NRMs.

Religious movements as social movements

The lack of attention paid to NRMs by theorists of NSMs may be short-sighted or ill advised but it is easily understandable in the light of the quasi-Marxist assumptions about emancipation that many of them share. It is more difficult, however, to explain the fact that other social scientists specialising in the study of *any* kind of social movements have, with some significant exceptions, shown relatively little interest in religious movements. In fact, the lack of entries on 'religious movements' in the textbooks and edited collections on social movements appears to be almost perverse. This supports Craig Calhoun's (1999: 237) claim that 'the field of social movements offers a strong example of the general pattern of devaluation and neglect' of religion, in spite of the 'cultural turn' that began to take place in social movement research in the late 1980s (Hart 1996). Significant exceptions include John Lofland's (1979, 1985, 1987) work on religious movements, especially the Unification Church, and Christian Smith's (1996) corrective view of religion's capacity to underpin protest and social movements. Major empirical investigations have also documented the religious in-put to a wide variety of movements including far right-wing politics in the US (Aho 1990; Barkun 1994), the Campaign for Nuclear Disarmament in the UK (Byrne 1988), the Sanctuary movement in the US (Golden & McConnell 1986), anti-pornography campaigns (Zurcher & Kirkpatrick 1976), pro-choice activism (Williams and Blackburn 1996), anti-feminism (Somerville 1997), opposition to gay rights (Herman 1997), Promise Keepers (Lockhart 2000) and inner-city political mobilisation (Wood 1999).

A further irony of the relative neglect of religious movements in studies of social movements is that the study of NRMs has arguably been one of the most vibrant areas of the sociology of religion since the 1970s. There is a vast literature in many languages about the religious movements that have attracted notoriety and, in some cases, opprobrium as a result of their more or less simultaneous eruption in many relatively prosperous parts of the world (Beckford 1985a; Robbins 1988; Barker 1989, Bromley & Hadden 1993; Saliba 1995; Chryssides 1999). The movements most widely regarded as controversial in the 1980s and 1990s include ISKCON, the Church of Scientology, the Unification Church, the Children of God (now the Family), Soka Gakkai and a wide variety of neo-Hindu movements such as Sahaj Yoga and the neo-Sannyas movement of the Bhaghwan Shree Rajneesh. Attempts to portray controversial NRMs in the mass media have also given rise to extensive research (Van Driel & Richardson 1988, 1989; Beckford 1995, 1999b; Silk 1995, 1997). In addition, social scientists continue to examine the attempts made by State authorities, legislators, law enforcement agencies and voluntary organisations to investigate and to control the activities of NRMs (Robbins 1981, 1987; Beckford 1993; Richardson 1995; Champion & Cohen 1999).

Finally, John Hannigan (1990, 1991, 1993) has made a persuasive case for the usefulness of looking closely at the relations between NSMs and NRMs. One part of his argument is that many NSMs display spiritual and religious characteristics. The other part is that the theoretical ideas that have been advanced to account for NSMs are applicable to NRMs as well. In view of the potential for 'synergy' that he detected between the normally separate fields of NSM and NRM studies Hannigan could see the value of blurring the distinction between religious and socio-political movements, principally because both types of mobilisation centre on the collective negotiation and re-negotiation of identity. In his view, NSMs and NRMs have much in common, including the three main processes of contestation, globalisation and empowerment.

There is much to be gained, then, from exploring religious movements as if they were social movements and *vice versa* (Zald & McCarthy 1998). The benefits of such a strategy are plain to see in studies of movements as diverse as the YMCA (Zald 1970), Nichiren Shoshu Buddhism (Snow 1976) and the International Society for Krisna Consciousness (Rochford 1985, 1997). Indeed, I have argued elsewhere (Beckford 1989, 2001a) that it has become all the more important these days to conduct research on religious movements because the influence of many of the major religious organisations is in decline.

'[A]s the influence of religious organizations has waned, religious symbols, meanings and values have been de-regulated and made more exploitable. "Religion has come adrift from its former points of anchorage" (Beckford 1989: 170) and is increasingly available for use in a bewildering variety of ways. This is why I described religion as a "free floating phenomenon". In this context, de-regulation means more than the relaxation of legal or constitutional restraints on religious activity. It also means that religious organizations are able to exercise less control over the uses made of their own religious symbols.' (Beckford 2001a: 232)

In other words, the 'free space' in which religious entrepreneurs can cultivate and promote novel forms of religious belief, experience, action, solidarity and organisation has expanded significantly since the mid-twentieth century.[3] Nowhere is this more evident than in the so-called Third World where religious movements such as Pentecostalism, Hindu nationalism and Islamic 'purity' movements have been expanding for several decades. This has prompted Jenkins (2002: 8) to ask, 'Since there were only a handful of Pentecostals in 1900, and several hundred million today, is it not reasonable to identify this as perhaps the most successful social movement of the past century?'. The buoyancy and vitality of certain religious movements are evidence of the extent to which they have been able to take advantage of the new structure of opportunities available in religiously deregulated countries. There is ample support for this argument among the exponents of what is widely called 'rational choice theory'.

Rational choice theory

Students of religious movements who have drawn inspiration from, and have helped to refine, insights from the broad stream of diverse theorising in terms of 'rational choice', 'rational action' and 'subjective rationality' have tended to focus their work primarily on the strategies employed by individuals and collectivities for optimising their rewards and minimising their costs. Thus, the resource mobilisation perspective outlined by McCarthy and Zald (1977) and the issue of the free-rider analysed by Olson (1965) have influenced studies of a wide range of religious movements. Examples include Hall's (1988) study of the People's Temple as a 'poor people's movement', Bromley and Shupe's (1979) analysis of the strategies of the Unificationist movement, and Iannaccone's (1992, 1994, 1997) interpretation of how high-demand religious movements such as Jehovah's Witnesses seek to avoid the problems posed by free-riders.

The conviction that sociological analysis should begin with assumptions about the subjective rationality of religious actors has also led to numerous insights into the religious beliefs, practices and affiliations of individuals. The propositional theory of religion originally expounded by Stark and Bainbridge (1985, 1987) and later elaborated by Bainbridge (1997) and Stark and Finke (2000) is the most ambitious attempt to explore the rationality of both individuals and collectivities in the religious marketplace. And, although these writers rarely refer to the notion of 'opportunity structures', the importance that they attach to the degree to which religious markets are regulated indicates close parallels with studies of social movements in the 'political process' tradition (McAdam 1982). Thus, religious movements are expected to flourish in circumstances where formerly, actual or would-be monopoly religions are weak and where political or legal constraints on religious activity are also weak. Bainbridge (1997), regarding religion as 'eternal', has coined the phrase 'the perpetual system' to capture the allegedly never-ending, circular process of secularisation, revival and religious innovation.

In short, the *potential* for fruitful investigation of religious movements as social movements is at least as strong within the rational choice framework as within any other. In fact, Rodney Stark, the doyen of studies of religion within the rational choice 'tradition', has repeatedly asserted his belief that the choices that people make about religion are no less rational than are the choices that they make in other spheres of life. His emphasis on novel, deviant faiths further underlines his conviction that there are, in principle, no limits to the applicability of the notion of 'subjective rationality' in sociological analysis. Nevertheless, Stark and Finke (2000) have recently sought to distance themselves from the most rigid, economistic implications of rational choice theory by adopting the softer notion of 'subjective rationality'. This notion characterises 'all human actions that are based on what appear to the actor to be "good reasons", reasons being "good" to the extent to which they rest upon plausible conjectures' (Stark & Finke 2000: 37). Yet, even this softer version of rationality still 'assumes the presence of subjective efforts to weigh the anticipated rewards against the anticipated costs, although these efforts usually are inexact and somewhat casual'.

The potential benefit from analysing religious movements in terms of rational choice is high partly because the resource mobilisation perspective, with its leading assumptions about rationality, has already inspired a wide range of studies of social movements and is currently regarded as the dominant approach in the USA. It has also survived extensive criticism (Gusfield 1981; Jenkins 1983) and has undergone various developments and enhancements such as 'frame alignment' (Snow *et al.* 1986). And, in spite of the objection that the resource mobilisation perspective may not really be applicable outside the political and legal institutions of the USA (Klandermans 1986), it remains highly influential in the field of social movement studies. It is perhaps surprising, then, that the 'parent' perspective of rational choice theory has not had a more far-reaching influence on studies of religious movements.

The reason why rational choice theorising has not yet had a more profound effect on social scientific studies of religious movements is that there are strong objections to some of its psychological and philosophical underpinnings.[4] In this respect, the sociology of religion is no different from other sub-fields of sociology where opinion is sharply divided over the explanatory potential of rational choice theory (Goldthorpe 1998; Zafirovski 1999a, 1999b; Archer & Tritter 2000). The two principal objections are, first, to the *methodological individualism* inherent in the belief that sociological explanation must begin with knowledge of actors' preferences. The contrary arguments are that the very notion of 'actor' is both social and cultural and that actors' preferences are partly shaped by social and cultural factors (Bruce 1999). Consequently, so this line of reasoning against rational choice theory runs, the decision to regard individual actors as the basic components of social life is arbitrary and at odds with what is known about the reality of social forces. Yet, the research of Sherkat and Wilson (1995) on religious 'switching' and apostasy shows that it *is* both possible and profitable to abandon the economistic assumption that actors' preferences are necessarily stable and, instead, to explain the ordering of preferences in terms of the social factors that influence them whilst still remaining true to the rational choice paradigm. Research by Ellison and Sherkat (1995: 1416) also shows that 'the decisions of rural southern Blacks about participation in congregational activities have been shaped to a considerable degree by social norms and expectations'. In fact, their argument is that the shaping of decisions was so powerful that the Black Church amounted to a 'semi-involuntary institution'. And my own research on chaplaincies in the prisons of England and Wales (Beckford 1999c) documents the structural constraints that shape the rational, yet paradoxical, decisions made by Christian chaplains about acting as 'brokers' for members of faith traditions other than Christianity.

A second objection to rational choice theory is that it operates with a narrow and exclusively instrumental conception of *rationality*. The capacity to calculate an efficient relation between means and ends is certainly characteristic of most human beings in most circumstances, but there is no reason to believe that they necessarily have the desire or the opportunity always to make use of this capacity. Nor does it make sense to preclude the possibility that, in certain circumstances, human beings do not actually optimise their individual utility but pursue, instead, collective goods, altruistic ends or transcendental values.[5] If the defendants of rational choice theory define these collective or self-sacrificial actions as disguised or surreptitious expressions of individual utility, their reasoning comes close to being vacuous. They would in effect be arguing that *all* human action is instrumentally rational, including acts of compassion, love, selflessness, hate and bigotry. This would make it virtually impossible to explain patterns of difference in social life. And it would lead to the ironic conclusion that rational choice theory's attempt to counter the tendency of social scientists to reduce human action to the mechanistic outcome of deterministic and irrational forces ends up crediting human beings with a threadbare form of purely instrumental rationality. This is a strange way to seek to restore dignity and autonomy to human actors (Jasper 1997).

There is a world of difference, then, between on the one hand insisting as a matter of methodological principle on recognising the capacity of human beings to act rationally and, on the other, reducing human rationality to cost-benefit calculus. My criticism of rational choice theorising is levelled not so much at the methodological principle as at the impoverished meaning that it tends to attribute to 'rationality'. To adapt a cliché, rationality is too important to be left to rational choice theorists. And this is the basis of my misgivings about the particular way in which some sociologists of religion operating within a rational choice tradition have tried to account for the propensity for human beings to engage in religion. The sticking point for me is the set of psychological assumptions about the association between religion and compensators for unattainable rewards (Beckford 2001b).

In early attempts to apply RCT to religion, Stark and Bainbridge (1987: 36, 39) postulated that 'Religion refers to systems of general compensators based on supernatural assumptions'. My criticism is that this assumption entailed a confusion between compensation and the procedures to be followed for achieving the desired goal. The notion of compensation does not appear in the theorising of Stark and Finke (2000), but these authors retain the view that 'Religion is the only plausible source of certain rewards for which there is a general and inexhaustible demand' and that 'Religion consists of very general explanations of existence, including the terms of exchange with a god or gods' (Stark & Finke 2000: 85, 91). The way in which people conduct the exchange with gods is allegedly as rational as the way in which they 'go about everything else', that is, they 'bargain, shop around, procrastinate, weigh costs and benefits, skip installment payments, and even cheat' (Stark & Finke 2000: 113). This appears to be a refreshing challenge to theoretical perspectives that reduce religion to ideological error or illusion. Indeed, RCT has generated interesting research findings about, for example, the strategies pursued by 'strict churches' for the avoidance of the free-rider problem (Iannaccone 1994); the effects of deregulation on the levels of religious vitality in the US (Finke 1990); the consequences of competition for religious change in the US (Finke 1997); the conditions in which weak church-type organisations might evolve towards the status of the sect-type (Stark & Finke 2000);[6] and the importance of studying 'whole religious economies' in any attempt to explain Europe's receptivity to cults and sects (Stark & Bainbridge 1995).

However, I question whether RCT perspectives are indeed based on a fair characterisation of human action. Subjective rationality is certainly an essential component of human thought and action – but so are wishful thinking, error, inconsistency, delusion, imagination, hope, creativity and fear. In other words, the exclusive focus on rationality can undoubtedly be helpful in sociological analysis of religious movements and should never be ignored, but it is rarely capable of providing well-rounded explanation in isolation from other considerations.

The value of rational choice theory lies not just in its capacity to stimulate debates in the philosophy of the social sciences (Hollis 1987, 1994, 1996; Barnes 1995; Goldthorpe 1998) but also in its ability to contribute towards well-rounded social scientific explanation. Rational choice theory has considerable *heuristic* value in the sense of generating models and hypotheses for testing. It is particularly useful as a source of 'thought experiments' or 'rational ideal-types', as Max Weber would have described their function as explanatory strategies. Michael Hechter's (1997: 157) assessment is therefore fair: the rational choice 'approach will motivate studies on religion that otherwise never would have been carried out, for it will suggest questions that had never been considered by scholars of religion'. Of course, the advocates of, and the enthusiasts for, applying rational choice theory to the scientific study of religion are unlikely to be content with my argument about the perspective's heuristic value alone. But this does not alter my view that examining the supply-side of the various religious economies in which religious movements operate can bring to light many important considerations that would probably be overlooked or omitted in studies based on different theoretical assumptions. I am confident that, in due time, selected elements of rational choice theory will be accepted without demur into the array of theoretical and conceptual tools of the social scientific study of religion. But I doubt whether the individualistic, instrumental and psychological assumptions about religion and compensators will be among the selection.

Culture and identity

One of the reasons why the study of religious movements has become more relevant to some current streams of social theory is that issues of culture and identity are central to them both. As the tendency to associate 'cults' and 'sects' with nothing but anomie, alienation, deprivation and crises of legitimacy has weakened, so students of religious movements (as well as non-religious social movements) have begun to tackle questions about the affinity between religious movements and broader movements of social and cultural sensibility concerning identity and spirituality. At the core of many of these questions are high-level theoretical concerns with the nature of post-modern, late-modern or new-modern society. There are also suggestions that the very concept of 'society' is becoming redundant under pressure from changes in technology, the economy, social relations and meaning systems (Urry 2000).

My aim here is to chart the mutual implications between these theoretical ideas and social scientific interpretations of religious movements. It goes without saying that religious movements are only one small 'site' on which these implications are working themselves out, but I want to argue that they carry a significance that belies the relatively small number of the movements' followers. This is because religious movements are quasi-laboratories in which profound social and cultural experiments can be relatively easily observed on a small scale. It is not difficult, in fact, to observe the processes whereby religious movements construct distinctive codes of meaning and modify them over time, often in conflict with the rest of society. Examples of movements born in conflict include the Kimbanguist movement in Central Africa (Martin 1975), the Children of God in the USA (Van Zandt 1991) and the formative years of Mormonism in Illinois (Hampshire 1985). Yet, religious movements are rarely free to construct their cultural codes in complete independence from existing codes and social structural constraints. In fact, they often develop a form of intense, inward-looking solidarity that is articulated and celebrated through controversies and conflicts with external agencies. Lethal violence was the tragic outcome in the case of movements as diverse as the People's Temple, the Solar Temple, the Branch Davidians and Aum Shinrikyo (Robbins & Palmer 1997; Wessinger 2000).

Studies of conversion to religious movements also provide a useful window on to the construction of collective, discursive frameworks that legitimate the movements' distinctiveness and separateness (Beckford 1978a; Machalek & Snow 1993). The discourses of ex-members or apostates, and about ex-members, are further resources for studies of biographical reconstruction and of collective self-defence through the anathematisation of perceived enemies (Beckford 1985a Chapters 4–6; Wright & Ebaugh 1993; Bromley 1998). In these respects, religious movements offer exceptionally clear and sometimes dramatised examples of cultural processes that are common and, for that very reason, likely to be overlooked. Moreover, in some cases, religious movements are bellwethers of impending transformations on a much larger scale. This is why the study of religious movements ought to be more strongly integrated into social theory. I shall expand this argument in three ways. The first point relates to the struggle of religious movements for free space and 'identity spaces'. The second point situates 'cult controversies' in the context of social and cultural uncertainties. And the third point explores connections between religious movements and theoretical ideas about self-reflexive identity and post-modernity.

(a)   Free space

The first nexus of theoretical ideas that help to explain the continuing interest in religious movements, especially in technologically advanced societies, has to do with the contested availability of *'free space'* in which religious experimentation can take place. The opportunity exists for religious experimentation partly because the religious organisations that used to control most public religious activities in the early modern period, often in alliance with agencies of the State, have now lost much of their power. The mobility of populations and the rapid circulation of ideas have also helped to foster in a minority of people a more experimental and voluntary attitude towards religious beliefs and activities. Thus, while many theorists agree that post-industrial, post-modern or late-modern societies have witnessed the increasing stranglehold of the State and of transnational corporations over wide swaths of social and cultural life, there still seems to be considerable scope for individuals to cultivate their own religious interests. Indeed, Daniel Bell (1980) expected that the 'return of the sacred' would occur in the 'radically disjunctive societies' where the forces of the 'techno-economic realm' were at odds with the polity and culture, and where a space would open up for 'existential predicaments' to elicit religious responses in the form of a return to tradition. According to the different logic of rational choice theory, as we saw earlier in this chapter, a 'market' for new religious 'products' has developed in the space vacated by the formerly dominant religious organisations – or, at least, left vacant by their former members. Religious 'entrepreneurs', new and old alike, have tried to exploit these opportunities, in many cases making use of the latest communications technologies (Brasher 2001), business strategies (Bromley & Shupe 1980) and networking capabilities (Heelas 1999).

There is also scope within theories of civil society for an argument about the value of competing religious visions for societal wellbeing, but theorists such as Casanova (1994) tend to restrict their attention to large, transnational churches and, with less confidence, to Islam in some countries (Casanova 2002). There is no doubt in my mind, however, that transnational religious movements like the Unificationist movement, the Church of Scientology and Soka Gakkai International consider themselves to be increasingly powerful actors in civil society. As these movements carry none of the historical and ideological 'baggage' of the racism and colonialism with which the Roman Catholic Church has been associated in, especially, Latin America and West Africa, their chances of influencing civil society may be correspondingly greater in the long run.

There is nothing inevitable or mechanical about these developments. My argument is definitely not the same as the rational choice thesis of 'the perpetual system' whereby older religious organisations are allegedly replaced in a never-ending cycle by upstart sects (Bainbridge 1997). Nor is it entirely compatible with the thesis that religion is somehow being 'restructured' (Hervieu-Léger 1999). Instead, my argument is simply about the availability of 'free space', within limits, where religious movements can operate with varying degrees of success. And it has to be added that, with the exception of the Pentecostal and Charismatic movements and a small number of other 'religious multinationals' (Beckford 1986), the number of people being mobilised is relatively small in comparison with the size of, for example, the audiences for mass market films and TV programmes or the spectators for major sporting events. Nevertheless, it is important to take proper account of the activities of religious movements because they can have a profound effect on their followers' lives.

A variety of theoretical ideas can claim to explain the availability of the 'free space' that religious movements occupy. The notion of 'mass society', for example, was an influential concept in attempts to explain the growing popularity of the Soka Gakkai movement in Japan in the 1960s (White 1970). The severe strain imposed by the Second World War on Japanese institutions – at the level of family, company and neighbourhood – was said to have left individuals vulnerable to the mobilising efforts of the New Religions. They allegedly exploited the opportunity to create new forms of religious practice cutting across social categories of social class, gender, age, level of education and type of occupation. In other words, the war and its aftermath created social spaces in which the New Religions were able to mount their campaigns for recruiting individuals whose relations to kin, company and community had been destroyed or weakened.

An alternative, less pathological, approach to understanding the free space occupied by religious movements involves an examination of the 'political opportunity structure' in which they operate. This approach emphasises, first, the constraints imposed on movements by the political, legal and economic contexts within which they work and, second, the opportunities for development that these contexts offer. The value of assessing the political opportunity structure available to religious movements was established by studies of African-American networks during the Civil Rights movement in the USA (McAdam 1982; Morris 1984). The Solidarity movement in Poland and numerous movements of religiously-motivated resistance and protest in the former Soviet Union and Latin America (Van Vugt 1991; Martin 1993) can also be understood, in part, by reference to their perception of, and responses to, the structure of political opportunities available to them. And there are grounds for speculating that the Falun Gong movement in China and 'Islamist' movements in the Middle East and North Africa may currently be in the process of testing the limits of the political opportunities open to them. Meanwhile, Jehovah's Witnesses have been struggling since the early twentieth century for the right to distribute their literature door-to-door and in public places, often in the face of hostile opposition (Lawson 1995; Côté & Richardson 2001). Other religious movements such as

ISKCON and the Church of Scientology also see themselves as engaged in a constant struggle to gain access to public places and to the broadcasting media for the purposes of proselytism.

In all these cases, religious movements are contending for the possibility of creating and exploiting free space. This is a further reason why social theorists of modernity and its evolution need to give more attention to the paradoxical situation in which religious movements simultaneously press for the extension or defence of free, public space *and*, in some cases, make use of it in order to create inward-looking communities that appear to isolate their members from public life. It is as if such religious movements demand the rights and freedoms associated with modernity for the purpose of living separately from it. This is an aspect of the 'inconsistency' remarked by Robertson (1979) but rarely reflected in social theorising about modernity. Another way of expressing this idea is to say that religious movements not only reflect the ambiguities of modernity but also agitate for a variety of modern freedoms whilst feeling threatened by other modern developments. Examples include the sophisticated legal campaigns of Jehovah's Witnesses to be exempt from laws and medical practices requiring them to accept or to sanction blood transfusions, and the resistance of the Exclusive Brethren in the UK to the opportunity to file certain tax documents by means of computers. As I shall show later, these campaigns for the freedom to extend, or to fend off, the advances of modern freedom can have important implications for gender relations in some religious movements.

In this connection, religious movements also illustrate some of the interesting complexities and ambiguities concerning the mapping of public and private spheres of social life in modernity. In one sense, religious movements are 'public' because they are part of neither the State nor the economy. They belong to the realm of 'civil society'. Indeed, movements such as Scientology, the Unificationists and some of the New Religions of Japan have repeatedly offered to serve the interests of wider society by providing drug rehabilitation programmes, schemes to reduce levels of crime and environmental pollution, and support for human rights campaigns. But their offers to contribute towards strengthening civil society, as a sphere of non-State and not-for-profit-seeking enterprises aimed at generating societal solidarity, are routinely blocked or criticised by their opponents. Furthermore, many religious movements conduct their activities in ways that are not visible to 'the public'. Some religious movements, particularly in countries with an established Church or officially recognised religions, even defend their right to operate on the grounds that religion is a matter of 'private' conscience or of the individual's right to freedom of private belief. Where institutions of civil society are weak,

religious movements are part of the 'private' sphere. True, religious movements are far from unique in this respect, but the energetic and sometimes
high profile campaigns that some of them wage for the right to operate
in public whilst remaining private are unusually clear illustrations of ambiguity in the public/private distinction (Weintraub & Kumar 1997). In
other words, the study of religious movements is a good way of exploring
the puzzling and changing geography of the public and the private. They
illustrate the multi-layered complexity of the public/private boundary in
late-modern societies.

Recent social theory offers at least two promising points of departure
for ways of exploring free space by using religious movements as 'trace elements' or 'analysers'. The first is Kevin Hetherington's (1998) 'cultural
geography' of new social movements in the fields of peace, environmentalism and human rights. His thesis is that such movements seek to exploit
'identity spaces' in which to practise resistance to dominant structures
and meanings. Moreover, these transgressive identity spaces are 'chosen
as sites for "eclectic" rites of passage [and] are not generally integrated
within the rituals of modern societies; they are out of the ordinary, out of
place, uncertain and anomalous – heteroclite – like the identities themselves' (Hetherington 1998: 18). He emphasises the importance of the expressive 'performative repertoires' through which new social movements
articulate their various identities in their particular identity spaces. For,
the 'relationship between expressivism, belonging and identity is a major feature of the quest for identity that runs through modern society'
(Hetherington 1998: 6). His own research was focused on countercul-
tural 'travellers' and protesters against road building programmes, among
other campaigns, but the central points about elective identities, identity spaces, protest practices and performative repertoires would apply
just as well to religious movements. For they are also a clear instance of
what Hetherington, after Schmalenbach (1977), terms a *Bund* or form of
communal grouping sealed by a covenant. The *Wandervogel* youth groups
and kibbutzim are further instances of the 're-communitisation of social
relations' in otherwise depersonalised societies. Hetherington shows no
awareness of the Bund-like character of many religious movements, but
the literature on this topic is extensive (Bromley 1988). The opportunities
for further testing and refinement of his conceptual scheme are therefore
many and diverse. By the same token, students of religious movements
stand to benefit from a conceptual scheme that, instead of marginalis-
ing or pathologising Bund-like groupings, explains their significance for
modern or late-modern societies.

The second point of departure for using religious movements as 'trace
elements' or ways of exploring free spaces in late-modern societies is

superficially allied to Hetherington's thesis. For one of his arguments is that

While the modern world promotes greater individuation through its weakening of the 'organic' tie of community, it also promotes elective and collective (neo-tribal) conditions of association – Bund – that act to promote individuality as well as provide an intense experience of communion into which that individuality is subsumed. (Hetherington 1998: 95)

One finds similar arguments in Maffesoli's (1988) thesis of neo-tribalism and in Mellor and Shilling's (1997) account of the tension between banality and carnality.

In fact, all these theorists work within a neo-Durkheimian logic of individuality and collectivity. Yet, there is also a less communal, less solidary way of interpreting the relations between individual and collectivity in what Ulrich Beck calls 'second modernity'. I suggest that this line of reasoning has the potential to cast religious movements in a theoretically interesting light and that, conversely, a careful study of religious movements could help to test the usefulness of Beck's theorising. The starting point is that processes of 'individualization' have become institutionalised (Beck & Beck-Gernsheim 2002). But, far from heralding either the disintegration of society or the formation of solidary communities of resistance, the structural individualisation that characterises second modern societies actually facilitates a form of societal integration rooted in standardisation. Moreover, '[t]his simultaneous individualization and standardization of our lives is not simply a private experience. It is institutional and structural' (Beck & Beck-Gernsheim 2002: 203). It also involves an enhancement of freedom, for '[i]ndividualization liberates people from traditional roles and constraints', albeit at the cost of making them dependent upon the labour market and, consequently, on markets affecting all areas of life. Thus, '[t]he individual is removed from traditional commitments and support relationships, but exchanges them for the constraints of existence in the labour market' (Beck & Beck-Gernsheim 2002: 203).

While Beck and Beck-Gernsheim are undoubtedly right to emphasise the crucial character of the labour market, I believe that their thesis about individualisation and standardisation could also be applied to other spheres of life such as religion. Numerous pieces of research have confirmed the point that traditional bonds of loyalty to, participation in, and identification with, mainstream religious organisations have been weakened since the 1960s, particularly in Western Europe.[7] At the same time, the market for non-traditional forms of religious activity has expanded and diversified. To describe individuals as 'consumers' of religion is no longer to borrow an analogy from the sphere of economics: it is a plausible description of the new relationships that a growing number of people really have with religious organisations and religious 'products'. The implications of this shift of perspective for social scientific studies of religion could be serious. It might call into question, for example, the thesis of the 'privatisation of religion' and its associated claims about the development of diversity and pluralism as guarantors of social order. It might also cast doubt on the idea that religious organisations form intermediary associations that buffer the individual from the State and the market. It would certainly contribute some new considerations to explanations of apostasy or switching between religious organisations.

But perhaps one of the most intriguing possibilities of adopting the individualisation perspective on religion as a market would be to force further debate about rational choice theories of religion. For example, if the Stark and Bainbridge (1985, 1987) and the Stark and Finke (2000) propositions about the psychology of compensation for unattainable rewards are set aside in favour of the view that religious products are consumed in the same way as other commodities, does that alter the perception of the market for religion? How can one reconcile the belief that unregulated religious markets promote religious vitality and diversity with the view that standardisation is a concomitant of markets? And can one really talk about the subjective rationality of religious consumers if their consumption patterns are shaped by market forces, advertising and marketing strategies? These questions are associated with fresh thinking about the tension within Max Weber's work between his conception of rationality as a defining characteristic of human beings and his belief that the process of rationalisation has trapped modern human beings in a hardened steel casing of disenchantment and bureaucracy (Locke 2001).

Conversely, the theory of individualisation would benefit from being tested against the evidence about religion in general and religious movements in particular. It would be necessary not only to establish the facts about religious markets and patterns of consumption but also to test the claim that

[b]eing an individual does not exclude caring for others . . . In the old value system the ego always had to be subordinated to patterns of the collective. A new ethics will establish a sense of 'we' that is like a co-operative or altruistic individualism. Thinking of oneself and living for others at the same time, once considered a contradiction in terms, is revealed as an internal, substantive connection. (Beck & Beck-Gernsheim 2002: 212)

New Age movements may provide evidence of this 'new ethics' (Heelas 1996a), but one wonders how far other religious movements are likely to support the optimistic claim that 'tolerance for other types of people and marginal groups, whether foreigners, homosexuals, handicapped people or the socially disadvantaged, has steadily increased as values have changed' (Beck & Beck-Gernsheim 2002: 162). It is precisely because the proponents of the individualisation thesis show very little awareness of religion in their writings that it is all the more important for students of religious movements to respond critically and, if necessary, to expose the weaknesses of an ambitious theoretical scheme. For example, the 'new ethics' is not yet evident in attitudes towards religious minorities in France, Belgium or Germany.

(b)   Cult controversies

A second nexus of theoretical ideas concerns the resistance that is widely shown to many religious movements' efforts to create the free spaces in which they can operate. The 'cult controversies' (Beckford 1985a) that have attracted so much attention among sociologists of religion relate mainly to disputes about the shifting boundary between what is regarded as 'normal' and 'abnormal' in late-modern religion (Beckford 2001d). For, whenever religious movements lay claim to free space they meet with challenges to their authenticity and *bona fides*. The sociological literature on controversies involving religious movements is huge. This is partly because sociologists have a wide range of theoretical reasons for being interested in them and partly because other interested parties, such as journalists, ex-members, politicians, State officials and anti-cult activists, have tried hard to keep the controversies in the public eye. This is not the place to review the controversies in full, but a good impression of the diversity of issues at stake can be obtained from Bromley & Richardson 1983; Beckford 1985a; Robbins 1988; Richardson 1988; Champion & Cohen 1999; Zablocki & Robbins 2001; and Kent 2001. Moreover, the differential salience of cult controversies and the wide variations in their causes, courses and consequences in different countries accentuate the need to understand them in relation to their local contexts. This is not to deny that ideas about why religious movements are controversial do not circulate between countries: it is merely to argue that such 'external' ideas are received, interpreted and assimilated differently in different countries (Beckford 1983b; Shupe, Hardin & Bromley 1983).

The first point of relevance to social theory thrown up by 'cult controversies' is that the persistence and growth of religious movements present a challenge both to assumptions about the privatisation and individualisation of life in late modernity (Beck & Beck-Gernsheim 2002) *and* to claims about the neo-tribal quality of post-modern identity (Maffesoli

1988). For religious movements fall under suspicion precisely because, on the one hand, they seem to isolate individuals by extracting them from networks of kin and friendship. On the other hand, religious movements seem to foster artificial, alternative forms of kinship, friendship and loyalty. Accusations of brainwashing are therefore rife in this area (Bromley & Richardson 1983; Barker 1984). Notions of brainwashing, coercive persuasion and milieu control are all deployed to explain the capacity of religious movements, first, to dissolve the 'normal' bonds of social life and, second, to cement 'abnormally' strong bonds of exclusive commitment to a religious group. The figures of the brainwashed zombie and of the manipulative all-controlling cult are iconic, particularly in popular culture. They represent, in a compressed and extreme form, two of the tendencies that are said to characterise late modernity, namely, hyper-individualisation or atomisation and 'destructive *Gemeinschaft*' (Sennett 1977). The success of religious movements is thereby implicitly contrasted to the liberal modern assumption that rational, self-interested individuals are normally integrated into the fabric of society by means of kinship relations and crosscutting, intermediary associations. This pluralistic image of 'the strength of weak ties' (Granovetter 1973) stands in theoretical opposition to the contrary image of the 'weakness of strong ties' in religious movements. Controversial religious movements are one of the battlegrounds on which the struggle between the notions of individualisation and collectivisation takes place.

Debates about the dynamic between individuals and collectivities have taken some particularly interesting turns in regard to gender relations in religious movements. Questions about gender relations arise in all spheres of social life but, once again, my case is that religious movements offer an especially sharp focus on phenomena that can be complex and elusive unless located in concrete contexts. Another way of putting this is to say that religious movements are not a microcosm of the societies in which they operate but that, in some crucial respects, they provide unusually clear-cut disclosure of issues that are virtually universal. Yet, social theorists have paid relatively little attention to gender relations in religion – and even less to gender relations in religious movements. Even feminist social theorists have tended to content themselves with analyses of the patriarchal, and therefore oppressive, exploitation of women by men in religious organisations and in styles of living heavily influenced by religions without inquiring more deeply into women's responses to sexism in religions. There are exceptions, however, and they are found mainly among feminist scholars in the Sociology of Religion, Religious Studies and Theology (Jacobs 1991; Erickson 1993; Neitz 1993; King 1994; Wallace 1996; Woodhead 2001). These scholars represent a minority among feminists, but their arguments raise interesting questions for social theory – especially in relation to studies of religious movements.

Feminist-inspired studies of religious movements have confirmed and reinforced a point that has recurred in this chapter, namely, that religious movements are analogous to laboratories of experimental living. But feminist researchers have added the equally important observation that religious movements permit or encourage some dramatically extreme forms of gendered social relations and innovative approaches to sexuality among their members. In simplified terms, movements such as the Unification Church, ISKCON (Rochford 1985, 1997; Knott 1995) and Promise Keepers (Donovan 1998) seem to favour a heightened form of the subordination of women to men. At the other extreme there are religious movements such as the Shakers (Brewer 1986) and the Bahai's (McMullen 2000) that have aspired towards unusually high degrees of equality between male and female followers in some respects. Variations on the theme of different, but complementary, relations between the genders are also common in movements such as Orthodox Judaism (Davidman 1991) – as in other spheres of life.

But religious movements ought to be especially interesting to social theory because many of them are micro-societies where radical experiments in sexuality and gender relations are theorised, enacted and fought over in dramatic fashion alongside thoroughly conservative patterns of gender and sexuality. In the intense, emotionally charged atmosphere of movements that are relatively isolated from the rest of society the degree of critical and continuous self-reflection on the forms of gendering and sexuality can be extremely high. According to Neitz (2000), for example, some feminist witchcraft practices offer the opportunity for a complete break with the categorical distinction between heterosexuality and homosexuality, thereby enabling a radically new nexus between body, emotion and religious identity. The stakes are high for movements that deliberately set themselves apart from societal conventions for religious reasons. Compromise is difficult; and the danger of fissiparousness is ever present. These factors help to make questions of gender roles and relations unusually vivid in religious movements.

The history of religious movements is marked by radical experimentation in a wide range of different relations between men and women not only with regard to sexual behaviour, the division of domestic labour or the public/private boundary but also with regard to responsibility for such things as prophecy, healing, preaching, leadership, prayers and teaching (Jules-Rosette 1975). This is another area in which social theorists, especially those with interests in social relations of trust and intimacy, stand to learn from social scientific studies of religious movements. Research has repeatedly demonstrated the importance that female participants in religious movements attribute to negotiating for themselves the symbolic and social resources needed to cope with their relative disadvantage in hierarchical organisations (Ozorak 1996). Discourses of empowerment are prominent, for example, among women campaigning for change in mainstream Christian churches just as much as among the activists in marginal movements such as feminist Wicca. Moreover, the power that is sought is not always the capacity to achieve one's ends regardless of resistance. It is just as likely to be the capacity to foster supportive, solidary relationships as a basis for self-realisation and collective wellbeing. This is what Linda Woodhead (2001: 78) terms 'a shift of weight towards the relational in religion', echoing Georg Simmel and Carol Gilligan among others. Feminist studies of religious movements have therefore extended and clarified notions of empowerment, often on the basis of strategies and methods of research embodying feminist principles (Oakley 2000).

It is also partly under the inspiration of feminist principles of research that social scientific studies of religious movements have begun serious exploration of the fact that religious activity is not only cognitive but is also embodied and emotional (Griffin 1995; 2000). Again, my point is that religious movements, especially those embroiled in controversies, represent a stage on which relatively common issues to do with human bodies and emotions are dramatised and thereby thrown into sharp relief. The most eye-catching examples concern the members of movements such as ISKCON who wear highly distinctive clothing and hairstyles, restrict sexual relations to the purpose of procreation, practise meditation for long periods of time and follow a vegetarian or vegan diet. In short, the bodily regime of ISKCON devotees is integral to their religious convictions, their feelings of loyalty to the movement and their sense of identity. The nexus between body, emotions and convictions is also at the heart of feminist Wicca, which, according to Susan Greenwood, is a positive response to the post-modern condition:

The issue of identity in relation to postmodernism is therefore problematic in a study of feminist Witchcraft because feminist Witchcraft draws extensively on notions of an essential 'true self'. This is often conceptualised as a project of self-discovery within a politics of shared oppression. Feminist Witchcraft's ideal of an essential true self is firmly located within a *primordial* holistic world-view of the Goddess embodied in Nature. The issue of finding the true self (through the feminist Witchcraft ritual process) is central to the 'postmodern condition' – which may be experienced as fragmentation and discontinuity . . . Bodily experience is the very essence of feminist spirituality and is seen as the locus of women's power. The body is thus the source of self-affirmation and identity. (Greenwood 2001: 138, 139)

The nexus between body, convictions and emotions is also central to Sufi forms of Islamic spirituality and to the prophetic and healing movements of West Africa and Southern Africa in which the wearing of uniforms assumes special significance.

At the same time, these bodily and emotional regimes are the focus of extensive criticism and opposition. Particular concern is expressed about the risks to which women may be exposed in movements that cultivate intense relations of dependence on charismatic gurus, teachers or prophets in social settings where countervailing pressures or interests are relatively weak (Feuerstein 1992; Puttick 1996, 1999), although not all scholars share this view (see Palmer 1994). In short, opinions are divided about the threats allegedly posed to women by religious movements – just as they are divided about the gender-related issues that arise in other religious organisations (Nason-Clark 2001) and in society at large.[8] The main point for present purposes is that the issues can be amplified and made more clearly visible in religious movements than in other settings. The fact that the movements range from the extremes of conservatism to libertarianism only increases their potential interest to social theorists concerned with change and continuity in gender relations.

Cult controversies are relevant to social theory in a second general sense. They challenge the widely held belief that modernity has undermined religion and that States in late-modernity are now neutral towards religion. As we saw in Chapter Two, however, there are many reasons for social scientists to be wary of simplistic notions of secularisation. Cult controversies are a reminder that questions about religion remain problematic even, or especially, in supposedly secular societies. This is ironic in view of the fact that struggles to achieve constitutional and other legal protection for the individual's freedom to choose religion or no religion was at the heart of many projects to create modern societies. As a result, religion enjoys certain privileges even in countries such as the USA, France and Italy where different forms of separation between State and religion are in operation.

Religious movements have an important bearing on our thinking about the relations between religion and the State in late-modernity because some of their activities challenge the limits of current thinking about the nature of religion for the purposes of the law. Questions arise, therefore, about the qualification of movements as truly 'religious' if, for example, they are economically successful; if they claim to be therapeutic; if they discourage their devotees from engaging in sexual relations or completing their education; if they forbid their members to avail themselves of certain medical treatments or to use computers; and so on. In other words, agencies of the State and courts of law find themselves obliged to decide where the boundary lies between religion and non-religion or between acceptable and unacceptable expressions of religion (Beckford 2001d). Moreover, the growth of religious diversity and of indifference to religion in most technologically advanced societies makes these boundary issues even more interesting from the point of view of theories of late-modernity. It is not too fanciful to suggest that what I shall call, following Habermas (1996), the 'juridification of religion' will, in turn, elicit further deviance or resistance from those religious movements that are dissatisfied with its outcome. In some respects, this is what happened in the period leading to the Iranian Revolution of 1979, in the emergence of the Islamist armed rebellion in Algeria in the 1990s, and in the consolidation of religious opposition to abortion in the USA.

However, there is no echo of Habermas' rationalist faith in the potential of juridification to resolve boundary disputes concerning religious move-ments in Michel Foucault's historically-informed scepticism about the whole range of cultural, social, political and legal devices for governing human populations through the conversion of knowledge into power. In-deed, Foucault's work on governmentality is a potentially rich, although not unproblematic, vein of insights into various aspects of religious move-ments. Yet, researchers have made very little use of these insights. This is unfortunate for two main reasons. The first is that Foucault's explo-rations of the centrality of confession in early and medieval Christianity could generate interesting hypotheses about the ways in which conver-sion and recruitment to religious movements take place. Indeed, it may seem surprising, in view of Foucault's account of the power of the psy-chological disciplines to control human subjectivity and action, that his work has not been influential in anti-cult circles. But the problem is that his approach undermines the credibility of the psychological sciences no less effectively than it would expose 'cultic mind control' techniques. The second reason for considering the lack of attention to Foucault's work in this area as unfortunate is that an opportunity has been missed to conduct an 'archaeological' investigation of the explanatory categories deployed in anti-cult and counter-cult discourses. Foucault's archaeological methods of disinterring the intimate connections between knowledge and power could help to shed new light on, for example, the medicalisation of the 'cult' problem (Robbins & Anthony 1982). Exponents of Foucault's dis-tinctive style of social theory do not yet seem to have realised that religious movements would constitute a potentially rewarding field of investigation from their point of view.

A third reason for social theorists to take better account of 'cult con-troversies' is that the representation of religious movements in the mass media casts light on some key aspects of late-modern society and culture. For, although today's religious movements, with the exception of the

Pentecostal and Charismatic movements, some movements in Western and Southern Africa and some of Japan's New Religions, do not attract huge numbers of followers, the theme of controversial cults is widely deployed in the mass media and popular culture. Relatively few people have any personal experience of religious movements, but journalists and programme makers keep the image of 'cults' in the public eye. It is as if the degree of public receptivity to the portrayal of religious movements in the news, in feature articles and in fiction is inversely related to the rate of public participation in religious activities. In part, this situation is perfectly understandable because a handful of religious movements have achieved notoriety for egregious incidents of deviance, abuse, violence and self-destruction. The cases of the People's Temple, the Branch Davidians, Aum Shinrikyô, the Solar Temple and Heaven's Gate are only the most notorious ones (Hall 2000; Wessinger 2000). But specialists in the study of religious movements are aware that many other movements have been controversial without being associated with murder or suicide (Bainbridge 1997; Saliba 1995). On the other hand, the mass media have a tendency to 'lump all cults together' (Barker 1989) and to foster a generic notion of them as uniformly dangerous and deceptive. The depiction of religious movements in films, novels, plays, comics, TV dramas and soap operas follows the same pattern.

The fascination that journalists and programme makers have for controversial religious movements is not only heavily patterned but is also a reflection of some of the social and cultural 'fault lines' and dilemmas of late-modern social life. The tug-of-love theme that concerns relatives' attempts to remove someone from a 'cult', for example, plays on uncertainties about the responsibility that parents feel for their adult children. The theme of the manipulative, charismatic guru or cult leader highlights general uncertainties about authority relations. The theme of economic exploitation plays on fears about unscrupulous sales techniques and marketing strategies. The theme of brainwashing plays on current anxieties about levels of surveillance, the pressure from advertising and the pervasiveness of political propaganda in supposedly free societies. Indeed, 'cults' are the setting for updated versions of 'The Invasion of the Body Snatchers', according to Thomas Robbins. Moreover, the strength of hostility expressed towards religious movements in France since the 1980s is evidence that they represent a kind of 'dystopia' in which some 'normal' features of late-modern life are amplified to the point where they tip over the edge into frightening scenarios of intensive manipulation and external control (Beckford 2001d).

In short, the pathological features projected on to religious movements in the mass media and fiction symbolise dilemmas, uncertainties and anxieties that are widespread in the early twentieth century. Religious movements have a direct effect on the lives of relatively few people in technologically advanced societies but they serve as a convenient stage on which to caricature and to dramatise situations that have extensive resonance. The grounds for anxiety nowadays include mediatised images of dangerous religious movements. 'Moral panic' (Jenkins 1992) is not too strong as a conceptual label for public sentiment towards controversial religious movements. There is an opportunity for social theorists to investigate the reasons why, at a time of declining interest in religion, the idea of deviant and deceptive religious movements continues to exercise a powerful influence over the popular imagination. It seems to me that this influence is stronger than that of the image of corrupt or abusive clerics in mainstream religious organisations.

(c)   Late-modern or post-modern selves and identities?

One might have expected that the 'cultural turn', which began to affect the human and social sciences profoundly in the 1970s, would have helped to raise the level of interest in studies of religion, but, aside from some pioneering efforts by Roland Robertson (1978, 1980) to calibrate changing conceptions of self-identity to broader shifts in culture and authority and some programmatic statements (Wuthnow 1987, 1991; Wuthnow & Witten 1988; Crane 1994), the early effect was relatively slight. In recent years, however, a growing number of scholars have reaped the benefits of applying insights from the sociology of culture and cultural studies to the social scientific analysis of religion (Beckford 2001e).[9] Again, one of the virtues of framing studies of religion in terms that make connections with broader social and cultural phenomena is that religion can be shown to dramatise these phenomena and throw them into sharper relief. Indeed, the analysis of religion provides particularly clear insights into cultural processes. At the same time, the case of religion poses challenging questions to analyses of cultural change and continuity.

Assuming that 'culture' refers to the meanings that are generated, transformed, challenged and transmitted in the course of social interaction over time and codified in symbolic forms, religion is unquestionably one of its major aspects. This holds true regardless of whether we prefer to think of culture as a way of life, a social institution, a set of meanings, a framework for action or a set of procedures. Similarly, distinctions between elite, mass and popular forms of culture do not affect the importance of religion; nor do the finer distinctions between sub-culture, counter-culture and hybrid culture.

The main reason for arguing that religious movements are particularly interesting from the point of view of culture is that they thrive in the cracks and interstices of mainstream ways of life. That is, religious movements probe the boundaries and limits of conventional meanings and practices. They deliberately explore alternative meanings and different ways of expressing them in, for example, dress codes, gender relations, sexual conduct, child rearing, diet, language, physical deportment, attitudes towards politics, ways of making a living and forms of communal organisation. Some religious movements also present challenges to systems of 'governmentality' or the apparatuses deployed by the State and other powerful agencies for translating scientific knowledge into categories of 'truth' about human subjectivity that serve to regulate them (Rose 1989). Given the sharp differences that distinguish some religious movements from their surrounding societies, they permit exceptionally clear views of the processes whereby culture is not only constructed but also embodied, charged with emotion, performed, controlled and often challenged.

There is nothing new or unusual about this aspect of religious movements, but it took on special significance in the latter part of the twentieth century when, according to various social theories, formerly dominant and authoritative cultural complexes began to fragment under pressure from, for example, 'the cultural contradictions of capitalism' (Bell 1976), 'the cultural logic of late capitalism' (Jameson 1991), the combination of 'flexible accumulation' and 'time-space compression' (Harvey 1989) or 'disorganised capitalism' (Offe 1985b). Despite the diversity of theoretical reasons given for the change, there was widespread agreement that, with the fragmentation of cultures that had previously appeared to be integrated, the transmission or inheritance of personal and collective identity could no longer be assumed to be smooth. Emphasis shifted, in fact, to the involvement of actors in negotiating their identities (in the plural) as a continuous process against a backdrop of constraints and opportunities, among which the effects of the human sciences as instruments for classifying and controlling people loomed large (Foucault 1977).

Notions such as post-modern simulation (Baudrillard 1993), post-modern ambivalence (Bauman 1991) and the decline of the meta-narrative of reason (Lyotard 1984) all draw attention to the moral and ideological frameworks of modernity and their apparent supersession by radical doubt, irony and transitoriness in post-modern conditions. Some theorists also detect considerable continuity with distinctly modern theorising about the power of commodification processes to shape human values and tastes in accordance with the forces of capitalist markets (Jameson 1991). Yet, at the same time as most theorists of post-modernity accentuate the decay of modern certainties, some of them recognise the possibility that creative vitality may also flourish in the cultural forms of hybridity and hyper-reality (Baudrillard 1990).

Studies of religion have found some evidence of these post-modern tendencies in, for example, ironic, self-parodying uses of religious symbolism or ritual on the Internet (Brasher 2001), in the growing number of Elvis Presley wedding chapels or in combinations of Christianity and astrology. Symbolic hybridity is also characteristic of some of the religious movements currently expanding in Latin America and Southern Africa (Lehmann 2001; Mary 2001). And David Lyon (2000) finds signs of a post-modern enthusiasm for conventional forms of Christianity.

Kieran Flanagan (1996a, 1996b) has taken the argument in a rather different direction with regard to the willingness of sociologists to take mainstream Christian ritual and tradition seriously. He detects a new openness to spirituality on the part of sociologists who are prepared to explore post-modernity's capacity to 'sacralise the secular'. More than this, he interprets this openness as a response to a deep theoretical crisis of confidence in the very purpose of sociology. The cultural turn, in Flanagan's opinion, brings not only aesthetics, ritual and ethics but also theology within sociology's range of concern. Hence, sociology's new-found interest in de-traditionalisation, the self, self-identity and self-reflexivity, as exemplified in the writings of Anthony Giddens (1990, 1991). Yet, Flanagan implicitly accuses Giddens of stopping short of taking the final step towards a 'felicitous marriage' of sociology and theology.

Giddens wants tradition but without the memory of the religious belief it might embody. He wants a believing without belonging, a faith without belief, a spirituality but without theological substance . . . It could be argued that postmodernity has its own theological imperatives which a sociological reflexivity uncovers. (Flanagan 1996b: 157)

For, if sociology's Enlightenment-inspired, modernist assumptions have proved to be empty deceptions, so this argument runs, there is no reason for theories of secularisation to hold sway any longer. Instead, post-modern conditions supposedly pave the way for a mingling of sociological and theological concerns with self-reflexivity and a re-engagement with tradition and orthodoxy, mediated by sacred rituals. Flanagan presents an intriguing scenario for a productive symbiosis of sociological and theological perspectives, but neither social theorists nor students of religious movements have yet adopted them in their own approaches to issues of culture and self-identity. On the contrary, Giddens and Zygmunt Bauman, for example, are more disposed to settle for modernist approaches to understanding religion that draw on Freud's view that religion represents 'the return of the repressed' – not a promising start to the re-sacralisation of the secular or the re-enchantment of sociology that Flanagan is anticipating.

In fact, studies of religious movements have also provided sound reasons for doubting whether post-modern manifestations of religion can represent the most successful, late-modern mobilisations of people and resources in the name of religion. This is not to say that post-modern tendencies do not exist. It is merely to put them in perspective and proportion. For the fact is that many of the religious movements that have flourished in the past few decades have been anything but post-modern. I am thinking of movements as diverse as the massive New Religions (Soka Gakkai, Rissho Kosei Kai and Reiyukai) and the so-called New New Religions of Japan (Agonshu and Shinnoyen) as well as the world-wide Unificationist Movement with its origins in South Korea, the highly variegated Pentecostal and Charismatic movements, the equally diverse Islamist movements of North Africa, the Near East, the Middle East, South Asia and South East Asia, and the American 'inventions' (Mormonism, Jehovah's Witnesses and Scientology). All these movements have tended to assert decidedly non-ironic, non-playful claims to non-relative truth and to communicate them through instrumentally rational means (Coleman 2000). In my view, the largest, fastest growing and most influential religious movements are resolutely modern in most respects. Very few social theorists appear to have taken this into account.

Perhaps the most significant omission from my list of religious movements with decidedly modern characteristics is the complex of religious and spiritual currents that flow into the New Age (York 1995; Hanegraaff 1996; Heelas 1996a; Rose 1998; Sutcliffe & Bowman 2000).[10] What most of these currents have in common is an optimistic belief that human beings and their cultures have developed to the point where unprecedented levels of enlightenment, tranquillity, insight, personal growth, healing and even prosperity (Heelas 1996b) are supposedly attainable. Progress or growth is conditional upon training and practice rather than revelation, divine grace or faith. Channelling, crystal healing, yoga, reflexology, acupuncture, aromatherapy and herbalism are some of the strongly embodied expressions of New Age spirituality. More abstract expressions include astrology, numerology and ufology. Expectations are high in some New Age circles that collective benefits will follow from the aggregation of individual attempts at personal growth. This helps to explain the relatively strong degree of imbrication between the New Age and other 'new' social movements such as feminisms, peace, human rights and, above all, environmentalism (Griffin 1988a, 1988b; Melucci 1996; Kearns 1996). It also helps to account for the pervasiveness of 'holistic' imagery throughout New Age thinking (Beckford 1984).

At first glance, then, the New Age movement may appear to have the post-modern characteristics of playfulness, pastiche, hybridity, bricolage and, in some respects, an air of magical fantasy. Moreover, New Age beliefs do not belong in the frameworks of Western rationalistic and positivistic epistemologies. And the supernatural and magical assumptions underlying many New Age beliefs, experiences and practices are premodern and/or post-modern for the most part.

On the other hand, there are good grounds for arguing that the New Age has features that appear to be thoroughly modern, non-ironic and rational, in an instrumental sense. For example, the New Age places a premium on the individual's acquisition of knowledge, insight, sensitivity and skills either through a system of apprenticeship or through processes of teaching, training and learning. Instructional courses, seminars, workshops, commercial exhibitions and vacation courses are the backbone of the movement. Books,[11] videocassettes, web sites and computer packages are no less central to the New Age than to modern educational systems. Some movements have formal systems of examination and certification. Payment of tuition fees is common. Indeed, the economic base of the New Age movement comprises a rational and modern system of entrepreneurialism, franchises, marketing and sales. There is a thriving transnational trade in commodified artefacts, services and resources such as crystals, dream catchers, massage oils, dowsing-rods and New Age retreats or tourism. Moreover, many business corporations and public authorities have built New Age perspectives into their management training programmes to such an extent that it would be no exaggeration to talk of the 'co-optation' of a supposedly 'alternative' form of spirituality into the mainstream (Heelas 1991; Roberts 2002). Consequently, Stark and Bainbridge (1985) place the New Age in their categories of 'audience cult' and 'client cult' on the grounds that participants are not so much members as consumers.

The case for regarding the New Age as modern rather than postmodern is reinforced by Paul Heelas' (1996b) characterisation of the movement as 'de-traditional' in the sense of not just celebrating the collapse of traditional cultural meta-narratives but also of amplifying an 'experiential meta-narrative'. The New Age meta-narrative revolves around notions such as 'an inner tradition' and a 'timeless wisdom' that, far from conveying depthless post-modern playfulness, fosters a clear sense of self-identity and a 'strong sense of collective identity' in its seekers. Thus,

[U]nlike the postmodern condition – the New Age has a relatively stable, uniform and prioritised set of values and experiences; inner tranquility [*sic*] *versus* outer distress; authenticity *versus* inauthenticity; creativity *versus* living life as a victim; and so on. (Heelas 1996b: 71)

In direct contradiction to much theorising about the disintegration of self among supposedly post-modern New Agers, Heelas emphasises the importance of codes of conduct, a canon of authoritative texts and relations of authority in New Age groups. The core teachings about what it means to be authentically human lead, in his view, to a shared ethic of humanity that underlies and belies the superficial diversity of New Age beliefs and values. In criticism of Turner's (1991) equation of expressivism, and hence the New Age, with post-modernity, Heelas notes the early modern origins of expressivism and includes it as one of the forces that shaped modernity, along with traditionalism and utilitarianism. The conclusion is that, since 'expressivism is as much a part of modernity as are the values of urban industrial civilisation' (Heelas 1996b: 71), there is no reason to describe the expressive features of the New Age movement as post-modern.

In keeping with the theoretical orientation of this book towards a form of theoretical pluralism that is self-reflexive and critical, I think it is important to remain alert to signs of post-modern developments among religious movements but without losing sight of the evidence that clearly depicts many of them as predominantly modern. There is cogent evidence of, for example, creedal claims to exclusive and absolute truth; rejection of relativistic beliefs; rational forms of organisation and management of resources; expectations that members will commit themselves fully to their movements; controls over the expression of emotion; and explicit guidance on personal morality and lifestyle. In short, religious movements present social theorists with some interesting challenges. The sheer variety of movements and the speed with which they proliferate, mutate and, in many cases, evaporate are a reproach to theories that claim to provide a single-stranded explanation of these changes. There is the additional complication that religious movements self-reflexively theorise their own place in history and are therefore contributors towards its explanation. And specialists in the study of religious movements have also offered many explanatory ideas, with and without the assistance of explicit social theories.

Conclusion

Social theorists have largely ignored religious movements in their reflections on the main tendencies in social and cultural life. Those exceptional theorists who *have* tried to explain the significance of religious movements have nevertheless tended to focus narrowly on a highly selective sub-set of movements that conveniently conform to theoretical expectations. Theorists have made very few attempts to 'test' the validity of their arguments against the full range of available empirical evidence. Taking these limitations into account, social theory has nevertheless furnished some important insights into the dynamics and social significance of selected movements.

Conversely, students of religious movements have made highly selective use of social theories and have made relatively few attempts systematically to relate their empirical investigations to social theories. This is an aspect of the insulation of the sociology of religion that I detected in the early 1980s (Beckford 1985b) and that Ebaugh (2002) can still detect nearly twenty years later. But the main argument of this chapter has been that developments in theories of social movements and of theoretical ideas about culture and identity tend to place religious movements near the centre of some currently important problems for social scientists. It is no longer appropriate, then, to consign religious movements to categories of deviant or marginal phenomena. The movements' beliefs, values, forms of organisation, kinds of activity, types of participation, societal reactions, and relations with agencies of social control all provide revealing insights into the dynamics of late modernity.

6　Constructing religion, self and society

I have made few attempts in this book to highlight themes that cut across, or run through, the topics of secularisation, pluralism, globalisation and religious movements. This is because my first priority was to indicate in detail the variety of ways in which social theorists have dealt with these particular aspects of religion *and* how specialists in the social scientific study of religion have theorised their work on them. There are very few studies of the interplay between these two sets of interests. My aim has therefore been to identify ways in which both social theory and social scientific studies of religion could benefit from greater exposure to the issues that each of them raises about the other.

The general framework within which I have presented the theoretical and analytical issues is social constructionism. This is a perspective that gives priority to questions about the processes involved in negotiating the meaning of social phenomena. It deploys systematic scepticism towards ontological claims about 'reality', preferring to study the means by which such claims are mounted, modified and challenged in everyday social life. In relation to religion, then, a social constructionist approach tries to discover how terms such as 'religion', 'religious', 'sacred' and 'spiritual' are used; how the usage varies across different categories of people, time and space; how it reflects collective interests; how human actors justify their usage of these terms; how social groups and organisations institutionalise the usage; and how social agencies try to regulate the activities to which the terms are applied.

It goes without saying that the social constructionist perspective is only one among many. There is no shortage of alternative viewpoints on religion and, in my opinion, no single Archimedean point from which to study it in the social sciences. On the other hand, I believe that the benefits of social constructionism in the study of religion have not been adequately acknowledged. In fact, there is a whiff of heresy about it that has probably deterred some students of religion from adopting it more extensively. And there are undoubtedly misgivings about the risk of entering a realm of infinite regress of 'social constructions of social constructions'.

My response to the point about an infinite regress is in two parts. First, I make no claims about the definitive character of social constructionist analyses. They are all provisional and relational in the sense of coming from particular points of view. As such, they are subject to re-interpretation from other viewpoints. This does not mean that they are necessarily arbitrary or solipsistic: it simply means that they are supported by what seems, from a certain point of view, to be appropriate evidence. Second, the analyses are not framed at a high level of abstraction. They usually attach significance to contextual and situational features for which good 'documentation' can be produced. This is a virtue of social constructionism but it also entails the corresponding requirement that its analyses be continually adjusted to different contexts and changing circumstances.

In defence of social constructionist perspectives, then, I regard them as indispensable to social scientific studies of religion but by no means exhaustive or definitive. They cast an interesting light on the use of religion in social and cultural life; and they provide a valuable antidote, or alternative, to the varieties of functionalism and essentialism that still tend to pervade the sociology of religion. Moreover, since they operate at an intermediary level of analysis between the micro and the macro, social constructionist analyses are compatible with some other theoretical perspectives. In other words, they provide partial insight into the complexity of social and cultural life; and they present a useful challenge to social scientific arguments that pretend to supersede or to bypass the processes of social construction. For this reason they make some social scientists uneasy by appearing to call in question their taken-for-granted categories of analysis.

My strategy has been to show that social theorists and specialists in the social scientific study of religion have tended to constitute religion as something other than a product of, and a contributor to, social construction. For some, religion amounts to an indispensable property of the human world. For others it is an institutional reality or an epiphenomenon of social forces. For still others it is a psychological or anthropological constant. Each of these ways of thinking about religion has distinct implications for deciding what needs explaining and how religion is likely to develop in the future. The meaning that social scientists and social theorists attribute to secularisation, for example, varies with their assumptions about whether it is a constitutive feature of social life, a contingent product of certain forms of social life, an anthropological constant or a psychological property. A characteristic logic or form of reasoning runs through each position making them virtually indifferent to arguments rooted in different positions. Social constructionism raises questions about the inner logic of these theoretical positions *and* about their implications for everyday social life. Thus, courts of law, school administrators, employers, broadcasting authorities, taxation officials, among others, all have to decide what counts as religion for their purposes. More subtly, religious organisations also have to decide for themselves where the boundary lies between 'really' religious activities and those that belong in the category of, say, tradition, superstition, culture or ethnicity. Opinions are often divided along lines of gender, age, generation, social class or nationality. In short, the social construction of religion is not only a theoretical topic but also an inescapable feature of everyday social interaction.

It was with this principle of social constructionism in mind that I selected the topics of secularisation, pluralism, globalisation and religious movements. While they are far from exhaustive of the range of topics concerning religion that interest social theorists and social scientists they are certainly central to many of these scholars' preoccupations. The omission of some topics may surprise some readers. For example, there is little concern here with the vast amount of research conducted in the USA on the dynamics of churches and denominations. The reason for this omission is that connections are relatively weak these days – unlike in the past – between this organisational research and the major themes of social theory (with the exception of rational choice theory). The same reason explains the relatively few references in this book to research on religions other than Christianity. Except for the currently fashionable interest in 'fundamentalism' in world religions, social theorists have made very few attempts to integrate Buddhism, Hinduism and Islam into their accounts of social change.

How can social constructionism contribute towards the improvement of social theorists' grasp of religion's significance? And how can social scientific studies of religion be enhanced by the adoption of social constructionist perspectives? I shall begin to answer these questions by summarising the four preceding chapters. Then I shall discuss the possibility that social scientific studies of religion may benefit from closer alignment with social theories with which they have so far had relatively few connections.

The discussion of debates about secularisation in Chapter Two tried to demonstrate the importance of social constructionist perspectives in two ways. The first argument was that, in the absence of an Archimedean position from which to gain a theory-free view of the growth and decline of religion, it is helpful to understand the philosophical and ideological assumptions that underlie the different conceptualisations of 'religion' and 'secularisation'. The history of these ideas throws interesting light on how the different problematics of secularisation have taken shape. The second argument was that, despite the increasing subtlety of many recent attempts to prove that religion is undergoing metamorphosis instead of decline, researchers could benefit from paying more attention to the social processes whereby the boundary between the religious and the secular is socially negotiated. The conclusion was that debates about secularisation are more valuable as sites for the exploration of these social constructs than they are as guides to the future of religion and non-religion.

The core of Chapter Three is an argument about the need for clarification of the different ways in which the term 'religious pluralism' is constructed in scholarly research and applied in everyday life. I drew distinctions between pluralism as religious diversity, pluralism as the acceptance of religious diversity, and pluralism as a positive evaluation of religious diversity. The reason for making these distinctions was to show that the liberal enthusiasm for pluralism in the 1960s tended to obscure some aspects of religious change that have subsequently assumed greater importance. On the one hand, some distinctly non-pluralistic religious tendencies have come to the fore in many places. On the other, it is clear that public authorities actively monitor and manage what they regard as acceptable forms of pluralism. The chapter concludes with a case study of the changing basis of prison chaplaincy in Britain that illustrates not only the tensions and conflicts that underlie the social construction of a supposedly multi-faith strategy but also the policy dilemmas associated with multiculturalism.

The central thesis of Chapter Four is that notions of globalisation are social constructs. Admittedly, they serve analytical purposes and may therefore appear to be objective tools in the hands of social scientists and theorists. But these notions are also 'active ingredients' in the changing ideologies of many religious organisations – even if only as targets of hostile criticism. It is not enough, then, to study religious responses to globalisation as if it were an objective, external force in the environment of religious collectivities. Rather, my argument is that social scientists would do well to examine the widely differing ways in which religious groups make sense of globalisation and reflexively use their own constructions of it. Indeed, a growing number of studies have already demonstrated the subtlety and complexity of the processes whereby religious organisations in many parts of the world have situated themselves in relation to perceived global forces. Social theorists, with few exceptions, have been slow to take proper account of these religious constructions of globalisation.

Social scientists have made major contributions to the understanding of religious movements in the modern world. Chapter Five explores the variety of theoretical ideas that convey their understanding, frequently expressed in terms such as class conflict, cognitive dissonance, anomie, church-sect dynamics and 'the new religious consciousness'. It surprises me, however, that relatively few attempts have been made to integrate studies of religious movements into theorising about other types of social movements. Nevertheless, there are several indications that inquiries into religious movements are becoming more closely aligned with theoretical ideas about macro-level social and cultural change. Discourse about 'new' social movements, the application of insights from rational choice theory, and many variants on the idea of modernity and post-modernity all represent promising ways forward. These broad developments of theoretical thinking are capable not only of throwing interesting theoretical light on religious movements but also of allowing evidence about the changing social constructions of religion to permeate debates about the kind of social world we now inhabit.

Construction and contestation

The *Leitmotiv* of the previous five chapters is the social construction of the meaning of religion. It is a continuous process of negotiation, reproduction and challenge, but the pace of change is variable in different times and places. The meanings attributed to religion are, in part, a product of social interaction and negotiation at the level of individuals, groups, organisations and whole societies. Moreover, global forces are currently shaping what counts as religion at a level above that of particular societies or regions of the world, thereby continuing a process with roots in ancient empires, trading systems and the modern capitalist world economy. Certain religious organisations have been able to sustain relatively uniform and stable models of religious belief and practice over long periods of time, in many cases with the active support of political, economic and military establishments. The indispensable counterpart to these authoritative models of religion is the construction of equally durable notions of religious deviance, heresy and apostasy. In other words, the social construction of religion also involves the social construction of false religion and non-religion.

To borrow military metaphors, the frontier separating religion from non-religion is the site of constant sniping and occasional pitched battles. At the same time, internal boundaries within the territory held by religion are the site of regular patrols and intermittent disputes over the question of what it means to be properly religious. Frontier skirmishes and border patrols have been constant features of the social process of constructing, defending, attacking, reforming and replacing ideas and institutions that claim to represent 'real' religion. Religion is no different in this respect from some other social and cultural institutions. Questions about the 'real' meaning of art, education and sport, for example, are equally matters of frontier wars and boundary disputes. But religion is distinctive because of the 'whole souled ardour' – to borrow a phrase from Karl Marx – with which some individuals, groups and political regimes promote particular constructions of religion as well as notions of religion as a supposedly universal property or practice. On the other hand, indifference and hostility to both the particular and the generic meanings attributed to religion are no less interesting from a social scientific point of view. For, when secularism finds expression in philosophical doctrines, political constitutions and state structures it can assume many of the characteristics of institutionalised religion.

Debates about secularisation, religious diversity and pluralism, globalisation and religious movements all centre on contested frontiers and boundaries between religion and non-religion, acceptable and unacceptable religions, local and global forms of religion, and authentic and inauthentic expressions of religion. The tendency is for social theorists to take very little account of these social processes of construction and contestation. My next question is, therefore, about the extent to which it could be beneficial for studies of religion to absorb the insights of social theorists – for most of whom religion seems to hold little intellectual interest – and for social theorists to build knowledge about the uses that are made of religion into their analyses of social life. In the limited space available here I can only outline the major points of emphasis in this potentially mutually beneficial relationship.

Religion, self and society – new theoretical leads

The focal point of social theories has long been the relationship between individual human beings and the collectivities in, and through, which they live. The conventional way of putting the matter is to talk of relations between the individual and society or between structures and agents. Starting from different questions about what needs explaining, and making different assumptions about the factors that influence the mutual interplay of individuals and collective phenomena, theorists have explored innumerable aspects of the dynamic intermingling of identity, culture, power and sociality. The most influential attempts to characterise particular forms of this intermingling in terms of 'capitalist', 'industrial', 'gesellschaftlich', 'modern', 'mass' and 'postindustrial' are associated with Marx and Engels, Durkheim, Tönnies, Weber, Parsons, Ortega y Gasset and Touraine or Bell. Only Durkheim, Marx and Parsons considered religion to be a significant aspect of changes in the mutual implication of individuals and society. And their theorising contributed strongly to the idea that secularisation, albeit with different nuances for each theorist, was an ineluctable trend.

The prospects for a different interpretation of religion's social significance improved in the latter half of the twentieth century with the development of theoretical perspectives such as phenomenology, symbolic interactionism, ethnomethodology, exchange theory and post-structuralism. This was because, in their different ways, they tended to soften the dualities of self and society, the one and the many, the micro and the macro, and so on. A range of different arguments converged on the idea that the 'individual' and 'society' were only abstractions from a reality that was more complex and perplexing. In particular, the apparently separate entities were shown to be mutually constitutive in the sense that individuals constructed social collectivities and cultural meanings, and, conversely, social and cultural configurations shaped the properties of individuals. As with earlier generations of social theorists, of course, the range of their understanding of religion was wide. At one extreme, the phenomenologically oriented work of Thomas Luckmann and the more eclectic work of Peter Berger held religion to be constitutive of humanness and central to the allegedly anthropological necessity for human beings to keep chaos at bay. At the other extreme, Michel Foucault laid bare the religious roots of the distinctly modern practices of surveillance and discipline that found their justification in the human sciences. The middle ground was suitable for adaptation to the investigation of, for example, the cognitive aspects of religious conversion, the indexical properties of religious discourse and texts, and the interactional frameworks of religious healing.

Self-reflexivity

More recent developments in social theorising have created further opportunities for seeing the social construction of religion and its uses in new terms. For example, the attention that Anthony Giddens (1991) gives to the trajectory of the *self and self-reflexivity* in his analysis of existential anxiety in conditions of high modernity seems to leave little room for religion except as the 'return of the repressed'. Yet, the findings of research on phenomena as diverse as New Age spirituality, 'prosperity Gospel' theology and the adaptations that many young Muslim women are making to the practice of Islam in Western countries indicate that religious self-reflexivity can take new forms that are not easily understandable in 'old' theoretical terms. There would be advantages to social theory *and* to the social scientific understanding of religion if the religious colouring of self-reflexivity could be brought into sharper focus.

It would be particularly rewarding to map the variety of attempts to build religious considerations into what Giddens calls 'life politics' or the politics of lifestyle. The current fashion for matching Pentecostalism to sober and industrious lifestyles in, say, Latin America or South Korea appears to challenge the idea that lifestyles are a luxury reserved for religion's 'cultured despisers' among Western intellectual elites. Moreover, the heavy investment of religious values and meanings in campaigns for human rights and pro-life and pro-choice mobilisations is further evidence that religion continues to inform lifestyle politics in the Western democracies. Religious voices are also central to public debates about contentious issues ranging from policies on cross-national migration and asylum seeking to the ethics of genetic engineering and new reproductive technologies.

Giddens is correct to claim that in high modernity the human body 'becomes a site of interaction, appropriation and reappropriation, linking reflexively organised processes and systematically ordered expert knowledge' (1991: 218). But he neglects to take account of the fact that religion, in this instance, claims to be one of these areas of expert knowledge. It is therefore misleading to talk of the 'remoralising of social life' following the 'repression' of moral and existential questions by the core institutions of modernity. The fact is that religion was used as a continuous source of normative guidance throughout the modern period but was often in conflict with more powerful interests in politics and business. It is a high modernist intellectual and ethnocentric conceit to believe that moral, spiritual or religious questions have only recently forced themselves back on to the public or private agenda. If these questions were invisible in modern social theory, it was because of the short-sightedness of the theorists. Nevertheless, there is certainly a valuable opportunity for social scientific studies of religion to pursue Giddens' line of reasoning about life politics by investigating present-day constructions of religion and spirituality as cultural resources on which some people choose to draw in certain circumstances.

'Post-modernity'

'Post-modernity' is a catch-all category that loosely covers a bewildering variety of claims about the alleged supersession of modernity by social and cultural conditions, including the erosion of faith in ideological grand narratives, the emancipatory power of reason and moral seriousness. Post-modernity is widely characterised by the celebration of playfulness, pastiche, hybridity, inter-textuality, the breaching of boundaries and genres, and the pervasiveness of virtual hyperreality. As such, it seemed to open up the possibility that the transcendental, the spiritual, the mystical, the emotional and the charismatic would enjoy wider currency than in strictly modern conditions. To some extent, this has indeed happened – albeit mainly in marginal areas of the New Age. No doubt, it would be helpful for further research to inquire more methodically into post-modern features of religious belief and practice. But the plausibility of claims about epochal change from modernity to post-modernity is under considerable strain from evidence showing that the most resilient and dynamic areas of religion are precisely those where clearly articulated doctrines, conservative ethics, tradition-centred lifestyles and authoritative patterns of leadership are dominant. In addition, the popularity of these conservative ways of expressing religion is not confined to marginal sections of the population but is most strikingly evident among relatively well educated people, many of whom have stakes in the technologically advanced sectors of the economy in both the advanced industrial democracies and the developing countries of Africa, Asia, Latin America and Eastern Europe. Although it makes very little sense in my view to characterise these developments as 'post-modern', there would be profit in examining the scope for post-modern developments alongside them. More importantly, it would be helpful if the social theorists of post-modernity confronted the evidence of vitality among distinctly modern forms of religion. My impression is that, when it comes to religion, theorists tend to ignore evidence that does not conform to their theoretical expectations.

An important exception to my argument about the lack of even-handedness among social theorists is the work of David Lyon (2000). He clearly believes that we live in what he calls 'postmodern times' and that the construction and use of religion are shaped by post-modern forces. Yet, he does not shrink from acknowledging the vitality of conservative forms of religion as well as of more experimental forms. It still amounts to post-modern religion, in his view, because it is all subject to 'the commodification of everyday life and the impact of mass consumer cultures' (Lyon 2000: xi). In their turn, consumerism and mass consumer culture depend on the new information technologies which have invaded everyday life with simulations and illusions that seem to defy the articulation of time and space. Lyon persuasively documents the post-modernist effects of these developments on formal and informal expressions of religion. The question in my mind, however, is whether it is enough to affix the label 'post-modernist' to meanings, symbols and experiences without taking proper account of the thoroughly modern, rational, business organisations and profit-seeking strategies that apply the new technologies to the task of creating hyperreal illusions such as 'instant heritage'. What is missing, in my view, is an analysis of the application of science and instrumental rationality, in a thoroughly modern fashion, to the creation of markets for simulation. The products may appear to be post-modern by virtue of their novelty or hybridity, but the methods and motives of their production are largely intensifications of modernity. In short, consumerism remains modern even when many consumer items have a post-modern appearance. Ideally, then, social scientific research on religion would investigate the modern 'drivers' of post-modern appearances without confusing the former with the latter.

Rational choice theory

Rational choice theory – or at least the notion of 'subjective rationality' – may be a helpful resource for researchers investigating the modern production of religious items for consumption in mass markets. As I argued in Chapter Five, there is no reason to reject 'supply side' accounts of the strategies that religious organisations adopt for the purpose of retaining or expanding their share of the market in religious goods. I also think that it makes good sense to analyse these organisational strategies in terms of rational ideal-types, that is, deliberately one-sided models that, for purely hypothetical purposes, make strong assumptions about rationality or complete information. These rational ideal-types are useful as benchmarks indicating the ways in which religious organisations could be expected to act if their actions were based on instrumental rationality and perfect information. The strategies and actions of real organisations can then be compared with the rational ideal-types in order to seek evidence that might help to explain the difference between the model and the reality.

The use of rational ideal-types of organisational strategies is particularly helpful in studies of religious organisations that acknowledge that they are involved in one or more markets and that they are, in effect, competing for consumers of their products. This is an aspect of collective self-reflexivity that is quite compatible with theoretical interest in the self-reflexivity of individuals. Ideally, in my view, social scientific studies of religion would make strong assumptions about rationality, for heuristic reasons, at the level of individuals *and* organisations.

It is precisely at the point of interface between the rationality of individuals and the rationality of organisations that there is wide scope for innovative research on religion in conditions of modernity or high modernity. This is a point of intersection between, on the one hand, notions of individualisation, subjectivisation and personal autonomy and, on the other, notions of marketing, advertising, brand loyalty and market segmentation. Research at the individual and collective levels of analysis needs to be pursued simultaneously if the tensions and paradoxes of the present are to be examined rather than obscured by an exclusive focus on one level or the other. This theoretical strategy is especially important from my point of view because it seeks to ensure that the social construction of religion is not confined within the kind of phenomenological framework that deals only with the inner experiences of individuals. Likewise, the strategy that I am proposing seeks to avoid any form of collective determinism by insisting on the need to study the *interaction* between the collective production of religion and individual responses. It is not about the analytical separation of structure and agency. On the contrary, it is an insistence on the necessity of recognising that the social construction of religion is simultaneously an individual and a collective process. This means, for example, that the religious beliefs that individuals report on questionnaires or in interviews should be understood in the context of the prevailing social and cultural models of what counts as religion. In this sense, the reported beliefs are 'indexical' without being determined. The challenge is, for example, to relate the increasing frequency of Westerners' reported beliefs in re-incarnation to such contextual factors as, say, the sequestration of birth and death in high modern hospitals and the public's faith in the efficacy of organ transplants and genetic therapy.

Emotion

A closely related theoretical development is the tendency to analyse the conceptualisation and expression of religious *experiences and emotions* in social, rather than individual, terms. In a departure from the common-sense view of experience and emotion as nothing but the products of individual psychology, various possibilities have emerged for analysing the social and cultural frameworks that shape the responses of individuals. For example, some theorists have re-asserted Durkheimian arguments about the capacity of 'effervescent' assemblies to generate strong feelings about the sacredness of social solidarity (Mellor & Shilling 1997). This is an interesting line of inquiry, although empirical investigation is needed to test the alternative hypothesis that notions of solidarity are not so much emergent properties of effervescent assemblies as products of pre-existing scene setting and management. In addition, the time is long gone when the behaviour of crowds can be plausibly explained solely by reference to forces such as contagion, imitation and suggestibility. The extent of publicity and stage management in advance of major public assemblies is now so great that neither 'crowd psychology' nor 'collective effervescence' is a good basis on which to try to explain their social dynamics. This is another illustration of the need to maintain a focus on individuals *and* their social contexts. It is not simply a matter of Durkheim's *homo duplex*; it is also a matter of the deliberate attempts made by various agencies to shape group responses.

In other words, effervescent assemblies such as the Million Man March organised by the Nation of Islam in Washington, DC in 1995 do not oc-cur in a social vacuum but are carefully designed, prepared and managed. This does not mean that the crowd's emotions are not genuine or heart-felt: it means that they are neither accidental nor the product of merely psychological forces. To take a very different example, the public and private expressions of grief at the time of the death and funeral of Diana, Princess of Wales in 1997 cannot be properly understood without tak-ing account of the massive publicity previously given to her life and of the artful dramatisation of her death by the mass media. The outpour-ing of public grief may have been genuine but by no means could it be fairly described as 'spontaneous', especially as local authorities in the UK, churches and even supermarkets were quick to provide books of condolence.

It is a short step from these debates about the possibility that late modern societies can still generate collective experiences of the sacred through the medium of effervescent assemblies to claims that all man-ner of events in the realms of sport and popular entertainment are also functional equivalents of religion with the capacity to sustain social sol-idarity with a sacred tinge. Again, my response is to acknowledge that intense feelings of solidarity and effervescence can indeed be stimulated by means of, for example, television programmes, rock concerts, shop-ping malls, sporting events and so on. But I also believe that it is no less important to analyse the commercial, political and cultural contexts in which these potential channels of the sacred are conceived, managed and marketed. I reject any functionalist 'law of the conservation of sacred matter' which holds that human societies must somehow continually pro-duce intimations of the sacred either in religious institutions or, failing that, in non-religious forms. There is no doubt in my mind, however, that a wide variety of individuals and agencies attempt to stimulate feel-ings of the sacred for an equally wide range of reasons. There are also receptive audiences and markets for these productions of the sacred. It is only the quasi-monopoly that some religions and religious organisations have at times been able to exercise over these audiences and markets that has sustained the idea that 'real' religion is given in the nature of things and that other expressions of the sacred are necessarily false, heretical or inauthentic. A social constructionist perspective on the sacred is a powerful antidote both to functionalist nostalgia or complacency and to the claims that some religious organisations make to the possession of exclusive truth.

'Postemotional society'?

Does it follow from my doubts about the possibility of unscheduled effervescence in late modernity that we live in a 'postemotional society' in which 'a new hybrid of intellectualised, mechanical, mass-produced emotions has appeared' (Meštrović 1997: 26)? Are the emotions that find expression in everyday life and popular entertainment merely nostalgic, re-cycled products from the past? Has the ubiquity of therapies stamped out authentic emotions by displacing them with vicarious emotions and with emotions designed to be consumed? Is it even possible for 'true' expressions of emotion to occur in a world dominated by the mass media, including advertising? These provocative questions are at the heart of Stjepan Meštrović's bathetic characterisation of 'postemotional society' in which 'genuinely collective experience has become almost impossible' because 'postemotional individuals are too cynical and too skilled at deconstruction to "let go" emotionally and experience collective effervescence' (Meštrović 1997: 118, 119). To the extent that postemotional society still permits any form of 'enchantment' it can only do so, according to Meštrović, on a basis of rational, instrumental calculation. He therefore denies that a Durkheimian notion of the sacred is credible any longer. This is because the sacred allegedly dried up when emotions atrophied in modernity along with the erosion of collective consciousness and the splintering of collective identity. As a result, Meštrović claims that nothing is sacred any more, although many attempts are made to induce a sense of the sacred mechanically, to induce a sense of totemic identity and to celebrate artificial rituals. Meštrović's depressing conclusion is that 'the real resistance front to postemotionalism' is 'the eruption of nationalism throughout the Western world' (Meštrović 1997: 154).

The notion of postemotional society is an intriguing challenge to social scientific students of religion for it calls into question the functionalist underpinnings of Durkheim's theoretical framework and it undercuts the credibility of Durkheim's 'cult of man'. It also deals a harsh blow to Bellah's notion of the American civil religion and, I believe, to Berger's notion of religious organisations as intermediary associations in a pluralist democracy. In fact, Meštrović's vision of postemotional society reduces religion to an empty shell or a simulacrum of 'real' religion. While I am critical of the implication in his work that religion used to be real in the sense of having roots in entirely non-manipulated emotion, I think that Meštrović is correct to draw attention to the extent to which the expression of emotion is shaped these days by interests and forces associated with consumerism and public relations. But I also believe that he exaggerates the extent to which the expression of emotion was previously direct and unmediated by social and cultural influences. The association between the expression of religion and the artful design of religious buildings, rituals, language, vestments, music, singing, bodily postures and lifestyles has always been close. This is no less true of the simplest and least formal expressions of religion than of its most formally and liturgically extravagant expressions. The term 'postemotional society' is therefore misleading, in my opinion, but still potentially helpful if it alerts us to recent changes in the social conditions that have invariably affected the expression of emotion. This is certainly one of the areas where the social scientific study of religion can provide insights into a more general social phenomenon *and* where developments in social theorising about emotion deserve to be scrutinised in studies of religion.

Embodiment

The social scientific study of religion has not often given prominence to the human body as a topic (Turner 1980, 1984; McGuire 1990; Simpson 1993; Mellor & Shilling 1997), but interest in the body as an object of religious concern or as a medium of religious expression has never been far beneath the surface. Indeed, studies of the social and cultural significance of the human body have much to gain from taking religion seriously. Thus, religious regulations of such things as diet, sexuality, illness, imprisonment, torture, 'mortification of the flesh', clothing and fasting have often been analysed. In turn, the influence of these religious regulations on more general cultural constructions of the body is also essential to an understanding of many forms of art, notions of wellbeing and categorisations of character and personality. Theories of mental wellbeing and ill health are particularly rich in religious influences – as in the history of strategies for monitoring and managing the wide range of symptoms associated with, for example, 'madness' and 'possession'. In short, investigations of religion and the body had borne fruit long before a new term, 'embodiment', became fashionable among social theorists.

Some dictionary definitions of 'embodiment' imply an opposition between physicality and spirituality, but social scientists who use the term strive to transcend body/mind dualisms by insisting that body and mind are partly constitutive of each other. That is, human experiences are grounded in physical bodies; and physical bodies are experienced through the human mind. From this perspective, then, the most interesting questions are not about the effects of mind on body or *vice versa*. Instead, the focus on embodiment challenges social scientists to consider the experience of living in a body – hence the use of such phrases as 'the lived body' and 'the mindful body'. It seems to me that 'embodiment', stressing the fact that all human meaning and activity is inescapably rooted in constructions of the human body, is a notion that could help to stimulate fresh thinking about religion. For example, a strong affinity exists between New Age spirituality and a wide range of bodily disciplines and practices aimed at training and disciplining minds *and* bodies. Indeed, many of these practices try to dissolve or to soften the mind-body distinction by cultivating a 'holistic' sense of their interdependence. Diet, exercise, meditation and mood management are all integral to the cultivation of distinctively New Age patterns of attitudes, dispositions and actions. Moreover, in so far as many profit-seeking and other organisations now offer management training programmes that draw on full-strength or diluted versions of New Age ideas, the time is ripe for empirical and theoretical investigation of this explicitly embodied spirituality's place in late modernity (Roberts 2002, chap 3).

No less distinctive, but different, are the embodied expressions of religion in the many forms of Pentecostalism and charismatic Christianity. They can be characterised not only by altered states of consciousness – or the loss of consciousness when believers are 'slain in the spirit' – but also by certain bodily postures and gestures during worship. Bodily manifestations of spirit possession are also common, and the practice of 'deliverance' from evil spirits is routine, in some branches of the wider Christian charismatic movement. One of the challenges facing social theorists and students of religion is to explain why these recognisably different forms of embodiment occur in virtually all the culturally different regions of the world where charismatic Christianity is practised. This question is notable by its absence from some of the most authoritative discussions of the charismatic movement. They tend, instead, to focus more on the moral and political implications of conversion to Pentecostalism without framing it as an embodied phenomenon (except indirectly in relation to the adoption of sobriety and marital fidelity).

Numerous studies of the association between spirituality or religion and health or wellbeing have claimed that people with strong religious beliefs are more likely to live longer and to display lower levels of morbidity than closely matched samples of people with few or no religious beliefs. Some of these studies are experimentally sophisticated and statistically sound, but they rest on a conventional biomedical assumption that the independent and dependent variables are clearly separable. The distinctive feature of the 'embodied' perspective, by contrast, is the belief that there is an 'internal' or meaningful connection between these two sets of variables. The physical body is also 'mindful' and emotional. Conversely, thoughts and emotions are part of the experience of inhabiting human bodies with all their genetic, chemical, electrical and mechanical particularities. Research drawing on the perspective of embodiment would investigate the embeddedness of religious or spiritual beliefs in indicators of health or wellbeing. This is already characteristic of research on New Age spiritualities, but studies of all kinds of religious belief and practice could benefit from the shift to a focus on embodiment.

Would such a shift in perspective be compatible with my advocacy of social constructionism? Is there not a contradiction between the recognition that human meanings and actions are rooted in physical bodies and my insistence on the need to understand how human experiences are shaped by social and cultural processes? My response is that, on the contrary, even the most brute physical 'facts' of birth, breathing and dying take place in social and cultural frameworks of meaning or contexts. They may be *merely* meaningless events in a purely physical dimension of reality; but they certainly have social and cultural meaning in abundance. They are experienced through bodily sensations as certain types of events – for which we have labels – the meaning of which can be both intensely personal and irremediably social. In this way, symptoms of physical and mental illness can carry a heavy charge of emotion and value in some circumstances. The experience of pain and suffering can also convey high status in some religious traditions. There is no question in my mind about the physical basis for these experiences. I am not denying that they are real in the sense of being based on phenomena that are independent of our capacity to conceptualise them. But at the same time their meaning varies with their social setting and with the (different) cultural frameworks applied to them by actors and observers. A streak of lightning, an episode of epilepsy or an outbreak of disease, for example, involve real forces in the non-human world, but human beings endow them with meaning and respond to them in culturally varied ways.

In short, I see no problem with my attempt to combine the theoretical perspectives of embodiment and social constructionism. Each stands to gain from the other. To assign priority to one over the other would not be acceptable. In other words, it is essential for social scientists to take account of the real constraints and possibilities associated with human lives lived in physical bodies that are also subject to threats from physical phenomena such as climate, viruses and scarcity. But it does not follow that these phenomena are unmediated by social and cultural meaning. Nor do these phenomena impose limitations alone on the 'lived body'. Sensitive studies of embodied religion would also focus on the positive experiences of joy, tranquillity, wholeness, mystery, reverence, love, healing, forgiveness, solidarity and so on. Indeed, it would be particularly interesting to investigate bodily practices that seek to cultivate the experience of leaving the body or inhabiting a different body. The social scientific study of embodiment and religion can, therefore, help to correct an imbalance that derives from medical sociology's understandable preoccupation with the vulnerability and deficiencies of human bodies or with the disciplinary implication of biomedical 'discourses'. It goes without saying that human lives are subject to real, physical constraints that result in death for everyone. This is part of the human condition. But it is no less characteristic of human beings to use religion for the purpose of interpreting their bodily circumstances and to use their bodies to celebrate life, to try to transcend scarcity and to create the conditions for hope.

Individualisation and context

Two general themes run in parallel through the theoretical leads that I have reviewed in this chapter. One theme stresses the importance of individualisation and subjective choice in a world where the variety of religious ideas and lifestyles seems to have increased. The other theme emphasises the contextual pressures that shape the choices that individuals make.

Individualisation

The first theme brings together a rich diversity of ideas about the increasing salience of individualisation, self-identity, self-reflexivity and subjective reason. It implies that ascribed identities and traditional beliefs are losing their capacity to retain loyalty. Advanced industrial societies in particular have supposedly become de-traditionalised, with the consequent weakening of the authority formerly vested in a broad range of organisations and institutions. Individual human beings are expected to exercise their autonomous judgement in choosing what to believe and how to implement their beliefs in practice. The notion of unconstrained choice is implicit in characterisations of individual beliefs as 'pastiches', 'bricolage' and 'pick-and-mix' varieties. Images of 'nomads', 'pilgrims' and 'new tribes' are deployed to capture the allegedly temporary, rootless, shifting and, above all, elective character of social relations among these individuals. 'Spirituality' is thought to be a more appropriate term than 'religion' as a label for their concerns with the overall meaning of things because it lacks any notion of obligation and of being permanently bound together with others. Some commentators also claim that late modernity favours the cultivation of forms of reflexive self-identity that turn the self into a project to be continually monitored with the aid, if necessary, of expert systems of therapy and counselling.

All these different attempts to seize the distinctiveness of the practice of religion in late-modern societies share the conviction that the most salient feature is the freedom of individuals to make choices about the kind of religious beliefs, if any, that they wish to hold. The scope of individual choice also extends to the ways in which individuals choose to express their religious beliefs and to use their religion. 'Individualisation' is therefore presented as the key process in religious change.

Empirical evidence in support of the individualisation theme is plentiful from sources as varied as opinion surveys, historical analyses, ethnographic accounts and (auto)biographies. The same theme finds echoes in arguments about the increasing popularity of subjective and emotional styles of religiosity. The interpretation of decisions to abandon religious beliefs and/or practices also tends to conform to the thesis of individualisation.

My argument is that the thesis of individualisation makes good sense of religious change – up to a point – but it needs to be brought into creative tension with my second general theme, namely, the contextual shaping of religion. What I have in mind here is an admittedly rather inclusive category of forces that bear upon the subjective choices that individuals supposedly make about religion these days. The social scientific study of religion, no less than social theory, runs the risk of being unbalanced if it fails to place the evidence of individualisation in a wider context of market forces and other pressures that facilitate and constrain individual choices.

Contexts

The second theme running through the theoretical leads reviewed in this chapter is that individual choices do not occur in a social or cultural vacuum. They take place in contexts that identify people as the kind of individuals who are capable of making certain choices. It goes without saying that these pressures are not new: there have always been pressures and inducements to believe certain religious things and to act in certain religious ways. Punishments for failing, or refusing, to comply with such pressures have also been a feature of many religious organisations and faith communities. Modernity and late modernity have rendered some types of pressure relatively ineffective or illegal *and* have created fresh opportunities for faith communities and religious organisations to influence individuals' lives.

The contexts within which human beings make their supposedly individual choices about religious belief, belonging and practice are too numerous for analysis here, but the following selection is indicative of their diversity. To begin with, international law and the constitutions of most states in the world now place religion in frameworks of human rights and legal entitlements. The degree of similarity, if not standardisation, among these regulatory frameworks is remarkable (Markoff and Regan 1987). Religious organisations can use the fact that some countries already recognise their activities as religious in terms of local interpretations of, say, international codes of human rights in order to gain recognition in other countries. In some cases, governmental and diplomatic agencies become involved in challenging or protecting the interests of religious organisations in foreign territories. The probability that individuals can enjoy the opportunity to exercise a choice between different religious ideas and groups varies with their countries' willingness to interpret international codes of law and human rights in certain ways.

The counterpart to claims to the right to practise a chosen form of religion is the argument that some *soi-disant* religions are not really religious and are not, therefore, eligible for protection from the law relating to religion. In effect, state agencies and courts of law have to determine a balance between the rights and the risks associated with certain religions. Another way of putting this is to say that consumerism is an undeniable feature of religion in late-modern societies but that consumer protection is equally important. The popular focus on individualisation tends to distract attention from the regulatory contexts in which individuals can or cannot make choices. The fact that individuals seem to have more choices to make about religion these days – as they do about their health and leisure – increases the pressure on them to choose responsibly, i.e. to avoid dangerous or harmful religious groups and practices. Public awareness of the risks stemming from clergy malfeasance has grown massively in recent decades. With the growing pressure to make responsible choices comes a greater likelihood of surveillance over the choices that individuals make. The preoccupation with 'cults' is the clearest illustration of the logic that connects notions of individual responsibility to processes of surveillance. Similar concerns now extend to involvement in any form of religion that entails altered states of consciousness or selfless devotion to a religious cause.

A second major part of the context within which individuals make religious choices today concerns the growth of transnational, if not global, networks of religious entrepreneurs, organisations and movements. New information technologies have intensified the efforts that some religious organisations have been making for thousands of years to extend their reach into all parts of the world. The rate at which people and ideas cross national boundaries now lags far behind the rate at which ideas, sentiments and money can be transmitted electronically. Migrants, refugees, political exiles and asylum seekers have been at the centre of many large-scale movements of religion across the world, but the Internet and satellite television are proving to be the most powerful media for the expansion of religious networks. Again, this means that individual choices are directly or indirectly influenced by events in cyberspace.

A third contextual feature of supposedly individualised choice in matters of religion is the impact of communal tensions and conflicts. Individual choices take place in many countries and regions against a background of conflictual relations between parties identified or self-identified by religious labels. Religion can serve as a – more or less accurate – marker of divisions based on 'race', ethnicity, nationality, culture, political sympathies and so on. In some circumstances, antagonists identify religious differences as the primary fault line between them. Leaving aside all questions about the 'real' causes of conflicts based on religious differences, there is no doubt that religious conflicts are real in their consequences. That is, they tend to polarise opinion and to exclude compromise. The people of Northern Ireland, Israel or the Punjab, for example, are legally free to choose to follow a religion other than those at the centre of their local conflicts, but it is questionable how far each polarised context would actually permit them to feel that they could escape from the conflicts. This explains the persistence of hoary ethno-religious jokes in Northern Ireland along the lines of: 'Are you a Protestant or a Catholic?'. 'I'm neither: I'm a Jew'. 'Yes, but are you a Protestant Jew or a Catholic Jew?'. It is as if the polarised context permits nothing but a particular kind of individuality.

A fourth context of powerful influences over individual choice is the increasing degree of exposure to the mass media of communication. Relatively little of the content of mass media materials has a direct bearing on religion except in media controlled by religious organisations, but that is not my point. I want to draw attention to the fact that, with variations linked to the age, gender, social class and ethnicity of audiences, the standardising effect of the mass media is massive. 'Lifestyle' topics, in particular, play on the paradoxical encouragement of individuality *and* conformity to fashion. Individuality in this context is about having the freedom to choose to follow a trend or fashion – and to avoid being ridiculed for being an outsider. It is also about mobility, change and 'makeovers' in all aspects of life – intimate relationships, employment, education, body shape, health and wealth. This form of individuality is clearly incompatible with conservative styles of religion that prize tradition and a rugged indifference to changing fashions. On the other hand, the mediatised form of individuality has strong affinities with the ethos of some other styles of religion. They include religious movements that offer the opportunity to opt for an entirely fresh self-identity as, for example, 'born again', 'saved', 'enlightened' or 'clear'. In some cases, individuals can also opt to undergo training or preparation for further changes of self-identity to 'sanctified', 'Operating Thetan' or 'enlightened Master'. Moreover, these changes follow from courses of instruction, thereby paralleling the trajectory of 'lifelong learning' that is central to the educational policies of late-modern societies. Another parallel between the ethos of late-modern individuality and the outlook of some religious movements is the sense that 'working' towards a new self-identity constitutes an investment that will produce practical benefits in everyday life for individuals. In other words, involvement in these individualised forms of religion is not so much a flight or escape from the pressure to make lifestyle choices as an expression of the same kind of 'standardised individuality'. An analogy with restaurants will make this point clearer. A wide range of cuisines is on offer in late-modern societies, thereby increasing the choices facing customers. But many restaurants belong to transnational corporations; and their menus reflect hybridised and standardised notions of taste. In short, the appearance of diversity and choice masks underlying pressures towards standardisation. Individual customers are certainly free to exercise their choice but they can only choose from items on the menu.

The evidence of increasing individualisation in religious beliefs and practices is persuasive. There is no reason to doubt that modernity and late-modernity have weakened the hold that traditional, communally oriented, ascriptive religious ideas used to have on many people's lives. The growing importance of subjective, self-regarding, elective ways of practising religion is also beyond doubt. At the same time, however, pressure to conform to various collective criteria and standards regarding the acceptable forms of religion remains strong in some contexts. Paradoxically, then, individualisation proves to be compatible with standardisation except in the case of those 'rugged individuals' or deviant individuals whose religion is truly idiosyncratic. It must be added that the conceptualisation of 'individualisation' and 'standardisation' is itself a matter of social construction as well as of social science and that it varies with time and place. To adapt Peter Wagner's (1994) characterisation of modernity, the most interesting challenge is to understand how liberty and discipline are mutually implicated.

Conclusion

The value of taking full account of individualisation *and* standardisation in religion is only the last of my arguments for even-handedness and balance in social theory and the social scientific study of religion. My aim throughout this book has been to show that these two fields of inquiry stand to benefit from mutual dialogue – provided that each of them remains open to the challenges and 'inconvenient' findings that the other delivers. A full-frontal confrontation between them will produce the most stimulating questions and the most radical claims. The effect will be much less rewarding if social theorists remain highly selective about the material that they take from studies of religion and if, in turn, social scientific students of religion refuse to consider seriously the diversity of social theoretical perspectives. It goes without saying that theological, philosophical and aesthetic perspectives can also contribute to a well-balanced account of religion as a social phenomenon.

Complexity, ambiguity and changeableness are characteristic of all the topics discussed in this book. Analysis of the subtlety of the social aspects of religion is conditional upon recognising that it is a social and cultural phenomenon. As such, its meaning is continuously under construction and is always revisable. There are no permanent points of anchorage for conceptualisations or definitions of religions. They depend on the active work of human beings – through the medium of institutions, organisations, movements and groups – to constitute religions as particular kinds of thing for particular purposes. Nevertheless, the situation is certainly not a chaotic free-for-all, for certain notions of what counts as religion are taken-for-granted; and they prevail in wide areas of social life. But tensions and conflicts with competing notions are also common. These issues of conceptualisation are at the heart of debates about secularisation, globalisation, religious diversity and religious movements, as I tried to show in the preceding chapters. Indeed, my argument is even more ambitious: it claims that these and other topics in the social scientific study of religion can make sense only if it is recognised that, at a basic level, they all involve prior questions about the social construction and use of religions. In other words, these particular topics should be of interest to social theorists and social scientific students of religion precisely because they concern, on the one hand, agreements and disagreements about competing conceptualisations of religions and, on the other, the implications of these competing conceptualisations for the uses to which people choose to put religions.

I have deliberately referred to 'religions' in the plural because I want to emphasise that the definition of religion in general is of interest only to academics and constitutional lawyers. 'Religion in general' is unlikely to interest the warring parties in Kashmir, Gujarat, Palestine, Northern Ireland or Sudan. Their primary concern is to promote highly particular notions of what it means to act in the name of particular religions. Of course, factors such as the distribution of political power, land, wealth and prestige may be closer to the centre of these conflicts, but the fact is that the conflicts are socially constructed as, at least in part, matters of religion.

The same argument about the social construction of religious particularities also applies to the less violent disputes concerning, for example, the Church of Scientology's claims to official recognition as a religion, the framing of debates about abortion, the legal restrictions placed on Christian movements that are not associated with Orthodox Churches in Eastern Europe and the former Soviet Union, the curriculum of Religious Education in British state schools, the controversy surrounding the Japanese state's apparent rehabilitation of the Yasukini Shrine honouring the spirits of Japan's war dead, and the long-running struggles for and against the permissibility of religious texts and religious activities in US public schools. These disputes all turn on assumptions about the meaning of 'real' religion and its appropriate uses in public life.

Social scientific studies that purport to explain religion without prior consideration of how the meaning of 'religion' is constructed and reconstructed in particular contexts cannot do justice to the phenomenon's complexity. The process of construction includes moral suasion, legal determination, political imposition, philosophical argument, historical reconstruction and, in some cases, casual violence and deadly force. John Caputo (2001: 1) may have good reason to stipulate that 'love of God' is the meaning of religion, but social scientists and social theorists still have the task of investigating the myriad of banal and bizarre ways in which human societies and cultures construct and use their particular versions of religion. *Pace* John Milbank (1990: 102), this is the very stuff of 'the social'. Unlike Milbank's parody of the sociologist, I do not assert that the social necessarily takes priority over the theological or the divine. Nor do I believe that it is worthwhile to search for a 'real' essence of religion. I merely assert that the social exists as a dimension of human life and that it calls for human understanding – especially when it concerns beliefs about the existence of a sacred domain.

Notes

INTRODUCTION

1. Calhoun (1999), Lemert (1999) and Ebaugh (2002) have subsequently reached similar conclusions about the marginality of the social scientific study of religion.

CHAPTER 1

1. Vedic text quoted by Wole Soyinka in Abramson 2002.
2. 'A "state", for example, ceases to exist in a sociologically relevant sense whenever there is no longer a probability that certain kinds of meaningfully oriented social action will take place' (Weber 1964: 118).

CHAPTER 2

1. I am well aware of the widely differing meanings that 'modernity' can carry; and I am sympathetic to Bernard Yack's (1997) argument for at least preferring 'modernities' in the plural. Since none of the formulations of 'secularisation' depends on the diversity of conceptions of modernity, however, I have left this term in the singular here.
2. Of course, other sociological investigations of religion followed avenues that displayed little or no association with ideas about secularisation. Indeed, some French, Japanese and Italian scholars argued that the concept of secularisation had very little relevance to developments in their countries.
3. 'By "religion" I mean an acceptance of a level of reality beyond the observable world known to science, to which are ascribed meanings and purposes completing and transcending those of the purely human realm' (Martin 1978: 12).
4. Founded as the CISR (la Conférence internationale de sociologie religieuse) in 1949, the name was changed to the International Society for the Sociology of Religion (ISSR) or, in French, la Société internationale de la sociologie des religions (SISR) in 1989. See Dobbelaere 1999.
5. Incidentally, Chaves does not apply his strictures against the vagueness of 'religion' to his own use of the term 'religious', opting for the decidedly vague definition of religious authority structures in terms of 'the fact that their claims are legitimated by at least a *language* of the supernatural' (Chaves 1991: 86, emphasis original).

6. In my opinion, 'pluralism' is an ideological or normative preference for the value of diversity. The idea would be more accurately rendered by 'religious diversity' or 'public recognition of more than one religion' in most contexts. See Beckford 1999a.
7. See Hornsby-Smith 1992 for cogent criticisms of this aspect of Davie's thesis.
8. See also Modood 2000.

CHAPTER 3

1. This elementary, but often overlooked, point was cogently made in a Council of Europe (2002: 8) report: 'It is true that religious diversity is a fact in central and eastern European – but this does not mean that religious pluralism (which is not the same thing) is increasing, at the same time and to the same extent, in all the countries of the region'.
2. The situation in the North of Ireland could be described as a 'plural society', however. For the relevance of this term to certain colonised societies and to South Africa under Apartheid, see Furnivall 1939 and Rex 1986.
3. Riis 1999 also criticises Berger for overlooking the possibility that 'a confrontation of different world views may lead to a clarification of their differences rather than to relativism' (§3.5).
4. Berger's failure to take account of differences in power between religious groups is one of the symptoms of his functionalist focus on harmony rather than conflict. See Beckford 1983a.
5. See the issue of the *MOST Journal on Multicultural Societies* 1 (2) 1999 on the public management of religious diversity.
6. See Beckford & Gilliat 1998; Beckford 1999a, 1999b, 2001 for more detailed discussion of the political economy of religion in British and American prisons.
7. See Davie 2000: 137, 188 for use of conjoint phrases such as 'pluralism and tolerance' and 'tolerant and pluralist society'.

CHAPTER 4

1. Beck makes remarkably few references to religion in any of his voluminous writings known to me, with the partial exception of Beck & Beck-Gernsheim 2002. See Beckford 1996.
2. Martin Albrow's 1996 sharply different sense of 'globality' will be discussed later in the chapter.
3. I am indebted to Jonathan Tritter for drawing my attention to the following, only slightly tongue-in-cheek claim about religion's role as a source of 'great global brands': 'Organised religion developed some of the first truly great global brands. They created powerful, globally recognisable symbols such as the cross, told great brand stories, used the mass media of churches, used brand ambassadors (clerics, missionaries), created a sense of identity by attacking rivals through various holy wars and created a sense of awe and spectacle through grand cathedrals and major festivities' (Brierley 2002: 23).
4. Robertson (1987: 40) attributes the special significance of Japanese religious movements, in the rise of global consciousness and action, to the

ancient tendency of Japanese culture 'to make an identity from various sources'.

5. 'Faith Christianity in Sweden therefore displays a Janus-face to the forces of globalisation' (Coleman 2000: 233).

6. This movement now operates under the umbrella name of the Family Federation for World Peace and Unification.

7. To take just one 'howler', Giddens asserts as a matter of fact that 'Jehovah's Witnesses reject much of the electronic technology of modernity' (1994: 90). Even a peremptory perusal of the relevant studies would have shown him that the Witnesses have actually been pioneers in the use of print-media, audio and visual technologies of mass communication.

8. 'Globalism' refers to 'values which take the globe as their frame or reference point' (Albrow 1996: 83).

9. Rosenberg (2000: 115–21) exposes this problem, with devastating effect, in Giddens' theory of globalisation. Albrow (1996: 85) also notes with disapproval that 'globalisation' is often used 'as an explanation, rather than as something to be analysed, explored and explained'.

10. I commend J-P Willaime's refusal to allow 'fundamentalism' to obliterate the distinctions between what he calls 'Catholic integrism', Protestant fundamentalism, integral Judaism, Islamist movements, Buddhist orthodoxy'. His reason for separating these different forms of radicalised religion is that 'each religious tradition is radicalised in accordance with its own logic, and the social effects of this radicalisation are not necessarily the same' (Willaime 1995: 64–5, trans. J.A.B.).

11. David Martin (2002: 1) has assembled a good list of reasons for 'rejecting this catch-all category' in studies of Pentecostal and charismatic groups. By contrast, Lawrence 1989 argues for retaining the category of 'fundamentalism' on condition that its many different forms can be analysed separately.

12. Albrow (1996) is an exception in so far as he does not lump all recent religious developments together under the 'global' label.

13. http://www.cec-kek.org/English/ChartafinE.htm

14. The list of distinguished contributions to research on religion and ethnicity, frequently with emphasis on changes that are associated with cross-national migration and return migration, has been growing in recent decades. It includes Williams (1988), Warner and Wittner (1997) and Ebaugh and Chavetz (2000), Ballard (1994), Khosrokhavar (1997) and Boyer (1998).

15. Martin Hollis (1999) might have gone even further by arguing that the notion of the particular makes no sense unless prior assumptions about the universal are in place.

16. See, for example, Robbins and Robertson 1987. In addition, a new journal *Religion-Staat-Gesellschaft* made its debut in 1999. The *Journal of Church and State* and *Religion, State and Society* have for many years been dealing more widely with issues of politics and religion as well as with relations between States and religions.

17. 'Everyone has the right to freedom of thought, conscience and religion; this right includes freedom to change his religion or belief and freedom,

either alone or in community with others and in public or private, to manifest his religion or belief in teaching, practice, worship and observance'.

18. The first part of Article 9 is a slightly rewritten version of Article 18 of the
UN Declaration. The second part stipulates that 'Freedom to manifest one's
religion or beliefs shall be subject only to such limitations as are prescribed by
law and are necessary in a democratic society in the interests of public safety,
for the protection of public order, health or morals, or for the protection of
the rights and freedoms of others'.

19. Mr Abdelfattah Amor was appointed in 1993 as the Special Rapporteur
in the field of religious freedom and tolerance. 'His appointment was
created by a United Nations Commission on Human Rights resolution
#1998/18. He functions independently, within the Office of the United
Nations High Commissioner for Human Rights in Geneva, Switzerland.
One of his tasks is to visit member States of the UN, assess their degree of religious freedom and tolerance, and write reports on his findings'.
http://www.religioustolerance.org/un_int02.htm, [accessed 16 April 2002].

20. International Religious Freedom Act (IRFA) 1998.

21. My reasons for being sceptical are similar to those given by McGovern (2002)
for doubting whether globalisation, rather than 'internationalisation', is responsible for post-1945 changes in the employment of professional soccer
players in England. Clearly, religion is not the only sphere of social life where
exaggerated claims have been made about globalisation.

CHAPTER 5

1. For general overviews of modern religious movements, see Wilson 1970;
Jules-Rosette 1989; Pereira de Queiroz 1989; Inoue 1991; Bainbridge 1997
and Bhatt 1997; Martin 2002.

2. For example, Cohen 1983; Kitschelt 1985; Offe 1985a and Brand 1990.

3. But see Nye 1998 for the problem that the ISKCON movement has had to
secure public access to the *physical* space of its principal temple in the UK.

4. For an extended account of these objections, see Beckford 2001b. See also
Robertson 1992a; Voyé 1992; Spickard 1998 and Bruce 1993, 1999.

5. See, for example, Waerness 1984 on the rationality of caring, and Voyé 1992
on the rationality of sacrifice.

6. 'The church-to-sect process is far more likely to occur in relatively unregulated religious economies where the survival of all religious groups rests on
market processes than in regulated economies featuring subsidized denominations' (Stark & Finke 2000: 262).

7. See Lambert 2002 for an overview of survey findings about changing patterns
of religious belief, practice and belonging.

8. For example, Brusco (1995) regards Pentecostalism in Latin America as
a movement that challenges 'machismo', whereas Mariz and Machado
(1997) consider it, in part, as a device for reproducing old patterns of
patriarchy.

9. A special issue of the journal *Sociology of Religion* was devoted to the 'Sociology
of Culture and Sociology of Religion' in 1996 (vol. 57 no. 1).

10. Bainbridge (1997: 363, 391) argues that 'the New Age movement permeates Western culture' and that 'with its ties to pseudo-science and Asian religion, the New Age is clearly the most formidable, thorough-going religious counterculture that currently exists in modern society'.
11. The publication and sale of books related to the New Age have been increasing in volume and commercial value for several decades. The amount of display shelving devoted to these books is a good, non-obtrusive measure of the interest that the reading public has for the New Age. See also Mears & Ellison 2000.

References

Aberle, D. F. 1970, 'A note on relative deprivation theory as applied to millenarian and other cult movements', in Thrupp, S. (ed.), *Millennial Dreams in Action*, New York: Shocken Books, pp. 209–14.

Abramson, J. (ed.) 2002, *The End of Tolerance*, London: Nicholas Brealey Publishing.

Aho, J. 1990, *The Politics of Righteousness. Idaho Christian Patriotism*, Seattle: University of Washington Press.

Aho, J. 1996, 'Popular Christianity and political extremism in the United States', in Smith, C. (ed.), *Disruptive Religion*, New York: Routledge, pp. 189–204.

Albrow, M. 1996, *The Global Age*, Cambridge: Polity Press.

Altglas, V. 2001, 'L'implantation du néo-hindouisme en Occident', in Bastian, J.-P., Champion, F. and Rousselet, K. (eds.) *La Globalisation du religieux*, Paris: L'Harmattan, pp. 49–60.

Ammerman, N. T. 1987, *Bible Believers. Fundamentalists in the Modern World*, New Brunswick, NJ: Rutgers University Press.

Anderson, B. 1991, *Imagined Communities*, London: Verso, revised.

Anon (ed.) 1988, *Voyage de Jean-Paul II en France*, Paris: Cerf.

Anthias, F. and Yuval-Davis, N. 1992, *Racialized Boundaries. Race, Nation, Gender, Colour and Class and the Anti-Racist Struggle*, London: Routledge.

Anthony, D. and Robbins, T. 1974, 'The Meher Baba movement: its effect on post-adolescent youthful alienation', in Zaretsky, I. I. and Leone, M. P. (eds.) *Religious Movements in Contemporary America*, Princeton University Press, pp. 479–511.

Antoun, R. T. and Hegland, M. E. (eds.) 1987, *Religious Resurgence. Contemporary Cases in Islam, Christianity, and Judaism*, Syracuse University Press.

Archer, M. S. and Tritter, J. Q. (eds.) 2000, *Rational Choice Theory. Resisting Colonization*, London: Routledge.

Arjomand, S. A. 1988, *The Turban for the Crown: The Islamic Revolution in Iran*, New York: Oxford University Press.

Asad, T. 1993, *Genealogies of Religion. Discipline and Reasons of Power in Christianity and Islam*, Baltimore: Johns Hopkins University Press.

Aubrée, M. 2001, 'Dynamiques comparées de l'Eglise universelle du royaume de Dieu au Brésil et à l'étranger', in Bastian, J.-P., Champion, F. and Rousselet, K. (eds.) *La Globalisation du religieux*, Paris: L'Harmattan, pp. 113–24.

Augé, M. 1992, *Non-Lieux. Introduction à une anthropologie de la surmodernité*, Paris: Seuil.

Ayubi, N. 1991, *Political Islam. Religion and Politics in the Arab World*, London: Routledge.

Bailey, E. 1997, *Implicit Religion in Contemporary Society*, Kampen: Kok Pharos.

Bailey, E. 1998, *Implicit Religion: an Introduction*, London: Middlesex University Press.

Bainbridge, W. S. 1997, *The Sociology of Religious Movements*, New York: Routledge.

Baird-Windle, P. and Bader, E. J. 2001, *Targets of Hatred: Anti-Abortion Terrorism*, New York: Palgrave.

Ballard, R. (ed.) 1994, *Desh Pardesh. The South Asian Presence in Britain*, London: Hurst.

Barker, E. V. 1984, *The Making of a Moonie*, Oxford: Blackwell.

Barker, E. V. 1989, *New Religious Movements. A Practical Introduction*, London: HMSO.

Barkun, M. 1994, *Religion and the Racist Right. The Origins of the Christian Identity Movement*, Chapel Hill: University of North Carolina Press.

Barnes, B. 1995, *Elements of Social Theory*, London: UCL Press.

Barr, J. 1977, *Fundamentalism*, London: SCM Press.

Barrett, D. V. 2001, *The New Believers: Sects, 'Cults' and Alternative Religions*, London: Cassell.

Bastian, J.-P., Champion, F. and Rousselet, K. (eds.) 2001, *La Globalisation du religieux*, Paris: L'Harmattan.

Baubérot, J. 1990a, *Un Nouveau pacte laïque?*, Paris: Seuil.

Baubérot, J. 1990b, *La Laïcité, quel héritage de 1789 à nos jours?*, Geneva: Labor et Fides.

Baubérot, J. (ed.) 1994, *Religions et laïcité dans l'Europe des douze*, Paris: Syros.

Baubérot, J. 1998, 'La laïcité française et ses mutations', *Social Compass* 45, 1: 175–87.

Baubérot, J. 1999, 'Laïcité, sectes, sociétés', in Champion, F. and Cohen, M. *Sectes et démocratie*, Paris: Seuil, pp. 314–30.

Baubérot, J. 2001, 'La laïcité française face au pluralisme et à ses mutations', in Côté, P. (ed.), *Chercheurs de Dieu dans l'espace public*, Ottawa: Presses de l'Université d'Ottawa, pp. 169–81.

Baudrillard 1990, *Cool Memories*, London: Verso.

Baudrillard 1993, *Symbolic Exchange and Death*, London: Sage.

Bauman, Z. 1991, *Modernity and Ambivalence*, Cambridge: Polity Press.

Bauman, Z. 1992, *Intimations of Postmodernity*, London: Routledge.

Bauman, Z. 1998, *Globalization. The Human Consequences*, Cambridge: Polity Press.

Baumann, G. 1996, *Contesting Culture: Discourses of Identity in Multi-Ethnic London*, Cambridge University Press.

Baumann, G. 1999, *The Multicultural Riddle. Rethinking National, Ethnic, and Religious Identities*, London: Routledge.

Beck, U. 2000, *What is Globalization?* London: Sage.

Beck, U. and Beck-Gernsheim, E. 2002, *Individualization*, London: Sage.

Beckford, J. A. 1978a, 'Accounting for conversion', *British Journal of Sociology* 29, 2: 249–62.

Beckford, J. A. 1978b, 'Cults and cures', *Japanese Journal of Religious Studies* 5, 4: 225–57.

Beckford, J. A. 1981, 'Functionalism and ethics in sociology: the relationship between "ought" and "function"', *The Annual Review of the Social Sciences of Religion* 5: 106–35.

Beckford, J. A. 1983a, 'The restoration of "power" to the sociology of religion', *Sociological Analysis* 44, 1: 11–31.

Beckford, J. A. 1983b, 'The cult problem in five countries: the social construction of religious controversy', in Barker, E.V. (ed.) *Of Gods and Men: New Religious Movements in the West*, Macon, GA: Mercer University Press, pp. 195–214.

Beckford, J. A. 1984, 'Holistic imagery and ethics in new religious and healing movements', *Social Compass* 31, 2–3: 259–72.

Beckford, J. A. 1985a, *Cult Controversies. The Societal Response to New Religious Movements*, London: Tavistock.

Beckford, J. A. 1985b, 'The insulation and isolation of the sociology of religion', *Sociological Analysis* 46, 4: 347–54.

Beckford, J. A. 1985c, 'The world images of new religious and healing movements', in Jones, R. K. *Sickness and Sectarianism*, Aldershot: Gower, pp. 72–93.

Beckford, J. A. (ed.) 1986, *New Religious Movements and Rapid Social Change*, London: Sage.

Beckford, J. A. 1989, *Religion and Advanced Industrial Society*, London: Unwin-Hyman.

Beckford, J. A. 1992, 'Religion, modernity and postmodernity', in Wilson, B. R. (ed.), *Religion: Contemporary Issues*, London: Bellew, pp. 11–23.

Beckford, J. A. 1993, 'States, governments and the management of controversial new religious movements', in Barker, E., Beckford, J. A. and Dobbelaere, K. (eds.), *Secularization, Rationalism and Sectarianism*, Oxford: Clarendon Press, pp. 125–43.

Beckford, J. A. 1995, 'Cults, conflicts and journalists', in Towler, R. (ed.) *New Religions and the New Europe*, Aarhus University Press, pp. 99–111.

Beckford, J. A. 1996, 'Postmodernity, high modernity and new modernity: three concepts in search of religion', in Flanagan, K. and Jupp, P. *Postmodernity, Sociology and Religion*, London: Macmillan, pp. 30–47.

Beckford, J. A. 1998, 'Secularization and social solidarity: a social constructionist view', in Laermans, R., Wilson, B. R. and Billiet, J. (eds.) *Secularization and Social Integration*, Leuven University Press, pp. 141–58.

Beckford, J. A. 1999a, 'The management of religious diversity in England and Wales with special reference to prison chaplaincy', *MOST Journal on Multicultural Societies* 1, 2: Online. [Available: http://www.unesco.org./most/vl1n2bec.htm]10pp. [accessed 25/1/00]

Beckford, J. A. 1999b, 'The mass media and new religious movements', in Wilson, B. R. and Cresswell, J. (eds.), *New Religious Movements. Challenge and Response*, London: Routledge, pp. 103–19.

Beckford, J. A. 1999c, 'Rational choice theory and prison chaplaincy: the chaplain's dilemma', *British Journal of Sociology* 50, 4: 671–85.

Beckford, J. A. 1999d, 'Social justice and religion in prison: the case of England and Wales', *Social Justice Research* 12, 4: 315–22.

Beckford, J. A. 2000, 'Religious movements and globalization', in Cohen, R. and Rai, S. (eds.), *Global Social Movements*, London: Athlone Press, pp. 165–83.

Beckford, J. A. 2001a, 'The tension between an Established Church and equal opportunities in religion: the case of prison chaplaincy', in Nesbitt, P. D. (ed.) *Religion and Social Policy*, Walnut Creek, CA: Alta Mira Press, pp. 29–53.

Beckford, J. A. 2001b, 'Social movements as free-floating religious phenomena', in Fenn, R. K. (ed.) *The Blackwell Companion to Sociology of Religion*, Oxford: Blackwell, pp. 229–48.

Beckford, J. A. 2001c, 'Choosing rationality', *Research in the Social Scientific Study of Religion*, 12: 1–22.

Beckford, J. A. 2001d, '"Dystopia" and the reaction to new religious movements in France', unpublished paper presented at the annual meeting of the Society for the Scientific Study of Religion, Columbus, OH, October.

Beckford, J. A. 2001e, 'The continuum between 'cults' and 'normal' religion', in Côté, P. (ed.), *Chercheurs de dieux dans l'espace public*, Les Presses de l'Université d'Ottawa, pp. 11–20.

Beckford, J. A. 2001f, 'Developments in the sociology of religion', in Burgess, R. G. and Murcott, A. (eds.), *Developments in Sociology*, London: Prentice-Hall, pp. 143–63.

Beckford, J. A. 2003, 'Sans l'état pas de transmission de la religion? Le cas de l'Angleterre', *Archives de Sciences Sociales des Religions*, 121: 57–67.

Beckford, J. A. and Cole, M. A. 1988, 'British and American responses to new religious movements', *Bulletin of the John Rylands University Library of Manchester*, 70, 3: 209–25.

Beckford, J. A. and Gilliat, S. 1998, *Religion in Prison. Equal Rites in a Multi-Faith Society*, Cambridge University Press.

Bell, D. 1976, *The Cultural Contradictions of Capitalism*, New York: Basic Books.

Bell, D. 1977, 'The return of the sacred', *British Journal of Sociology* 28, 4: 419–49.

Bell, D. 1980, *Sociological Journeys*, London: Heinemann.

Bellah, R. N. 1970, *Beyond Belief*, New York: Harper & Row.

Bellah, R. N. 1976, 'New religious consciousness and the crisis in modernity', in Glock, C.Y. and Bellah, R. N. (eds.) *The New Religious Consciousness*, Berkeley: University of California Press, pp. 333–52.

Bellah, R. N., Madsen R., Sullivan, W. M., Swidler, A., Tipton, S. M. 1985, *Habits of the Heart*, Berkeley: University of California Press.

Berger, P. L. 1969, *The Social Reality of Religion*, London: Faber & Faber, published in 1967 in the USA as *The Sacred Canopy*.

Berger, P. L. 1974, 'Some second thoughts on substantive versus functional definitions of religion', *Journal for the Scientific Study of Religion* 13, 2: 125–33.

Berger, P. L. 1999, 'The desecularization of the world: a global overview', in Berger, P. L. (ed.) *The Desecularization of the World*, Grand Rapids, MI: William B. Eerdmans, pp. 1–18.

Berger, P. L. 2001, 'Postscript', in Woodhead, L. (ed.), *Peter Berger and the Study of Religion*, London: Routledge, pp. 189–98.

Berger, Peter L. and Neuhaus, R. M, 1977, *To Empower People*, Boston: American Enterprise Institute.

Besier, G. (ed.) 1999, *The Churches, Southern Africa and the Political Context*, London: Minerva Press.

Beyer, P. 1994, *Religion and Globalization*, London: Sage.

Bhatt, C. 1997, *Liberation and Purity. Race, New Religious Movements and the Ethics of Postmodernity*, London: UCL Press.

Bibby, R. W. 1987, *Fragmented Gods. The Poverty and Potential of Religion in Canada*, Toronto: Irwin.

Birman, P. 1998, 'Cultes de possession et pentecôtisme au Brésil: passages', *Cahiers du Brésil contemporain*, 35–36: 185–208.

Bizeul, Y. 2001, 'Les stratégies oecuméniques dans un contexte de globalisation' in J.-P. Bastian, Champion, F. and Rousselet, K. (eds.) *La Globalisation du religieux*, Paris: L'Harmattan, pp. 197–208.

Blau, J., Land, K. and Redding, K. 1992, 'The expansion of religious affiliation', *Social Science Research*, 21: pp. 329–52.

Blumer, H. 1963, 'Collective behavior', in Lee, A. M (ed.) *Principles of Sociology*, New York: Barnes & Noble, pp. 166–220.

Bowker, J. 1973, *The Sense of God. Sociological, Anthropological and Psychological Approaches to the Origin of the Sense of God*, Oxford University Press.

Boyer, A. 1998, *L'Islam en France*, Paris: Presses Universitaires de France.

Brand, K.-W. 1990, 'Cyclical aspects of new social movements: waves of cultural criticism and mobilization cycles of new middle-class radicalism', in Dalton, R. and Kuechler, M. (eds.) *Challenging the Political Order: New Social and Political Movements in Western Democracies*, Cambridge: Polity Press: 23–42.

Brasher, B. 2001, *Give Me That Online Religion*, New York: Jossey Bass Wiley.

Breault, K. D. 1989, 'Reply to Finke and Stark', *American Sociological Review* 54: 1056–9.

Bréchon, P. 2000, 'L'enquête ISSP de 1998 en France: premiers résultats', *Institut d'Etudes Politiques*, Grenoble.

Brewer, P. 1986, *Shaker Communities, Shaker Lives*, Hanover, NH: University Press of New England.

Brierley, S. 2002, 'The Church of England – Is That Still Going Then?', *Marketing Week* 24 January: 23.

Bromley, D. G. 1988, 'Understanding the structure of covenantal and contractual social relations: implications for the sociology of religion', *Sociological Analysis* 49 S: 15–32.

Bromley, D. G. (ed.) 1998, *The Politics of Religious Apostasy: the Role of Apostates in the Transformation of Religious Movements*, Westport, CT: Praeger.

Bromley, D. G. and Hadden, J. K. (eds.) 1993, *The Handbook on Cults and Sects in America*, 2 vols, Greenwich, CT: JAI Press.

Bromley, D. G. and Hammond, P. E. (eds.) 1987, *The Future of New Religious Movements*, Macon, GA: Mercer University Press.

Bromley, D. G. and Richardson, J. T. (eds.) 1983, *The Brainwashing/ Deprogramming Controversy: Sociological, Psychological, Legal and Historical Perspectives*, New York: Edwin Mellen Press.

Bromley, D. G. and Shupe, A. D. Jr. 1979, *The Moonies in America*, Beverly Hills, CA: Sage.

Bromley, D. G. and Shupe, A. D. Jr. 1980, 'Financing the new religions: a resource mobilization perspective', *Journal for the Scientific Study of Religion* 19, 3: 227–39.

Brouwer, S., Gifford, P. et al. 1996, *Exporting the American Gospel. Global Christian Fundamentalism*, New York: Routledge.

Brown, C. G. 2001, *The Death of Christian Britain*, London: Routledge.

Bruce, S. 1984, *Firm in the Faith*, Aldershot: Gower.

Bruce, S. 1993, 'Religion and rational choice: a critique of economic explanations of religious behaviour', *Sociology of Religion* 54, 2: 193–205.

Bruce, S. 1999, *Choice and Religion. A Critique of Rational Choice*, Oxford University Press.

Bruce, S. 2002, *God is Dead: Secularization in the West*, Oxford: Blackwell.

Brusco, E. 1995, *The Reformation of Machismo*, Austin, TX: University of Texas Press.

Budd, S. 1973, *Sociologists and Religion*, London: Collier-Macmillan.

Budd, S. 1977, *Varieties of Unbelief. Atheists and Agnostics in English Society, 1850–1960*, London: Heinemann.

Butler, C. 2001, 'Reconstructing ethnicity and identity: the influence of second-generation Turkish-Cypriot and Pakistani women in London', unpublished PhD thesis, University of Warwick.

Byrne, P. 1988, *The Campaign for Nuclear Disarmament*, London: Croom Helm.

Calhoun, C. 1999, 'Symposium on religion', *Sociological Theory* 17, 3: 237–9.

Campbell, C. 1971, *Toward a Sociology of Irreligion*, London: Macmillan.

Campiche, R., Dubach, A., Bovay, C., Krügler, M. and Voll, P. 1992, *Croire en Suisse(s)*, Lausanne: L'Age d'Homme.

Caputo, J. D. 2001, *On Religion*, London: Routledge.

Casanova, J. 1994, *Public Religions in the Modern World*, University of Chicago Press.

Casanova, J. 2002, 'Civil society and religion: retrospective reflections on Catholicism and prospective reflections on Islam', *Social Research* 68, 4: 1041–80.

Castells, M. 1997, *The Power of Identity*, Oxford: Blackwell.

Césari, J. 1998, *Musulmans et Républicains. Les Jeunes, l'Islam et la France*, Paris: Complexe.

Chadwick, O. 1975, *The Secularization of the European Mind in the Nineteenth Century*, Cambridge University Press.

Champion, F. 1999, 'The diversity of religious pluralism', *MOST Journal on Multicultural Societies*, 1, 2. Online. [Available: http://www.unesco.org/most/v11n2cha.htm] 16pp. [accessed 25/1/00]

Champion, F. and Cohen, M. (eds.) 1999, *Sectes et Démocratie*, Paris: Seuil.

Chaves, M. A. 1997, *Ordaining Women: Culture and Conflict in Religious Organizations*, Cambridge, MA: Harvard University Press.

Chaves, M. A. 1991, 'Secularization in the twentieth-century United States', unpublished PhD dissertation, Harvard University.

Chaves, M. and Cann, D. E. 1992, 'Regulation, pluralism, and market structure: explaining religion's vitality', *Rationality and Society* 4: 272–90.

Chryssides, G. 1999, *Exploring New Religions*, London: Cassell.

Cipriani, R. 1989, '"Diffused religion" and new values in Italy', in Beckford, J. A. and Luckmann, T. (eds.) *The Changing Face of Religion*, London: Sage pp. 24–48.

Clark, D. 1982, *Between Pulpit and Pew. Folk Religion in a North Yorkshire Fishing Village*, Cambridge University Press.

Cohen, J. 1983, 'Rethinking social movements', *Berkeley Journal of Sociology* 28: 97–113.

Coleman, S. 2000, *The Globalisation of Charismatic Christianity. Spreading the Gospel of Prosperity*, Cambridge University Press.

Commission 2000, *Commission on the Future of Multi-Ethnic Britain*, London: Profile Books.

Coney, J. 1995, '"Belonging to a global religion": the sociological dimensions of international elements in Sahaja Yoga', *Journal of Contemporary Religion* 10, 2: 109–20.

Coney, J. 2000, *Sahaj Yoga*, London: Curzon Press.

Corten, A. 1995, *Le Pentecôtisme au Brésil. Emotion du pauvre et romantisme théologique*, Paris: Karthala.

Côté, P. and Richardson, J. T. 2001, 'Disciplined litigation, vigilant litigation, and deformation: dramatic organization change in Jehovah's Witnesses', *Journal for the Scientific Study of Religion* 40, 1: 11–25.

Council of Europe 1999, *Religion and the integration of immigrants*, Strasbourg.

Council of Europe 2002, 'Religion and change in Central and Eastern Europe', Parliamentary Assembly, Report of the Committee on Culture, Science and Education, Doc. 9399. Online. [Available: http://stars.coe.fr/Documents/WorkingDocs/Doc02/EDOC9399.htm] 14pp. [accessed 29/7/02]

Coward, H., Hinnells, J. and Williams, J. (eds.) 2000, *The South Asian Religious Diaspora in Britain, Canada, and the United States*, Albany, NY: State University of New York Press.

Crane, D. 1994, 'Introduction: the challenge of the sociology of culture to sociology as a discipline', in Crane, D. (ed.), *The Sociology of Culture*, Oxford: Blackwell pp. 1–19.

Dahl, R. A. 1967, *Pluralist Democracy in the United States: Conflict and Consent*, Chicago, IL: Rand McNally.

Davidman, L. 1991, *Tradition in a Rootless World*, Berkeley, CA: University of California Press.

Davie, G. 1990, 'Believing without belonging: is this the future of religion in Britain?' *Social Compass* 37, 4: 455–69.

Davie, G. 1999, 'Europe: The exception that proves the rule', in Berger, P. (ed.) *The Desecularization of the World. Resurgent Religion and World Politics*, Grand Rapids, MI: Eerdmans, pp. 65–83.

Davie, G. 2000, *Religion in Modern Europe*, Oxford University Press.

Davie, G. 2001a, 'Global civil religion: A European perspective', *Sociology of Religion* 62, 4: 455–73.

Davie, G. 2001b, 'Patterns of religion in Western Europe: an exceptional case', in Fenn, R. K. (ed.), *The Blackwell Companion to Sociology of Religion*, Oxford: Blackwell, pp. 264–78.

Davie, G. 2001c, 'The persistence of institutional religion in modern Europe', in Woodhead, L. (ed.) *Peter Berger and the Study of Religion*, London: Routledge, pp. 101–11.

Dawson, L. L. and Hennebry, J. 1999, 'New religions and the Internet: recruiting in a new public space', *Journal of Contemporary Religion* 14, 1: 17–39.

Deakin, N. 2001, *In Search of Civil Society*, Basingstoke: Palgrave.

Deigh, J. 1991, 'Freud's later theory of civilization: changes and implications', in Neu, J. (ed.) *The Cambridge Companion to Freud*, Cambridge University Press, pp. 287–308.

Demerath, N. J. III 2001, 'Secularization extended: from religious "myth" to cultural commonplace', in Fenn, R. K. (ed.) *The Blackwell Companion to Sociology of Religion*, Oxford: Blackwell, pp. 211–28.

Demerath, N. J. III 2002, 'Secularization', in Borgatta, E. F. (ed.) *Encyclopedia of Sociology* 2nd edn. vol. 4, New York: Macmillan, pp. 2482–91.

Demerath, N. J. III. and Schmitt, T. 1998, 'Transcending sacred and secular: mutual benefits in analyzing religious and nonreligious organisations', in *Sacred Companies. Organizational Aspects of Religion and Religious Aspects of Organizations*. N. J. Demerath III, P. D. Hall, T. Schmitt and R. H. Williams (eds.), New York: Oxford University Press, pp. 381–400.

Dillon, M. 1999, 'The authority of the holy revisited: Habermas, religion, and emancipatory possibilities', *Sociological Theory* 17, 3: 290–306.

Dobbelaere, K. 1981, 'Secularization: a multi-dimensional concept', *Current Sociology* 29, 2: 1–216.

Dobbelaere, K. 1987, 'Some trends in European sociology of religion: the secularization debate', *Sociological Analysis* 48, 2: 107–37.

Dobbelaere, K. 2002, *Secularization: An Analysis at Three Levels*, Brussels: P.I.E.-Peter Lang.

Donovan, B. 1998, 'Political consequences of private authority: Promise Keepers and the transformation of hegemonic masculinity', *Theory and Society* 27: 817–43.

Drahos, P. and Braithwaite, J. 2001, 'The globalisation of regulation', *Journal of Political Philosophy* 9, 1: 103–28.

Durkheim, E. 1964, *The Elementary Forms of the Religious Life*, trans. J. W. Swain, London: Allen & Unwin. First published in French 1912.

Durkheim, E. 1975, 'Individualism and the intellectuals', from Bellah, R. (ed.) *Emile Durkheim on Morality and Society*, University of Chicago Press, pp. 43–57. Trans. M. Traugott. First published in French 1898.

Durkheim, E. 1984, *The Division of Labour in Society*, trans. G. Simpson, New York: Macmillan. First published in French 1893.

Ebaugh, H. R. 2002, 'Return of the sacred: reintegrating religion in the social sciences', *Journal for the Scientific Study of Religion* 41, 3: 385–95.

Ebaugh, H. R. and Chafetz, J. S. (eds.) 2000, *Religion and the New Immigrants: Continuities and Adaptations in Immigrant Congregations*, Walnut Creek, CA: Alta Mira Press.

Eddy, P. R. 2002, *John Hick's Pluralist Philosophy of World Religions*, Aldershot: Ashgate.

Eder, K. 1985, 'The new social movements: moral crusades, political pressure groups, or social movements', *Social Research* 52, 4: 869–90.

Ellison, C. G. and Sherkat, D. E. 1995, 'The "semi-involuntary institution" revisited: regional variations in church participation among Black Americans', *Social Forces* 73, 4: 1415–37.

Erickson, V. L. 1993, *Where Silence Speaks: Feminism, Social Theory and Religion*, Minneapolis, MN: Fortress Press.

Evans, M. D. 2000, 'The United Nations and freedom of religion: the work of the Human Rights Committee', in Ahdar, R. (ed.), *Law and Religion*, Aldershot: Ashgate, pp. 35–61.

Fauset, A. H. 1944, *Black Gods of the Metropolis. Negro Religious Cults of the Urban North*, Philadelphia: University of Pennsylvania Press.

Featherstone, M. 1991, *Consumer Culture and Postmodernism*, London: Sage.

Feher, S. 1998, 'From the Rivers of Babylon to the Valleys of Los Angeles: the exodus and adaptation of Iranian Jews', in Warner, R. S. and Wittner, J. (ed.), *Gatherings in Diaspora*, Philadelphia, PA: Temple University Press, pp. 71–94.

Fenn, R. K. 1978, *Toward a Theory of Secularization*, Storrs, CT: Society for the Scientific Study of Religion.

Fenn, R. K. 1981, *Liturgies and Trials*, Oxford: Blackwell.

Ferrari, S. and Bradney, A. (eds.) 2000, *Islam and European Legal Systems*, Aldershot: Ashgate.

Feuerstein, G. 1992, *Holy Madness*, New York: Arkana Books.

Finke, R. 1990, 'Religious deregulation: origins and consequences', *Journal of Church and State* 32, 3: 609–26.

Finke, R. 1997, 'The consequences of religious competition. Supply-side explanations for religious change', in Young, L. (ed.) *Rational Choice Theory and Religion*, New York: Routledge, pp. 46–65.

Finke, R. and Iannaccone, L. R. 1993, 'Supply-side explanations for religious change', *The Annals of the American Academy of Political and Social Science* 527, May: 27–39.

Finke, R. and Stark, R. 1988, 'Religious economies and sacred canopies: religious mobilization in American cities, 1906', *American Sociological Review*, 53: 41–9.

Finke, R. and Stark, R. 1998, 'Religious choice and competition', *American Sociological Review*, 63: 761–6.

Flanagan, K. 1990, 'Theological pluralism. A sociological critique', in Hamnett, I. (ed.), *Religious Pluralism and Unbelief*, London: Routledge: 81–113.

Flanagan, K. 1991, *Sociology and Liturgy*, London: Macmillan.

Flanagan, K. 1996a, *The Enchantment of Sociology: a Study of Theology and Culture*, London: Macmillan.

Flanagan, K. 1996b, 'Postmodernity and culture: sociological wagers of the self in theology', in Flanagan, K. and Jupp, P. C. (ed.), *Postmodernity, Sociology and Religion*, London: Macmillan, pp. 152–73.

Flanagan, K. and Jupp, P. (eds.) 1996, *Postmodernity, Sociology and Religion*, London: Macmillan.

Foss, D. and Larkin, R. 1976, 'From "the Gates of Eden" to "Day of the Locust": an analysis of the dissident youth movement of the 1960s and its heirs in the 1970s - the post-movement groups', *Theory and Society* 3: 45–64.

Foss, D. and Larkin, R. 1979, 'The roar of the lemming: youth, post-movement groups, and the life construction crisis', in Johnson, H. W. (ed.), *Religious Change and Continuity*, San Francisco: Jossey-Bass, pp. 264–85.

Foucault, M. 1977, *Discipline and Punish: The Birth of the Prison*, London: Allen Lane.

Freston, P. 1994, 'Popular Protestants in Brazilian politics: a novel turn in church-state relations', *Social Compass* 41, 4: 537–70.

Freston, P. 1995, 'Pentecostalism in Brazil', *Religion* 25, 2: 119–33.

Furnivall, J. S. 1939, *Netherlands India – A Study of Plural Economy*, Cambridge University Press.

Furseth, I. 2000, 'Religious diversity in prisons and in the military – the rights of Muslim immigrants in Norwegian state institutions', *MOST Journal of Multicultural Societies* 2, 1. Online. [Available: http://www.unesco.org/most/vl2n1fur.htm] 12pp. [accessed 21/12/00].

Fustel de Coulanges, N. D. 1864, *La Cité antique*, Paris.

Gaborieau, M. 2001, 'De la guerre sainte (jihad) au prosélytisme (da'wa) ? Les organisations musulmanes transnationales d'origine indienne', in Bastian, J.-P., Champion, F. and Rousselet, K. (eds.) *La Globalisation du religieux*, Paris: L'Harmattan, pp. 35–48.

Galembert, C. de 2001, 'La régulation étatique du religieux à l'épreuve de la globalisation', in Bastian, J.-P., Champion, F. and Rousselet, K. (eds.) *La Globalisation du religieux*, Paris: L'Harmattan, pp. 223–34.

Gallie, W. B. 1955, 'Essentially contested concepts', *Proceedings of the Aristotelian Society* 56: 167–98.

Gatens, M. 1991, *Feminism and Philosophy: Perspectives on Difference and Equality*, Cambridge University Press.

Gay, P. 1988, *Freud: A Life For Our Time*, London: Macmillan.

Gergen, K. J. 1999, *An Invitation to Social Construction*, London: Sage.

Giddens, A. 1990, *The Consequences of Modernity*, Berkeley, CA: University of California Press.

Giddens, A. 1991, *Modernity and Self-Identity. Self and Society in the Late Modern Age*, Cambridge: Polity Press.

Giddens, A. 1994, 'Living in a post-traditional society', in Beck, U., Giddens, A. and Lasch, S. (eds.), *Reflexive Modernization*, Cambridge: Polity Press, pp. 56–109.

Gill, R. 1993, *The Myth of the Empty Church*, London: S.P.C.K.

Gill, R. 1999, *Churchgoing and Christian Ethics*, Cambridge University Press.

Gilliat, S. 1998, 'English cathedrals and civic rituals', *Theology* 101, 801: 179–88.

Gilliat-Ray, S. 1999, 'Civic religion in England: traditions and transformations', *Journal of Contemporary Religion*, 14, 2: 233–44.

Gilroy, P. 1987, *There Ain't No Black in the Union Jack: The Cultural Politics of Race and Nation*, London: Routledge.

Glasner, P. 1977, *The Sociology of Secularisation. A Critique of a Concept*, London: Routledge & Kegan Paul.

Glock, C. Y. and Bellah, R. N. (eds.) 1976, *The New Religious Consciousness*, Berkeley, CA: University of California Press.

Golden, R. and McConnell, M. 1986, *Sanctuary: the New Underground Railroad*, New York: Orbis.

Goldthorpe, J. H. 1998, 'Rational action theory for sociology', *British Journal of Sociology* 49, 2: 167–92.

Goulbourne, Harry 1991, 'Varieties of pluralism: the notion of a pluralist post-imperial Britain', *New Community* 17, 2: 211–27.

Granovetter, M. S. 1973, 'The strength of weak ties', *American Journal of Sociology* 78: 1360–80.

Greenwood, S. 2000, 'Feminist Witchcraft. A transformatory politics', in Griffin, W. (ed.), *Daughters of the Goddess. Studies in Healing, Identity and Empowerment*, Walnut Creek, CA: Alta Mira: 136–50.

Greil, A. and Robbins, T. (eds.) 1994, *Between Sacred and Secular: Research and Theory on Quasi-Religions. Religion and the Social Order*, New Brunswick, NJ: Transaction Publishers.

Griffin, D. R. (ed.) 1988a, *The Reenchantment of Science*, Albany, NY: SUNY Press.

Griffin, D. R. 1988b, *Spirituality and Society*, Albany, NY: SUNY Press.

Griffin, W. 1995, 'The embodied goddess: feminist witchcraft and female divinity', *Sociology of Religion* 56, 1: 35–48.

Griffin, W. (ed.) 2000, *Daughters of the Goddess. Studies in Healing, Identity and Empowerment*, Walnut Creek, CA: Alta Mira.

Gusfield, J. R. 1981, 'Social movements and social change: perspectives of linearity and fluidity', *Research in Social Movements, Conflict and Change* 4: 317–39.

Habermas, J. 1981, 'New social movements', *Telos* 49: 33–7.

Habermas, J. 1987, *The Theory of Communicative Action. Vol. 2 Lifeworld and System*, Boston: Beacon Press ['Trans T. McCarthy].

Habermas, J. 1996, *Between Facts and Norms*, Cambridge: Polity Press.

Hadden, J. K. 1987, 'Toward desacralizing secularization theory', *Social Forces* 65, 3: 587–611.

Hall, J. R. 1988, 'Collective welfare as resource mobilization in Peoples Temple: a case study of a poor peoples religious social movement', *Sociological Analysis* 49 S: 64–77.

Hall, J. R. 2000, *Apocalypse Observed*, London: Routledge.

Halliday, F. 1996, *Islam and the Myth of Confrontation*, London: I. B. Tauris.

Hamnett, I. 1973, 'Sociology of religion and sociology of error', *Religion* 3, 1: 1–12.

Hamnett, I., (ed.) 1990, *Religious Pluralism and Unbelief*, London: Routledge.

Hampshire, A. P. 1985, *Mormonism in Conflict. The Nauvoo Years*, New York: Edwin Mellen Press.

Hanegraaff, W. J. 1996, *New Age Religion and Western Culture*, Leiden: E. J. Brill.

Hannigan, J. A. 1990, 'Apples and oranges or varieties of the same fruit? The new religious movements and the new social movements compared', *Review of Religious Research* 31, 3: 246–58.

Hannigan, J. A. 1991, 'Social movement theory and the sociology of religion: toward a new synthesis', *Sociological Analysis* 52, 4: 311–31.

Hannigan, J. A. 1993, 'New social movement theory and the sociology of religion', in Swatos, W. H. J. (ed.), *A Future for Religion?* Newbury Park: Sage, pp. 1–18.

Harding, S. F. 2000, *The Book of Jerry Falwell: Fundamentalist Language and Politics*, Princeton University Press.

Hart, S. 1996, 'The cultural dimension of social movements: a theoretical re-assessment and literature review', *Sociology of Religion* 57, 1: 87–100.

Harvey, D. 1989, *The Condition of Postmodernity*, Oxford: Blackwell.

Hay, D. 1990, *Religious Experience Today. Studying the Facts*, London: Mowbray.

Haynes, J. 1998, *Religion in Global Politics*, London: Longman.

Hechter, M. 1997, 'Religion and rational choice theory', in Young, L. (ed.), *Rational Choice Theory and Religion*, New York: Routledge, pp. 147–59.

Hedges, E. and Beckford, J. A. 1999, 'Holism, healing and the New Age', in Sutcliffe, S. and Bowman, M. (eds.), *Beyond the New Age: Alternative Spirituality in Britain*, Edinburgh University Press, pp. 169–87.

Heelas, P. 1991, 'Cults for capitalism: self-religions, magic, and the empowerment of business', in Gee, P. and Jupp, P. C. (eds.), *Religion and Power*, London: BSA Sociology of Religion Study Group, pp. 27–41.

Heelas, P. 1992, 'The sacralization of the self and New Age capitalism', in Abercrombie, N. and Warde, A. (eds.), *Social Change in Contemporary Britain*, Oxford: Polity Press, pp. 139–66.

Heelas, P. 1996a, *The New Age Movement*, Oxford: Blackwell.

Heelas, P. 1996b, 'De-traditionalisation of religion and self: the New Age and postmodernity', in Flanagan, K. and Jupp, P. (eds.), *Postmodernity, Sociology and Religion*, London: Macmillan, pp. 64–82.

Heelas, P. 1999, 'Prosperity and the New Age movement: the efficacy of spiritual economics', in Wilson, B. R. and Cresswell, J. (eds.), *New Religious Movements: Challenge and Response*, London: Routledge, pp. 51–77.

Herman, D. 1997, *The Antigay Agenda. Orthodox Vision and the Christian Right*, University of Chicago Press.

Hervieu-Léger, D. 1986, *Vers un nouveau Christianisme?*, Paris: Cerf.

Hervieu-Léger, D. 1989, 'Tradition, innovation and modernity: research notes' *Social Compass* 36, 1: 71–81.

Hervieu-Léger, D. 1993, *La Religion pour Mémoire*, Paris: Cerf.

Hervieu-Léger, D. 1996, '"Une messe est possible": les double funérailles du Président', *Le Débat* 91: 23–30.

Hervieu-Léger, D. 1999, *Le Pèlerin et le Converti. La religion en mouvement*, Paris: Flammarion.

Hervieu-Léger, D. 2001a, 'The twofold limit of the notion of secularization', in Woodhead, L. (ed.) *Peter Berger and the Study of Religion*, London: Routledge, pp. 112–25.

Hervieu-Léger, D. 2001b, *La Religion en miettes ou la question des sectes*, Paris: Calmann-Lévy.

Hesse, Mary 1980, *Revolutions and Reconstructions in the Philosophy of Science*, Brighton: Harvester.

Hetherington, K. 1998, *Expressions of Identity. Space, Performance, Politics*, London: Sage.

Hexham, I. and Poewe, K. 1997, *New Religions as Global Cultures: The Sacralization of the Human*, Boulder, CO: Westview Press.

Hill, M. and Lian, K. F. 1995, *The Politics of Nation Building and Citizenship in Singapore*, London: Routledge.

Hobsbawm, E. and Ranger, T. (eds.) 1992, *The Invention of Tradition*, Cambridge University Press.

Hollis, M. 1987, *The Cunning of Reason*, Cambridge University Press.

Hollis, M. 1994, *The Philosophy of Social Science: An Introduction*. Cambridge University Press.

Hollis, M. 1996, *Reason in Action*, Cambridge University Press.

Hollis, M. 1999, 'Is universalism ethnocentric?', in Joppke, C. and Lukes, S. (eds.) *Multicultural Questions*, Oxford University Press, pp. 27–43.

Hornsby-Smith, M. P. 1992, 'Believing without belonging? The case of Roman Catholics in England', in Wilson, B. R. (eds.), *Religion: Contemporary Issues*, London: Bellew, pp. 125–34.

Hornsby-Smith, M. P., Lee, R. M. and Reilly, P. 1985, 'Common religion and customary religion: a critique and a proposal', *Review of Religious Research* 26, 3: 244–52.

Hurbon, L. 1992, 'Pratiques de guérison et religion dans la Caraïbe', in Lautman, F. and Maître, J. (eds.), *Gestion religieuse de la santé*, Paris: L'Harmattan, pp. 91–105.

Hurbon, L. 2001, 'Pentecôtisme et transnationalisation dans la Caraïbe', in Bastian, J.-P., Champion, F. and Rousselet, K. (eds.) *La Globalisation du religieux*, Paris: L'Harmattan, pp. 125–38.

Hutten, K. 1950, *Seher, Grübler, Enthusiasten. Sekten und religiöse Sondergemeinschaften der Gegenwart*, Stuttgart: Quell Verlag.

Iannaccone, L. R. 1992, 'Sacrifice and stigma: reducing free-riding in cults, communes, and other collectives', *Journal of Political Economy* 100, 2: 271–91.

Iannaccone, L. R. 1994, 'Why strict churches are strong', *American Journal of Sociology* 99, 5: 1180–211.

Iannaccone, L. R. 1997, 'Rational Choice. Framework for the scientific study of religion', in Young, L. (ed.), *Rational Choice Theory of Religion*, New York: Routledge, pp. 25–45.

Inoue, N. (ed.) 1991, *New Religions. Contemporary Papers in Japanese Religion*, Tokyo: Institute for Japanese Culture and Classics, Kokugakuin University.

Introvigne, M. 1995, 'L'évolution du "mouvement contre les sectes" chrétien 1978–1993', *Social Compass* 42, 2: 237–47.

Jacobs, J. L. 1991, 'Gender and power in new religious movements. A feminist discourse on the scientific study of religion', *Religion* 21 (4): 345–56.

Jacobson, J. 1997, 'Religion and ethnicity: dual alternative sources of identity among young British Pakistanis', *Ethnic and Racial Studies* 20, 2: 238–56.

Jacobson, J. 1998, *Islam in Transition: Religion and Identity among British Pakistani Youth*, London: Routledge.

Jameson, F. 1991, *Postmodernism, or the Cultural Logic of Late Capitalism*, London: Verso.

Jasper, J. M. 1997, *The Art of Moral Protest: Culture, Biography, and Creativity in Social Movements*, University of Chicago Press.

Jenkins, J. C. 1983, 'Resource mobilization theory and the study of social movements', *Annual Review of Sociology* 9: 527–53.

Jenkins, P. 1992, *Intimate Enemies. Moral Panics in Contemporary Great Britain*, New York: Aldine.

Jenkins, P. 2002, *The Next Christendom: The Coming of Global Christianity*, New York: Oxford University Press.

Jenkins, R. 1997, *Rethinking Ethnicity*, London: Sage.

Johnson, B. 1961, 'Do sects socialize in dominant values?' *Social Forces* 39, May: 309–16.

Juergensmeyer, M. 1993, *The New Cold War? Religious Nationalism Confronts the Secular State*, Berkeley, CA: University of California Press.

Juergensmeyer, M. 2000, *Terror in the Mind of God. The Global Rise of Religious Violence*, Berkeley, CA: University of California Press.

Jules-Rosette, B. 1975, *African Apostles*, Ithaca, NY: Cornell University Press.

Jules-Rosette, B. 1989, 'The sacred in African new religions', in Beckford, J. A. and Luckman, T. (eds.), *The Changing Face of Religion*, London: Sage, pp. 147–62.

Kearns, L. 1996, 'Saving the Creation: Christian environmentalism in the United States', *Sociology of Religion* 57, 1: 55–70.

Kent, S. 2001, *From Slogans to Mantras*, Syracuse University Press.

Kepel, G. 1994, *The Revenge of God*, Oxford: Blackwell.

Khosrokhavar, F. 1997, *L'Islam des Jeunes*, Paris: Flammarion.

King, U. 1994, 'Voices of protest and promise: women's studies in religion, the impact of the feminist critique on the study of religion', *Studies in Religion* 23, 3: 315–29.

Kitschelt, H. 1985, 'New social movements in West Germany and the United States', *Political Power and Social Theory* 5: 273–324.

Kitschelt, H. 1986, 'Political opportunity structures and political protest', *British Journal of Political Science* 16: 57–85.

Klandermans, B. 1986, 'The new social movements and resource mobilization: the European and the American approach', *International Journal of Mass Emergencies and Disasters* 4, 2: 13–37.

Knott, K. 1995, 'The debate about women in the Hare Krishna movement', *Journal of Vaishnava Studies* 3, 4: 85–109.

König, M. 2001, 'Identités nationales et institutions globales: la restructuration des relations entre religion et citoyenneté en Europe', in Bastian, J.-P., Champion, F. and Rousselet, K. (eds.) *La Globalisation du religieux*, Paris: L'Harmattan, pp. 211–22.

Kühle, L. 2002, 'Muslim prisoners in Denmark', unpublished paper presented at the seminar on 'Muslim prisoners in Europe', Swedish Muslim Council, Stockholm.

Kuhn, T. 1962, *The Structure of Scientific Revolutions*, University of Chicago Press.

Kurien, P. 1998, 'Becoming American by becoming Hindu: Indian Americans take their place at the multicultural table', in Warner, R. S. and Wittner, J. (eds.), *Gatherings in Diaspora*, Philadelphia, PA: Temple University Press, pp. 37–70.

Kurzman, C. 1996, 'Structural opportunity and perceived opportunity in social movement theory: the Iranian Revolution of 1979', *American Sociological Review* 61, 1: 153–70.

Kymlicka, W. (ed.) 1995, *The Rights of Minority Cultures*, New York: Oxford University Press.

La Barre, W. 1972, *The Ghost Dance. Origins of Religion*, London: George Allen & Unwin.

Ladrière, P. 1985, 'Sciences de la vie, éthique et religion', *Acts of the 18th International Conference for the Sociology of Religion*. CISR. Leuven, CISR, pp. 77–91.

Lambert, Y. 1985, *Dieu change en Bretagne*, Paris: Cerf.

Lambert, Y. 2002, 'Religion: L'Europe à un tournant', *Futuribles*, 277: 129–59.

Land, K., Deane, G. and Blau, J. 1991, 'Religious pluralism and church membership: a spatial diffusion model', *American Sociological Review* 56: 237–49.

Lapeyronnie, D. 1993, *L'Individu et les Minorités. La France et la Grande-Bretagne face à leurs Immigrés*, Paris: Presses universitaires de France.

Lasch, C. 1981, *The Culture of Narcissism*, New York: W. W. Norton.

Lash, S. and Urry, J. 1987, *The End of Organised Capitalism*, Cambridge: Polity Press.

Lawrence, B. 1989, *Defenders of God: The Fundamentalist Revolt Against the Modern Age*, San Francisco: Harper.

Lawson, R. 1995, 'Sect-state relations: accounting for the differing trajectories of Seventh-day Adventism and Jehovah's Witnesses', *Sociology of Religion* 56, 4: 351–77.

Lechner, F. 2000, 'Global fundamentalism', in Lechner, F. and Boli, J. (eds.), *The Globalization Reader*, Oxford: Blackwell, pp. 338–41.

Lee, R. S. 1967, *Freud and Christianity*, Harmondsworth: Penguin. First published 1948.

Lehmann, D. 1996, *Struggle for the Spirit: Religious Transformation and Popular Culture in Brazil and Latin America*, Cambridge: Polity Press.

Lehmann, D. 1998, 'Fundamentalism and globalism', *Third World Quarterly* 19, 4: 607–34.

Lehmann, D. 2001, 'Charisme et possession en Afrique et au Brésil', in Bastian, J.-P., Champion, F. and Rousselet, K. (eds.) *La Globalisation du religieux*, Paris: L'Harmattan, pp. 139–52.

Lehmann, D. 2002, 'Religion and globalization', in Woodhead, L. and Heelas, P. (eds.) *Religions in the Modern World*, London: Routledge, pp. 299–315.

Lemert, C. 1999, 'The might have been and could be of religion in social theory', *Sociological Theory* 17, 3: 240–63.

Lewis, I. M. 1986, *Religion in Context. Cults and Charisma*, Cambridge University Press.

Locke, S. 2001, 'Sociology and the public understanding of science: from rationalization to rhetoric', *British Journal of Sociology*, 52, 1: 1–18.

Lockhart, W. H. 2000, '"We are one life", but not of one gender ideology: unity, ambiguity, and the Promise Keepers', *Sociology of Religion* 61, 1: 73–92.

Lockwood, D. 1964, 'Social integration and system integration', in Zollschan, G. K. and Hirsch, W. *Explorations in Social Change*, Boston: Houghton Mifflin.

Lofland, J. 1979, 'White-hot mobilization: strategies of a millenarian movement', in Zald, M. and McCarthy, J. (eds.), *The Dynamics of Social Movements*, Cambridge, MA: Winthrop.

Lofland, J. 1985, *Protest*, New Brunswick, NJ: Transaction.

Lofland, J. 1987, 'Social movement culture and the Unification Church', in Bromley, D. G. and Hammond, P. E. (eds.), *The Future of New Religious Movements*, Macon, GA: Mercer University Press, pp. 91–108.

Luckmann, T. 1967, *The Invisible Religion*, London: Macmillan.

Luckmann, T. 1990, 'Shrinking transcendence, expanding religion', *Sociological Analysis* 50, 2: 127–38.

Luhmann, N. 1977, *Funktion der Religion*, Frankfurt: Suhrkamp.

Luhmann, N. 1984, *Religious Dogmatics and the Evolution of Societies*, New York: Edwin Mellen Press.

Luhmann, N. 1985, 'Society, meaning, religion – based on self-reference', *Sociological Analysis* 46, 1: 5–20.

Lyon, D. 2000, *Jesus in Disneyland. Religion in Postmodern Times*, Cambridge: Polity Press.

Lyotard, J-F. 1984, *The Condition of Postmodernity*, Manchester University Press.

McAdam, D. 1982, *Political Process and the Development of Black Insurgency, 1930–1970*, University of Chicago Press.

McCarthy, J. D. and Zald, M. N. 1977, 'Resource mobilization and social movements: a partial theory', *American Journal of Sociology* 82, 6: 1212–41.

McFarland, H. N. 1967, *The Rush Hour of the Gods. A Study of New Religious Movements in Japan*, New York: Macmillan.

McGovern, P. 2002, 'Globalization or internationalization? Foreign footballers in the English League, 1946–95', *Sociology* 36, 1: 23–42.

McGuire, M. 1990, 'Religion and the body: rematerializing the human body in the social sciences of religion', *Journal for the Scientific Study of Religion* 29, 3: 283–96.

McGuire, M. 2003, 'Contested meanings and definitional boundaries: historicizing the sociology of religion', in Greil, A. and Bromley, D. (eds.) *Religion and the Social Order*, Vol. 12 (in press).

McMullen, M. 2000, *The Baha'i: The Religious Construction of a Global Identity*, New Brunswick, NJ: Rutgers University Press.

Machalek, R. and Snow, D. A. 1993, 'Conversion to new religious movements', in Bromley, D. G. and Hadden, J. K. (eds.) *The Handbook on Cults and Sects in America*, Greenwich, CT: JAI Press. Part B: 53–74.

Maffesoli, M. 1988, *Le Temps des tribus. Le déclin de l'individualisme dans les sociétés de masse*, Paris: Klincksieck.

Mariz, C. and M. Das Dores Campos Machado 1997, 'Pentecostalism and women in Brazil' in E. Cleary and H. Stewart-Gambino (eds.) *Power, Politics and Pentecostals*, Boulder, CO: Westview, pp. 41–54.

Markoff, J. and D. Regan 1987, 'Religion, the state and political legitimacy in the worlds' constitutions', in T. Robbins and R. Robertson (eds) *Church-State Relations*, New Brunswick, NJ: Transaction Books, pp. 161–82.

Marshall, B. L. 1994, *Engendering Modernity. Feminism, Social Theory and Social Change*, Cambridge: Polity Press.

Martin, D. A. 1967, *A Sociology of English Religion*, London: S.C.M. Press.

Martin, D. A. 1978, *A General Theory of Secularization*, Oxford: Blackwell.

Martin, D. A. 1990, *Tongues of Fire. The Explosion of Protestantism in Latin America*, Oxford: Blackwell.

Martin, D. A. 1999, 'The evangelical upsurge and its political implications', in Berger, P. L. (ed.) *The Desecularization of the World. Resurgent Religion and Worldly Politics*, Grands Rapids, MI: Eerdmans, pp. 37–49.

Martin, D. A. 2002, *Pentecostalism: The World Their Parish*, Oxford: Blackwell.

Martin, L. (ed.) 1993, *Religious Transformations and Socio-Political Change. Eastern Europe and Latin America*, Berlin: Mouton de Gruyter.

Martin, M.-L. 1975, *Kimbangu. An African Prophet and His Church*, Oxford: Blackwell.

Marty, M. and Appleby, S. 1992, *The Glory and the Power*, Boston: Beacon Press.

Marty, M. and Appleby, S. (eds.) 1991, *Fundamentalisms Observed*, University of Chicago Press.

Marty, M. and Appleby, S. (eds.) 1993a, *Fundamentalisms and Society: Reclaiming the Sciences, the Family and Education*, University of Chicago Press.

Marty, M. and Appleby, S. (eds.) 1993b, *Fundamentalisms and the State: Remaking Polities, Economies and Militance*, University of Chicago Press.

Marty, M. and Appleby, S. (eds.) 1994, *Accounting for Fundamentalisms: The Dynamic Character of Movements*, University of Chicago Press.

Marty, M. and Appleby, S. (eds.) 1995, *Fundamentalisms Comprehended*, University of Chicago Press.

Marx, K. 1977, *Selected Writings*, Edited by D. McLellan. Oxford University Press.

Mary, A. 1994, 'Bricolage Afro-Brésilien et bris-collage post-moderne', in Laburthe-Tolra, P. (ed.) *Roger Bastide ou le réjouissement du l'abîme*, Paris: L'Harmattan, pp. 85–98.

Mary, A. 1999, 'Culture pentecôtiste et charisme visionnaire au sein d'une Eglise indépendante africaine', *Archives de Sciences Sociales des Religions* 105: 29–50.

Mary, A. 2001, 'Globalisation des pentecôtismes et hybridité du christianisme africain', in Bastian, J.-P., Champion, F. and Rousselet, K. (eds.) *La Globalisation du religieux*, Paris: L'Harmattan, pp. 153–68.

Mears, D. P. and Ellison, C. G. 2000, 'Who buys New Age materials? Exploring sociodemographic, religious, network, and contextual correlates of New Age consumption', *Sociology of Religion* 61, 3: 289–313.

Mellor, P. and Shilling, C. 1997, *Re-Forming the Body. Religion, Community and Modernity*, London: Sage.

Melton, J. G. 1987, 'How new is new? The flowering of the "new" religious consciousness', in Bromley, D. G. and Hammond, P. E. (eds.) *The Future of New Religious Movements*, Macon, GA: Mercer University Press, pp. 46–56.

Melucci, A. 1989, *Nomads of the Present: Social Movements and Individual Needs in Contemporary Society*, Philadelphia: Temple University Press.

Melucci, A. 1995, 'The new social movements revisited: reflections on a sociological misunderstanding', in Maheu, L. *Social Movements and Social Classes*, London: Sage, pp. 107–19.

Melucci, A. 1996, *Challenging Codes. Collective Action in the Information Age*, Cambridge University Press.

Meštrović, S. 1997, *Postemotional Society*. London: Sage.

Milbank, J. 1990, *Theology and Social Theory. Beyond Secular Reason*, Oxford: Blackwell.

Modood, T. 1994, 'Establishment, multiculturalism and British citizenship', *Political Quarterly* 65, 4: 53–73.

Modood, T. (ed.) 1997, *Church, State and Religious Minorities*, London: Policy Studies Institute.

Modood, T. 1998, 'Anti-essentialism, multiculturalism and the "recognition" of religious groups', *Journal of Political Philosophy* 6, 4: 356–77.

Modood, T. 2000, 'La place des musulmans dans le multiculturalisme laic en Grande-Bretagne', *Social Compass* 47, 1: 41–55.

Mol, J. J. 1976, *Identity and the Sacred*, Agincourt: Book Society of Canada.

Moon, G. and Allen, R. 2000, 'Substantive rights and equal treatment in respect of religion and belief: towards a better understanding of the rights and their implications', *European Human Rights Law Review* 6: 580–602.

Moore, R. L. 1986, *Religious Outsiders and the Making of Americans*, New York: Oxford University Press.

Morier-Genoud, E. 2000, 'The 1996 "Muslim Holidays" affair: religious competition and state mediation in contemporary Mozambique', *Journal of Southern African Studies* 26, 3: 409–27.

Morioka, K. 1975, *Religion in Changing Japanese Society*, Tokyo University Press.

Morris, A. D. 1984, *The Origins of the Civil Rights Movement*, New York: Free Press.

Morris, B. 1987, *Anthropological Studies of Religion*, University of Cambridge Press.

Motta, R. 2001, 'Déterritorialisation, standardisation, diaspora et identités: à propos des religions afro-brésiliennes', in Bastian, J.-P., Champion, F. and Rousselet, K. (eds.) *La Globalisation du religieux*, Paris: L'Harmattan, pp. 61–72.

Mouzelis, N. 1995, *Sociological Theory: What Went Wrong?*, London: Routledge.

Mullins, M. R. 1994, 'The empire strikes back. Korean Pentecostal mission to Japan', in Poewe, K. (ed.), *Charismatic Christianity as a Global Culture*, Columbia, SC, University of South Carolina Press, pp. 87–102.

Nason-Clark, N. 2001, 'Woman abuse and faith communities: religion, violence, and the provision of social welfare', in Nesbitt, P. D. (ed.), *Religion and Social Policy*, Walnut Creek, CA: Alta Mira Press, pp. 128–45.

Neitz, M. J. 1993, 'Inequality and difference. Feminist research in the sociology of religion', in Swatos Jr., W. H. (ed.), *A Future for Religion?*, London: Sage, pp. 165–84.

Neitz, M. J. 2000, 'Queering the Dragonfest: changing sexualities in a post-patriarchal religion', *Sociology of Religion* 61, 4: 369–91.

Nielsen, J. S. 1992, *Muslims in Western Europe*, Edinburgh University Press.

Nye, M. 1998, 'Hindus old and new: problems of sacred space in Britain', in Barker, E. V. and Warburg, M. (eds.), *New Religions and New Religiosity*, Aarhus University Press, pp. 222–42.

Oakley, A. 2000, *Experiments in Knowing. Gender and Method in the Social Sciences*, Cambridge: Polity Press.

Offe, C. 1985a, 'New social movements: challenging the boundaries of institutional politics', *Social Research* 52, 4: 817–68.

Offe, C. 1985b, *Disorganized Capitalism*, Cambridge: Polity Press.

Olson, D. V. 1998, 'Religious pluralism in contemporary US counties', *American Sociological Review* 63: 759–61.

Olson, D. V. 1999, 'Religious pluralism and US church membership: a reassessment', *Sociology of Religion* 60, 2: 149–73.

Olson, M. 1965, *The Logic of Collective Action*, Cambridge, MA: Harvard University Press.

O'Toole, R. 1984, *Religion: Classic Sociological Approaches*, Toronto: McGraw-Hill Ryerson.

Ozorak, E. W. 1996. 'The power, but not the glory: how women empower themselves through religion', *Journal for the Scientific Study of Religion* 35, 1: 17–29.

Palmer, S. 1994, *Moon Sisters, Krishna Mothers, Rajneesh Lovers*, Syracuse University Press.

Parekh, B. 1992, 'The Concept of Fundamentalism', University of Warwick Centre for Research in Asian Migration. *Occasional Papers in Asian Migration Studies*, no.1.

Parekh, B. 2000, *Rethinking Multiculturalism. Cultural Diversity and Political Theory*, Basingstoke: Macmillan.

Parker Gumucio, C. 1998, 'Catholicismes populaires urbains et globalisation: étude de cas au Chili', *Social Compass* 45, 4: 595–618.

Parmly, M. E. 2001, 'Religious liberty in transatlantic perspective.' Presentation made at the Institute for Religion and Public Policy's conference on "Transatlantic conversations on religious coexistence", Washington, DC. [Available: http://www.cesnur.org/2001/fr_may02.htm]

Pereira de Queiroz, M. I. 1989, 'Afro-Brazilian cults and religious change in Brazil', in Beckford, J. A. and Luckman, T. (eds.), *The Changing Face of Religion*, London: Sage, pp. 88–108.

Poblete, R. 1960, 'A sociological approach to the sects', *Social Compass* 1, 5–6: 383–406.

Poewe, K. (ed.) 1994, *Charismatic Christianity as a Global Culture*, University of South Carolina Press.

Poloma, M. 1989, *Assemblies of God at the Crossroads*, Knoxville, TN: University of Tennessee Press.

Poloma, M. 1998, 'Reviving Pentecostalism at the millennium: the Harvest Rock story.' Unpublished paper presented at a conference at Southern California College. [Available: http://www.hirr.hartsem.edu/research/research_pentecostalism_polomaart4.html]

Poulat, E. 1987, *Liberté, Laïcité: La guerre des deux Frances et le principe de la modernité*, Paris: Cerf.

Prozesky, M. (ed.) 1990, *Christianity in South Africa*, Bergvlei: Southern Book Publishers.

Putnam, H. 1981, *Reason, Truth and History*, Cambridge University Press.

Puttick, E. 1996, *Women in New Religions*, London: Macmillan.

Puttick, E. 1999, 'Women in new religious movements', in Wilson, B. R. and Cresswell, J. (eds.) *New Religious Movements. Challenge and Response*, London, Routledge, pp. 143–62.

Rémond, R. 1976, *L'Anticléricalisme en France de 1815 à nos jours*, Paris: Fayard.

Rex, J. 1986, *Race and Ethnicity*, Milton Keynes: Open University Press.

Richardson, J. T. (ed.) 1988, *Money and Power in New Religious Movements*, New York: Edwin Mellen Press.

Richardson, J. T. 1995, 'Legal status of minority religions in the United States', *Social Compass* 42, 2: 249–64.

Richardson, J. T. and Introvigne, M. 2001, ' "Brainwashing" theories in European parliamentary and administrative reports on "cults" and "sects" ', *Journal for the Scientific Study of Religion* 40, 2: 143–68.

Rieff, P. 1966, *Triumph of the Therapeutic*, London: Chatto & Windus.

Riesebrodt, M. 1993, *Pious Passion: The Emergence of Modern Fundamentalism in the United States and Iran*, Berkeley, CA: University of California Press.

Riis, O. 1999, 'Modes of religious pluralism under conditions of globalisation', *MOST Journal on Cultural Pluralism* 1, 1: 1–14. Online. [Available: www.unesco.org/most/vl1n1edi.htm]

Robbins, T. 1981, 'Church, state and cult', *Sociological Analysis* 42, 3: 209–26.

Robbins, T. 1987, 'Church-state tension in the United States', in Robbins, T. and Robertson, R. (eds.), *Church-State Relations*, New Brunswick, NJ: Transaction Books, pp. 67–75.

Robbins, T. 1988, *Cults, Converts and Charisma: the Sociology of New Religious Movements*, London: Sage.

Robbins, T. and Anthony, D. 1972, 'Getting straight with Meher Baba: a study of drug-rehabilitation, mysticism, and post-adolescent role-conflict', *Journal for the Scientific Study of Religion* 11, 2: 122–40.

Robbins, T. and Anthony, D. 1982, 'The medicalization of new religions', *Social Problems* 29, 3: 283–97.

Robbins, T., Anthony, D., Doucas, M. and Curtis, T. 1976, 'The last Civil Religion: Reverend Moon and the Unification Church', *Sociological Analysis* 37, 2: 111–25.

Robbins, T. and Palmer, S. (eds.) 1997, *Millennium, Messiahs and Mayhem. Contemporary Apocalyptic Movements*, New York: Routledge.

Robbins, T. and Robertson, R. (eds.) 1987, *Church-State Relations. Tensions and Transitions*, New Brunswick, NJ: Transaction Books.

Roberts, B. R. 1968, 'Protestant groups and coping with urban life in Guatemala City', *American Journal of Sociology* 73, 6: 753–67.

Roberts, R. H. 1995, 'Globalised religion? The "Parliament of the World's Religions" Chicago 1993 in theoretical perspective', *Journal of Contemporary Religion* 10, 2: 121–37.

Roberts, R. H. 2002, *Religion, Theology and the Human Sciences*, Cambridge University Press.

Robertson, R. 1978, *Meaning and Change*, Oxford: Blackwell.

Robertson, R. 1979, 'Religious movements and modern societies: toward a progressive problemshift', *Sociological Analysis* 40, 4: 297–314.

Robertson, R. 1980, 'Aspects of identity and authority in sociological theory', in Robertson, R. and Holzner, B. (eds.), *Identity and Authority*, Oxford: Blackwell, pp. 218–79.

Robertson, R. 1987, 'Globalization and societal modernization: a note on Japan and Japanese religion', *Sociological Analysis* 47 S: 35–42.

Robertson, R. 1992a, 'The economization of religion? Reflections on the promise and limitations of the economic approach', *Social Compass* 39, 1: 1147–57.

Robertson, R. 1992b, *Globalization: Social Theory and Global Culture*, London: Sage.

Robertson, R. and Chirico, J. 1985, 'Humanity, globalization and worldwide religious resurgence: a theoretical exploration', *Sociological Analysis* 46, 3: 219–42.

Robertson-Smith, W. 1889, *Lectures on the Religion of the Semites*, Edinburgh: Black.

Rochford, E. B. 1985, *Hare Krishna in America*, New Brunswick, NJ: Rutgers University Press.

Rochford, E. B. 1997, 'Family formation, culture and change in the Hare Krsna movement', *ISKCON Communications Journal* 5, 2: 61–82.

Rochford, B. E. 2000, 'Analysing ISKCON for twenty-five years: a personal reflection', *ISKCON Communications Journal* 8, 1: 33–6.

Rose, N. 1989, *Governing the Soul. The Shaping of the Private Self*, London: Routledge.

Rose, S. 1998, 'An examination of the New Age movement: who is involved and what constitutes its spirituality', *Journal of Contemporary Religion* 13, 1: 5–22.

Rosenberg, J. 2000, *The Follies of Globalisation Theory. Polemical Essays*, London: Verso.

Saliba, J. A. 1995, *Perspectives on New Religious Movements*, London: Geoffrey Chapman.

Samad, Yunus 1997, 'The plural guises of multiculturalism: conceptualizing a fragmented paradigm', pp. 240–60 in Modood, T. and Werbner, P. (eds.) *The Politics of Multiculturalism in the New Europe*, London: Zed Books.

Schmalenbach, H. 1977, 'Communion – A sociological category', in Lüschen, G. and Stone, G. (eds.) *Hermann Schmalenbach: On Society and Experience*, University of Chicago Press, pp. 64–125.

Scholte, J. A. 2000, *Globalization. A Critical Introduction*, Basingstoke: Macmillan.

Searle, J. 1995, *The Construction of Social Reality*, New York: Free Press.

Séguy, J. 1980, *Christianisme et société. Introduction à la sociologie de Ernst Troeltsch*, Paris: Cerf.

Séguy, J. 1996, 'Les spiritualités dans le catholicisme récent: projet d'une recherche', in Voyé, L. (ed.), *Figures de dieux. Rites et mouvements religieux*, Paris et Bruxelles: De Boeck Université, pp. 247–69.

Sennett, R. 1977, 'Destructive Gemeinschaft', in Birnbaum, N. (ed.), *Beyond the Crisis*, New York: Oxford University Press, pp. 171–95.

Sharot, S. 1992, 'Religious fundamentalism: neo-traditionalism in modern societies', in Wilson, B. R. (ed.), *Religion: Contemporary Issues*, London: Bellew, pp. 24–45.

Sherkat, D. E. and Wilson, J. 1995, 'Preferences, constraints, and choices in religious markets: an examination of religious switching and apostasy', *Social Forces* 73, 3: 993–1026.

Shiner, L. E. 1967, 'The concept of secularization in empirical research', *Journal for the Scientific Study of Religion* 6, 2: 207–20.

Shupe, A. D., Jr., Hardin, B. and Bromley, D. G. 1983, 'A comparison of anti-cult groups in the United States and West Germany', in Barker, E. V. (ed.), *Of Gods and Men: New Religious Movements in the West*, Macon, GA: Mercer University Press, pp. 177–93.

Silk, M. 1995, *Unsecular Media. Making News of Religion in America*, Urbana, IL: University of Illinois Press.

Silk, M. 1997, 'Journalists with attitude: a response to Richardson and Van Driel', *Review of Religious Research* 39, 2: 137–43.

Simmel, G. 1905, 'A contribution to the sociology of religion', *American Journal of Sociology* 11, 3: 359–76.

Simpson, J. 1993, 'Religion and the body. Sociological themes and prospects' in W. H. Swatos, Jr. (ed.) *A Future for Religion? New Paradigms for Social Analysis*, Newbury Park, CA, Sage, pp. 149–64.

Smelser, N. 1962, *Theory of Collective Behaviour*, London: Routledge & Kegan Paul.

Smith, C. (ed.) 1996, *Disruptive Religion. The Force of Faith in Social Movement Activism*, New York: Routledge.

Smith, C. (ed.) 1998, *American Evangelicalism*, University of Chicago Press.

Smith, G. 2000, 'Global systems and religious diversity in the Inner City – migrants in the East End of London', *MOST Journal of Multicultural Societies* 2, 1: Online. [Available: http://www.unesco.org./most/vl2n1smi.htm]. 21 pp. [Accessed 21/12/00]

Snow, D. A. 1976, 'The Nichiren Shoshu Buddhist movement in America: a sociological examination of its value orientation, recruitment efforts and spread', unpublished PhD dissertation, University of California, Los Angeles.

Snow, D. A. and Machalek, R. 1982, 'On the presumed fragility of unconventional beliefs', *Journal for the Scientific Study of Religion* 21, 1: 15–26.

Snow, D. A. *et al.* 1986, 'Frame alignment processes, micromobilization and movement participation', *American Sociological Review* 51(4): 464–81.

Somerville, J. 1997, 'Social movement theory, women and the question of interests', *Sociology* 31, 4: 673–95.

Soysal, Y. 1994, *Limits of Citizenship. Migrants and Postnational Membership in Europe*, University of Chicago Press.

Soysal, Y. 1997, 'Changing parameters of citizenship and claims-making: organized Islam in European public spheres', *Theory and Society* 26, 4: 509–27.

Spencer, H. 1893, *Principles of Sociology*, vol. III, 3rd edition, London.

Spickard, J. V. 1998, 'Rethinking religious social action: what is "rational" about rational choice theory?', *Sociology of Religion* 59, 2: 99–115.

Stark, R. 1997, 'Bringing theory back in', in Young, L. (ed.), *Rational Choice Theory and Religion*, New York: Routledge, pp. 3–23.

Stark, R. and Bainbridge, W. S. 1985, *The Future of Religion. Secularization, Revival and Cult Formation*, Berkeley, CA: University of California Press.

Stark, R. and W. S. Bainbridge 1987, *A Theory of Religion*, New York: Peter Lang.

Stark, R. and Finke, R. 2000, *Acts of Faith: Explaining the Human Side of Religion*, Berkeley, CA: University of California Press.

Surin, K. 1990, 'Towards a "materialist" critique of "religious pluralism"', in Hamnett, I. (ed.), *Religious Pluralism and Unbelief*, London: Routledge, pp. 114–29.

Sutcliffe, S. and Bowman, M. (eds.) 2000, *Beyond New Age. Exploring Alternative Spirituality*, University of Edinburgh Press.

Swatos, W. H. (ed.) 1994, *Gender and Religion*, New Brunswick, NJ: Transaction Books.

Tamney, J. B. 1992, 'Conservative government and support for the religious institution in Singapore: an uneasy alliance', *Sociological Analysis* 53, 2: 201–17.

Ter Haar, G. 1998, *Halfway to Paradise. African Christians in Europe*, Cardiff Academic Press.

Thomas, G. M. 2001, 'Religions in Global Civil Society', *Sociology of Religion* 62, 4: 515–33.

Thrupp, S. L. 1970 (ed.), *Millennial Dreams in Action*, New York: Schocken.

Tipton, S. 1984, *Getting Saved from the Sixties. Moral Meaning in Conversion and Cultural Change*, Berkeley, CA: University of California Press.

Tönnies, F. 1955, *Community and Association*, Trans. C. P. Loomis, London: Routledge & Kegan Paul. First published in Germany as *Gemeinschaft und Gesellschaft* in 1887.

Touraine, A. 1981, *The Voice and the Eye*, University of Cambridge Press.

Touraine, A. 1985, 'An introduction to the study of social movements', *Social Research* 52, 4: 749–87.

Touraine, A., Dubet, F., Wieviorka, M. and Strzelecki, J. 1983, *Solidarity. Poland 1980–81*, University of Cambridge Press.

Touraine, A. and Khosrokhavar, F. 2000, *La Recherche de Soi. Dialogue sur le Sujet*, Paris: Fayard.

Towler, R. 1974, *Homo Religiosus: Sociological Problems in the Study of Religion*, London: Constable.

Towler, R. 1984, *The Need for Certainty. A Sociological Study of Conventional Religion*, London: Routledge.

Tschannen, O. 1991, 'The secularization paradigm: a systematization', *Journal for the Scientific Study of Religion* 30, 4: 395–415.

Tshcannen, O. 1992, *La Théorie de la Sécularisation*, Geneva: Droz.

Turner, B. S. 1980, 'The body and religion: towards an alliance of medical sociology and sociology of religion', *Annual Review of the Social Sciences of Religion* 4: 247–86.

Turner, B. S. 1984, *The Body and Society*, Oxford: Blackwell.

Turner, B. S. 1991, *Religion and Social Theory*, London: Heinemann.

Turner, B. S. 2001, 'Cosmopolitan virtue: on religion in a global age', *European Journal of Social Theory* 4, 2: 131–52.

Turner, R. and Killian, L. 1972, *Collective Behavior*, 2nd edn., Englewood Cliffs, NJ: Prentice-Hall.

Urry, J. 2000, 'Mobile sociology', *British Journal of Sociology* 51, 1: 185–203.

Van der Veer, P. 1994, *Religious Nationalism: Hindus and Muslims in India*, Berkeley, CA: University of California Press.

Van der Veer, P. 2000, 'Religious nationalism in India and global fundamentalism', in Guidry, J. A., Kennedy, M. D. and Zald, M. N. (eds.), *Globalizations and Social Movements*, Ann Arbor: University of Michigan Press, pp. 315–36.

Van Driel, B. and Richardson, J. T. 1988, 'Print media coverage of new religious movements: a longitudinal study', *Journal of Communication* 38, 3: 37–61.

Van Driel, B. and Richardson, J. T. 1989, 'Journalistic attitudes towards new religious movements', paper presented at the 20th International Conference of the Sociology of Religion, Helsinki.

Van Vugt, J. P. 1991, *Organizing for Social Change. Latin American Christian Base Communities and Literacy Campaigns*, New York: Bergin & Harvey.

Van Zandt, D. 1991, *Living in the Children of God*, Princeton University Press.

Velody, I. and Williams, R. (eds.) 1998, *The Politics of Constructionism*, London: Sage.

Vertovec, S. 1994, 'Multicultural, multi-Asian, multi-Muslim Leicester: dimensions of social complexity, ethnic organization and local government interface', *Innovation* 7, 3: 259–76.

Vertovec, S. 1996, 'Multiculturalism, culturalism and public incorporation', *Ethnic and Racial Studies* 19, 1: 49–69.

Vidich, A. J. and Lyman, S. M. 1985, *American Sociology. Worldly Rejections of Religion and Their Directions*, New Haven, CT: Yale University Press.

Voyé, L. 1992, 'Religion et économie: apports et limites de l'analyse du religieux à partir de cadres théoriques empruntés à l'économie', *Social Compass* 39, 1: 159–69.

Waerness, K. 1984, 'The rationality of caring', *Economic and Industrial Democracy* 5: 185–211.

Wagner, P. 1994, *A Sociology of Modernity. Liberty and Discipline*, London: Routledge.

Wallace, R. A. 1996, 'Feminist theory in North America: new insights into the sociology of religion', *Social Compass* 43, 4: 467–79.

Wallace, W. L. 1969, *Sociological Theory*, London: Heinemann.

Wallerstein, I. 1974, *The Modern World-System*, New York: Academic Press.

Wallerstein, I. 1990, 'Culture as the ideological battleground of the modern world-system', *Theory, Culture and Society* 7, 2–3: 31–56.

Wallis, R. 1984, *The Elementary Forms of the New Religious Life*, London: Routledge & Kegan Paul.

Wallis, R. and Bruce, S. 1992, 'Secularization: the orthodox model' in Bruce, S. (ed.), *Religion and Modernization*, Oxford University Press, pp. 8–30.

Walter, T. 2001, 'From cathedral to supermarket: mourning, silence and solidarity', *Sociological Review* 49, 4: 494–511.

Warburg, M. 1999, 'Baha'i: a religious approach to globalisation', *Social Compass* 46, 1: 47–56.

Warner, R. S. 1993, 'Work in progress toward a new paradigm for the sociological study of religion in the United States', *American Journal of Sociology* 98 March: 1044–93.

Warner, R. S. 1997, 'Convergence toward the new paradigm. A case of induction', in Young, L. (ed.), *Rational Choice Theory and Religion*, New York: Routledge, pp. 87–101.

Warner, R. S. 1998, 'Immigration and religious communities in the United States', in Warner, R. S. and Wittner, J. (eds.), *Gatherings in Diaspora. Religious Communities and the New Immigration*, Philadelphia: Temple University Press, pp. 3–34.

Warner, R. S. and Wittner, J. (eds.) 1997, *Gatherings in Diaspora. Religious Communities and the New Immigration*, Philadelphia: Temple University Press.

Waters, M. 2001, *Globalization*, London: Routledge.

Weber, M. 1964, *The Theory of Social and Economic Organization*, Trans A. M. Henderson and T. Parsons, New York: Free Press [First published 1947].

Weintraub, J. and Kumar, K. (eds.) 1997, *Public and Private in Thought and Practice*, University of Chicago Press.

Wessinger, C. 2000, *How the Millennium Comes Violently*, New York: Seven Bridges Press.

Westerlund, D. (ed.) 1995, *Questioning the Secular State. The Worldwide Resurgence of Religion in Politics*, London: Hurst.

White, J. R. 1970, *The Soka Gakkai and Mass Society*, Stanford University Press.

Wieviorka, M. 2001, *La Différence*, Paris: Balland.

Willaime, J.-P. 1995, *Sociologie des Religions*, Paris: Presses Universitaires de France.

Willaime, J.-P. 1996, 'Laïcité et religion en France' in Davie, G. and Hervieu-Léger, D. (eds.) *Identités religieuses en Europe*, Paris: La Découverte, pp. 153–71.

Williams, R. B. 1988, *Religions of Immigrants from India and Pakistan*, New York: Cambridge University Press.

Williams, R. H. 2000, 'Introduction: Promise Keepers: a comment on religion and social movements', *Sociology of Religion* 61, 1: 1–10.

Williams, R. H. and Blackburn, J. 1996, 'Many Are Called but Few Obey? Ideological Commitment and Activism in Operation Rescue', in Smith, C. (ed.) *Disruptive Religion. The Force of Faith in Social Movement Activism*, New York: Routledge.

Wilson, B. R. 1961, *Sects and Society*, London: Heinemann.

Wilson, B. R. 1970, *Religious Sects*, London: Weidenfeld & Nicolson.

Wilson, B. R. 1973, *Magic and the Millennium*, London: Heinemann.

Wilson, B. R. 1985, 'Secularization: the inherited model', in Hammond, P. E. (ed.), *The Sacred in a Secular Age*, Berkeley, CA: University of California Press, pp. 9–20.

Wilson, B. R. 1992, 'Reflections on a many sided controversy' in Bruce, S. (ed.), *Religion and Modernization*, Oxford University Press, pp. 195–210.

Wilson, B. R. 1995, 'Religious toleration, pluralism and privatization', *Kirchliche Zeitgeschichte* 8, 1: 99–116.

Wilson, B. R. and Cresswell, J. (eds.) 1999, *New Religious Movements: Challenge and Response*, London: Routledge.

Wilson, J. F. 1973, 'The historical study of marginal American religious movements', *Religious Movements in Contemporary America* in Zaretsky, I. I. and Leone, M. P. (eds.) Princeton University Press, 596–611.

Witte, J. J. and van der Vyver, J. D. (eds.) 1996, *Religious Human Rights in Global Perspective*, The Hague: Martinus Nijhoff.

Wood, R. L. 1999, 'Religious culture and political action', *Sociological Theory* 17, 3: 307–32.

Woodhead, L. 2001, 'Feminism and the sociology of religion: from gender-blindness to gendered difference', in Fenn, R. K. (ed.) *The Blackwell Companion to Sociology of Religion*, Oxford: Blackwell, pp. 67–84.

Wright, S. A. and Ebaugh, H. R. 1993, 'Leaving new religions' in Bromley, D. G. and Hadden, J. K. (eds.), *The Handbook of Cults and Sects in America*, Greenwich, CT: JAI Press. Part B, pp. 117–38.

Wuthnow, R. 1976, *The Consciousness Reformation*, Berkeley, CA: University of California Press.

Wuthnow, R. 1978, *Experimentation in American Religion*, Berkeley, CA: University of California Press.

Wuthnow, R. 1982, 'World order and religious movements', in Barker, E. V. (ed.), *New Religious Movements: a Perspective for Understanding Society*, New York: Edwin Mellen Press, pp. 47–65.

Wuthnow, R. 1987, *Meaning and Moral Order: Exploration in Cultural Analysis*, Berkeley, CA: University of California Press.

Wuthnow, R. 1991, 'Religion as culture', in Bromley, G. (ed.), *Religion and Social Order*, Greenwich, CT: JAI Press, pp. 267–83.

Wuthnow, R. 2001, 'Spirituality and spiritual practice', in Fenn, R. K. (ed.) *The Blackwell Companion to Sociology of Religion*, Oxford: Blackwell, pp. 306–20.

Wuthnow, R. and Witten, M. 1988, 'New directions in the study of culture', *Annual Review of Sociology* 11: 111–33.

Wydmusch, S. 2001, 'Intégration européenne et réseaux transnationaux: le lobbying européen des Eglises', in Bastian, J.-P., Champion, F. and Rousselet, K. (eds.) *La Globalisation du religieux*, Paris: L'Harmattan, pp. 249–62.

Yack, B. 1997, *The Fetishism of Modernities: Epochal Self-consciousness in Contemporary Society*, South Bend, IN: University of Notre Dame Press.

York, M. 1995, *The Emerging Network. A Sociology of the New Age and Neo-Pagan Movements*, Lanham, MD: Rowman & Littlefield.

Young, L. A. (ed.) 1997, *Rational Choice Theory and Religion*, New York: Routledge.

Yuval-Davis, N. 1994, 'Fundamentalism, multiculturalism and women in Britain', in Goldberg, D. T. (ed.), *Multiculturalism. A Critical Reader*, Oxford: Blackwell, pp. 278–91.

Zablocki, B. and Robbins, T. (eds.) 2001, *Misunderstanding Cults. Searching for Objectivity in a Controversial Field*, University of Toronto Press.

Zafirovski, M. 1999a, 'Unification of sociological theory by the rational choice model: Conceiving the relationship between economics and sociology', *Sociology* 33, 3: 495–514.

Zafirovski, M. 1999b, 'What is really rational choice? Beyond the utilitarian concept of rationality', *Current Sociology* 47, 1: 47–113.

Zald, M. N. 1970, *Organizational Change: the Political Economy of the YMCA*, University of Chicago Press.

Zald, M. N. and McCarthy, J. D. 1998, 'Religious groups as crucibles of social movements', in Demerath, N. J. I., Hall, P. D., Schmitt, T. and Williams, R. H. (eds.), *Sacred Companies. Organizational Aspects of Religion and Religious Aspects of Organizations*, New York: Oxford University Press, pp. 24–49.

Zetterberg, H. L. 1965, *On Theory and Verification in Sociology*, Totowa, NJ: The Bedminster Press, third enlarged edn.

Zurcher, L. A. J. and Kirkpatrick, R. G. 1976, *Citizens for Decency. Antipornography Crusades as Status Defense*, Austin, TX: University of Texas Press.

Zylberberg, J. 1995, 'Laïcité, connais pas: Allemagne, Canada, Etats-Unis, Royaume Uni', *Pouvoirs* 75: 37–52.

Index